AMERICA'S GREATEST LIBRARY

AMERICA'S GREATEST LIBRARY

An Illustrated History of the Library of Congress

John Y. Cole, Library of Congress Historian
Foreword by Carla D. Hayden, Librarian of Congress

LIBRARY OF CONGRESS

The Library of Congress, Washington, DC, in association with D Giles Limited, London

Copyright © 2017 The Library of Congress

First published in 2017 by GILES
An imprint of D Giles Limited
4 Crescent Stables,
London SW15 2TN, UK
www.gilesltd.com

Library of Congress cataloguing data

Names: Cole, John Young, 1940- author.
Title: America's greatest library : an illustrated history of the Library of
  Congress / John Y. Cole, Library of Congress Historian ; foreword by Carla
  D. Hayden, Librarian of Congress.
Description: Washington, DC : The Library of Congress, Washington, DC, in
  association with D Giles Limited, London, 2017. | Includes index.
Identifiers: LCCN 2017022031| ISBN 9781911282136 (hardcover) | ISBN
  9780844495750 (softcover)
Subjects: LCSH: Library of Congress–History. | Library of
  Congress–History–Pictorial works.
Classification: LCC Z733.U6 C563 2017 | DDC 027.573–dc23 LC record available at
  https://lccn.loc.gov/2017022031

ISBN: 978-1-911282-13-6 (Publisher's hardcover edition)
ISBN: 978-0-844495-75-0 (Library's softcover edition)

For the Library of Congress
Managing Editor: Margaret Wagner
Editor and Photo Editor: Amy Pastan
Editor: Aimee Hess

For D Giles Limited
Copy-edited and proof-read by Jodi Simpson
Designed by Alfonso Iacurci
Produced by GILES,
an imprint of D Giles Limited, London
Printed and bound in China

Frontispiece: View of the US
Capitol at sunrise, from a
window in the North Corridor
of the Great Hall of the Library
of Congress Thomas Jefferson
Building. Above the window is
a mural by Charles Sprague
Pearce with a quotation from
Confucius.

This page: The Library of
Congress Thomas Jefferson
Building, as seen from the
dome of the US Capitol.

FOREWORD

The Library of Congress occupies an important crossroads in American life, a place where the nation's political and literary cultures intersect. Created by Congress in 1800, it is the major research arm of the US Congress, as well as the nation's copyright agency and the world's largest library. Since the opening of its Jefferson Building in 1897, it has served as America's de facto national library, a multifaceted cultural institution, an international leader in library and copyright matters, and an important innovator and partner in electronic and digital network development.

The Library's unparalleled book, manuscript, music, map, sound recording, television, film, and graphic arts collections are the heart of the institution. The Library holds some of the world's largest collections, from sheet music to comic books; founding documents like Thomas Jefferson's handwritten draft of the Declaration of Independence; the full papers of 23 presidents; and the works of eminent Americans such as Samuel Morse, Frederick Douglass, Clara Barton, Leonard Bernstein, Bob Hope, and Thurgood Marshall. Just as important as the collections is the Library's unsurpassed staff, comprised of dedicated specialists and skilled and loyal individuals who each year respond to millions of requests and visitors, both in person and online.

In *America's Greatest Library*, John Y. Cole highlights the history, personalities, collections, and events that have created and sustained this unusual institution. Most importantly, the Library could not have flourished without the continuous support provided by the US Congress since the Library's creation in 1800. Its purchase in 1815 of Thomas Jefferson's wide-ranging personal library became the foundation of the modern Library of Congress. The Jeffersonian concept of a universal library covering all subjects is the basis of the Library's comprehensive collecting policies. Jefferson's belief that democracy depends on free access to knowledge eventually ensured the availability of the Library's rich collections and extensive services not only to Congress, but also to the nation and to the entire world. Simply put, the Library of Congress is one of the greatest gifts and legacies the Congress has given to the American people.

The vision of a national library to serve members of Congress and the communities they represent continues the legacy of my 13 predecessors as Librarian of Congress. For over 200 years, each librarian's experiences and contributions reflected the country's social and historical landscape and advanced the progress of this library. Over time these leaders have expanded the scope of materials collected, advocated successfully to bring the federal copyright system here, and overseen construction of the facilities necessary to house and preserve the collections and the services offered here.

It feels like yesterday that I began my career at a store-front branch of the Chicago Public Library. Forty years later, it is an honor to lead one of the greatest institutions of our nation, and of the world. As a descendant of people who were denied the right to read, to now have the opportunity to serve and lead the institution that is our national symbol of knowledge is a historic moment for which I am grateful.

The 6th Librarian of Congress Ainsworth Rand Spofford famously called the Library "the book palace of the American people" when the Jefferson Building opened in 1897. But the Library of Congress is so much more than beautiful architecture wrapped around bookshelves. It is, in fact, the second part of Spofford's quote—used less often—that is truly powerful: the Library, he said, is "the book palace of the American people in which you all have equal rights with me . . . in which the works of all of you will be welcomed and forever preserved."

The Library of Congress is a place where we grow scholars, where we inspire young authors, where we connect with those individuals outside the limits of Washington and help them make history themselves. This is a place where you can touch history and imagine your future. I invite you to visit the Library of Congress—through this book and our other publications, in person, or through the Internet. There never has been a library—or an institution—quite like it.

Carla D. Hayden
Librarian of Congress

The second floor of the Great Hall in the Library of Congress Thomas Jefferson Building.

AUTHOR'S NOTE
AND ACKNOWLEDGMENTS

I am grateful to several individuals who helped make this publication possible, particularly Julie Chrystyn Opperman, a member of the James Madison Council, the Library's private-sector donor group. Her generous contribution in support of this volume was a vote of confidence that came just at the right time.

In the Library's Publishing Office, editor Amy Pastan's assistance with illustrations and text was invaluable. Support from Director of Publishing Becky Clark and editors Aimee Hess and Margaret Wagner was much needed and appreciated.

Cheryl Fox, collections specialist in the Library's Manuscript Division, helped with both photos and textual questions. Raymond White and Peter Stark traced acquisition dates for several specific collections. Additional help in locating images came from Katherine Blood, Ann Brener, Kia Campbell, Glen Cooper, Barbara Dash, Peter Devereaux, Jeffrey Flannery, Paul Fraunfelter, Eric Frazier, Jennifer Gavin, Grant Harris, Megan Harris, Todd Harvey, Martha Kennedy, Michelle Krowl, Harold Leich, Shawn Miller, Barbara Natanson, Robin Rausch, Cheryl Regan, Marietta Sharpeson, and Georgia Zola.

I want to thank several people at D Giles Ltd., first of all publisher Dan Giles, who persistently pursued the idea of a publication that would build on my first book, *For Congress and the Nation: A Chronological History of the Library of Congress* (1979). Also, for their skilled work, managing editor Allison McCormick, production manager Louise Ramsay, designer Alfonso Iacurci, and copy editor Jodi Simpson.

I am fortunate to have served on the staff of the Library of Congress since 1966 and to have been learning and writing about this unusual institution for nearly as long. Sarah L. Wallace, a former director of publishing, suggested my first article, which was published in the *Quarterly Journal of the Library of Congress* in 1971.

In the decades following, I worked closely and with pleasure on various projects with publishing directors Dana Pratt (1978–1993) and W. Ralph Eubanks (1995–2013) and staff members Joanna Craig, Frederick B. Mohr, Evelyn Sinclair, and Blaine Marshall, among others.

Two historically minded Library officials stimulated my interest in the Library's history. David C. Mearns, a distinguished staff member from 1918 until 1967, served as Assistant Librarian from 1949 to 1951 before becoming chief of the Manuscript Division. Dan Lacy started his career at the National Archives and was Assistant Librarian of Congress from 1950 to 1951 before joining McGraw-Hill Publishing. We met in 1976 when I headed Librarian Boorstin's Task Force on Goals, Organization, and Planning, and Dr. Boorstin appointed Lacy to be chair of the Task Force's advisory group on publishing. As a publisher Lacy also played a leadership role in two reading and book promotion organizations that preceded the Library of Congress Center for the Book: the American Book Publishers Council and its successor, the National Book Committee (1954–1974).

Other Library officials and administrators who have encouraged me along the way are listed below in rough chronological order. Before the year 2000, they included Charles D. Goodrum, Paul L. Berry, John G. Lorenz, Mary Lethbridge, Alan Fern, William Matheson, John C. Broderick, and Carol Nemeyer. In recent years, encouragement has come from Ralph E. Ehrenberg, Roberta Shaffer, and David Mao.

Former staff members to whom I am grateful for their interest, ideas, and occasional personal "LC history" files are listed below, also roughly in chronological order. Before the year 2000, they included Marlene D. Morrisey, Helen-Anne Hilker, Don Reines, Robert D. Stevens, Robert Zich, Connie Carter, Nancy E. Gwinn, Janet Chase, Lucia S. Rather, Warren Tsuneishi, Arthur J. Lieb, Margaret Shannon, Kurt Maier, William Sittig, John Knowlton, Mary Wolfskill, John Wolter, Lou Jacob, John Wayne, Alice D. Schreyer, and Lynda Corey Claassen. In recent years encouragement came from Helen D. Dalrymple, Frank Evina, Kathy Woodrell, Maurvene D. Williams, Evelyn Timberlake, Josephus Nelson, Judith Farley, C. Ford Peatross, Helena Zinkham, Abby Yochelson, George Thuronyi, Maria Pallante, Carl Fleischhauer, Giulia Adelfio, Peter Armenti, Cheryl Adams, and Audrey S. Fischer.

Finally, I value the friendship of four library historians whose own work—about the Library of Congress and library history more widely—has encouraged me to expand my interest in the multiple roles the Library of Congress has played in American life and culture. In particular, Donald G. Davis, Jr., and Wayne Wiegand invited me to contribute to several reference works they planned and edited; Jane Aikin co-edited and helped me plan the *Encyclopedia of the Library of Congress*, a ten-year project that concluded in 2004; and Mary Niles Maack planned and edited *The Library of Congress and the Center for the Book*, a festschrift published in my honor in 2011.

The ceiling of the Reading Room in the Library of Congress Thomas Jefferson Building.

PART ONE

★

FOR CONGRESS
1800–1897

This ca. 1800 watercolor of the planned
US Capitol shows the future home of
the Library of Congress.

INTRODUCTION

Books and libraries were essential to America's founding generation. Most of the founders received vigorous, classical educations. It follows, then, that the members of the First Continental Congress, which convened in Philadelphia in 1774, were also avid readers. So were the first congressmen. When the early US Congresses met in New York and Philadelphia, the legislators were able to use both the New York Society Library and the Library Company of Philadelphia. But proposals to establish a library specifically for the use of Congress repeatedly met with failure. However, the 1790 agreement among Alexander Hamilton, James Madison, and Thomas Jefferson to locate the permanent federal capital in the small town of Washington on the Potomac River—a location without libraries or bookstores—forced the government's hand.

In 1800, as part of an act of Congress providing for the removal of the new national government from Philadelphia to Washington, President John Adams approved a $5,000 appropriation for the founding of a Library of Congress. A Joint Committee on the Library (Joint Library Committee) was formed to oversee the purchase of the books, furnish a catalog, and manage the institution. Thomas Jefferson's presidency, from 1801 to 1809, gave the Library early prominence. During his term he approved a compromise act concerning the appointment of the Librarian of Congress, and the House of Representatives agreed to the Senate preference that the president of the United States appoint the Librarian. Jefferson named the first two Librarians of Congress, each of whom also served as the clerk of the House of Representatives.

It was also former President Jefferson, long retired from office, who came to the Library's rescue during the War of 1812. In 1814, the British torched Washington, deliberately destroying the unfinished Capitol and the small congressional library in its north wing. To "replace the devastations of British Vandalism," Jefferson wrote to his friend Samuel Smith, asking him to offer Congress Jefferson's comprehensive collection of books because "there is in fact no subject to which a member of Congress may not have occasion to refer." And Congress agreed. They purchased 6,487 books from Jefferson for $23,950.

Despite the attention of Jefferson and other politicians, the Library struggled for legitimacy. Was it intended to serve Congress alone, or to be the repository of knowledge for the entire country? Although it was created by a national legislature to serve the national government, the Library's early decades were marked by uncertainty about its national role. Perennially underfunded, its primary function was to serve the Congress and, only secondarily, make popular literature accessible to the general public.

The Library played an important but limited role in assisting Congress in its work of making political decisions in the 1840s and 1850s. Its books and maps, for example, were especially useful for research and legislation, helping shape America's westward expansion. The Library also was consulted on topics such as slavery, trade and tariffs, the European revolutions of 1848, and new and developing technologies. Senator James A. Pearce, who dominated the Joint Library Committee from the mid-1840s until the 1860s, was both protective of the Library and quite content with its limited role.

After the Civil War, the American economy improved rapidly, and both the federal government and the city of Washington expanded as well. The Library of Congress entered a period of unprecedented growth under the leadership of Ainsworth Rand Spofford, Librarian of Congress from 1864 to 1897. Spofford appealed to a growing cultural nationalism in pursuing his ambitious plan to turn the Library of Congress into a national library. In Jeffersonian terms, he advocated a single, comprehensive collection of American publications for use by both Congress and the American people. The centralization of copyright at the Library, achieved in 1870, was essential for the growth of these collections, as was the construction of a separate Library building. When the impressive new structure opened to the public across from the Capitol in 1897, Spofford called it "The Book Palace of the American People."

In 1897, the Library moved from the US Capitol into its own building, a monumental structure immediately east of the Capitol. Today known as the Jefferson Building, it is a powerful and impressive symbol of both classical learning and American cultural nationalism. This photograph of the Great Hall's second floor north corridor depicts an exuberant recognition of the Five Senses, the Eight Virtues, and six contemporary American publishing and printing firms.

1800

APRIL 24 - President John Adams approves an "act to make provision for the removal and accommodation of the Government of the United States," which establishes the Library of Congress. Five thousand dollars is appropriated "for the purchase of such books as may be necessary for the use of Congress" after it moves from Philadelphia to the new capital city of Washington. The books will be housed in the Capitol, and a Joint Library Committee will oversee the purchase of the books, furnish a catalog, and "devise and establish" the Library's regulations.

1801

MAY 2 - The initial collection, consisting of 152 titles in 740 volumes and three maps, arrives and is stored in the office of the Secretary of the Senate.

1802

JANUARY 26 - President Thomas Jefferson approves a compromise act of Congress "concerning the Library for the use of both Houses of Congress." The Librarian of Congress, who will be paid "two dollars per diem," will be appointed by the President of the United States. The Joint Library Committee will supervise the expenditure of funds. Its rules and regulations will be established by the president of the Senate and the Speaker of the House of Representatives. "For the time being, its use is restricted to members of Congress and the President and Vice President of the United States."

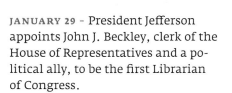

John Adams, who in 1800 signed the first appropriation to provide books for the use of Congress.

JANUARY 29 - President Jefferson appoints John J. Beckley, clerk of the House of Representatives and a political ally, to be the first Librarian of Congress.

APRIL - The first Library catalog, *Catalogue of the Books, Maps, and Charts Belonging to the Library of the Two Houses of Congress*, is printed by William Dunne. It lists the collection of 964 volumes according to their size and appends a list of nine maps.

The Library of Congress
looks to Thomas
Jefferson as one of its
principal founders. His
concept of universality
is the rationale for the
comprehensive collecting
policies of today's Library
of Congress.

"A SUITABLE APARTMENT" — THE LIBRARY'S FIRST HOME

In the country's early years, the growing pains of the new democracy naturally affected the fledgling library that was to serve it—even in terms of its physical space. In accordance with the law of April 24, 1800, that created the Library of Congress, it was assigned "a suitable apartment" in the Capitol to be its first home. On June 20 the Joint Library Committee placed an order for 740 books with the London booksellers Cadell & Davis. But when the valuable purchase arrived in the new City of Washington in early spring 1801, the Capitol was still under construction, so the precious volumes were temporarily housed in the office of the Secretary of the Senate.

Eventually, the act of January 26, 1802, which established the rules and procedures "concerning the Library for the use of both Houses of Congress," provided for the move of the Library into a room on the west side of the north wing of the Capitol, a site formerly occupied by the House of Representatives. Measuring 86 feet long and 35 feet wide with a 36-foot ceiling, the attractive chamber had upper galleries and two ranges of windows for natural lighting. For visitors to the Capitol, it was a must-see attraction. In June 1804, Librarian John Beckley proudly showed it off to artist Charles Willson Peale and Peale's guest, the famous German naturalist Baron Alexander von Humboldt. Local citizens gathered there as well, especially as the new capital city was still sparsely settled and lacked churches, schools, and other public facilities. The Library remained in those lavish quarters until December 1805, when the space was refitted to accommodate a growing House of Representatives.

For the next few years, the Library occupied a series of committee rooms. However, when the British invaded Washington during the War of 1812, much of the city was burned in the attack, including the Capitol. The Library was destroyed. Thankfully, Thomas Jefferson, the founding father who famously declared that he could not "live without books," understood the loss to the nation and offered to sell his personal library to Congress to "recommence"

its own. It was purchased on January 30, 1815, and a law approved on March 3, 1815, authorized the preparation of a "proper apartment" for the volumes. Blodgett's Hotel at Seventh and E Streets, NW, served as the temporary Capitol, and a room on the third floor became the new site for the Library of Congress. There, Jefferson's library was received and organized by Librarian of Congress George Watterston.

The Library moved back to the Capitol in 1818. However, its new quarters in the attic story of the Capitol's north wing proved inadequate. Architect of the Capitol Charles Bulfinch soon developed plans for a spacious library room in the center of the west front of the Capitol. The new room, which measured 90 feet long by 30 feet wide, was occupied on August 17, 1824. This fitting home was threatened on December 22, 1825, when a candle left burning in the gallery ignited the room. Representative Edward Everett first noticed the fire, and firemen were able to get the blaze under control before it could cause serious damage. According to the *National Intelligencer*, Representatives Sam Houston and Daniel Webster were among the members of Congress who aided the firemen and "vied with one another in their exertions to save the Library." Later investigations into fireproofing the room concluded that the expense would be too great. It was an ill-fated decision.

On Christmas Eve, 1851, the Library of Congress suffered a truly disastrous fire. Approximately 35,000 of its 55,000 volumes, as well as two-thirds of Jefferson's personal library, were destroyed in flames, accidentally caused by a faulty chimney flue. In its detailed story, *The Farmer's Cabinet* newspaper reported that President Millard Fillmore, along with "numerous members and officers of Congress" were "early on the grounds, rendering all the service in their power." The only good news that Librarian of Congress John Meehan could convey to Joint Library Committee chairman James A. Pearce of Maryland was that the Library's unique copy of Audubon's *Birds of America* was "saved and uninjured."

Congress agreed to replace the lost volumes and

Following a disastrous accidental fire in 1851 that destroyed two-thirds of the Library's collections, this elegant and enlarged new Library of Congress room was opened across the west front of the Capitol building on August 23, 1853. Designed by Architect of the Capitol Thomas U. Walter to be completely fireproof, it was said to be "the largest room made of iron in the world." It measured 91 feet long, 34 feet wide, and 38 feet high. Each of the encircling galleries was 9 feet 6 inches high, rendering the use of stepladders unnecessary. The furniture was made expressly for the location, "in harmony with the surroundings."

rebuild its Library. Architect of the Capitol Thomas U. Walter presented a plan, approved by Congress, to repair and enlarge the Library room, this time using fireproof materials throughout. Called by the press the "largest room made of iron in the world," it filled the entire west front of the Capitol. A month before its opening on August 23, 1853, President Franklin Pierce inspected the new Library in the company of British scientist Sir Charles Lyell, who pronounced it "the most beautiful room in the world."

In 1865, Librarian of Congress Ainsworth Rand Spofford, determined to convince Congress that its library was also the national library, obtained approval for expanding the Library's room by adding two new fireproof wings, each 95 feet long by 35 feet wide. They were completed in 1866 and soon filled, one by the transfer of the science library of the Smithsonian Institution, the other by the purchase of the Peter Force Library of incunabula and Americana. In addition, the Copyright Law of 1870 brought two copies of all copyrighted items to the Library; the resulting flood of books, maps, newspapers, prints, printed music, and photographs led Spofford to suggest construction of a separate building for the Library in his 1871 annual report. In his 1872 report he presented a detailed plan for such a structure. Three years later he reported that the Library not only had exhausted all existing shelf space, but also that "books are now, from sheer force of necessity, being piled on the floor in all directions."

Spofford's struggle for a new building continued until 1886 when, with congressional support, the first Library of Congress building finally was authorized. When it opened to the public on November 1, 1897, the Library of Congress—established, destroyed, rebuilt, and developed during its 97 years in the US Capitol—entered a new era.

JAMES MADISON,
4TH PRESIDENT OF THE UNITED STATES.

PHILADELPHIA.
Published by C. S. WILLIAMS, N.E. corner of Market & 7th St.

1806

JANUARY 2 - Joint Library Committee Chairman Samuel Latham Mitchell urges the expansion of the Library: "Every week of the session causes additional regret that the volumes of literature and science within the reach of the national legislature are not more rich and ample."

MARCH 31 - Joint Library Committee member John Quincy Adams notes in his diary that most of the Library's acquisitions funds will be spent during the recess by himself, Chairman Mitchell, and member Henry Clay "in collecting books in Boston, New York and Philadelphia, as the occasion may offer."

1807

APRIL 8 - John J. Beckley, clerk of the House of Representatives and Librarian of Congress, dies.

NOVEMBER 7 - President Jefferson appoints Patrick Magruder, a Washington newspaperman who was made clerk of the House of Representatives on October 26, 1807, to the concurrent post of Librarian of Congress.

1811

DECEMBER 6 - President James Madison approves an act of Congress that renews the annual Library appropriation of $1,000 for a period of five years.

1812

The first classified catalog is issued, listing 3,076 volumes in 18 classes, subarranged by size, and 53 maps, charts, and plans.

MARCH 2 - President Madison approves a joint resolution of Congress that authorizes the judges of the Supreme Court to use the Library's books.

1813

APRIL 27 - American forces capture York (Toronto), the capital of Upper Canada, and burn the parliamentary building, including the small library of the Legislative Assembly.

President James Madison approved the purchase of Jefferson's personal library to restore the Library of Congress after the British burned it in 1814.

The British burned the US Capitol, seen here in its ruined state, on August 24, 1814.

"Every week of the session causes additional regret that the volumes of literature and science within the reach of the national legislature are not more rich and ample."

— Congressman Samuel Latham Mitchell, 1806

1814

AUGUST 24 - After capturing Washington, the British burn the Capitol, destroying the Library of Congress.

SEPTEMBER 21 - In retirement at his Virginia estate, Monticello, Thomas Jefferson offers to sell his comprehensive personal library to the Joint Library Committee in order to restore the congressional library.

NOVEMBER - Georgetown bookseller and binder Joseph Milligan provides the Joint Library Committee with an evaluation of Jefferson's books: the price of the 6,487 volumes is $23,950.

DECEMBER 3 - The Senate approves a bill to purchase Jefferson's personal library.

1815

JANUARY 26 - By a vote of 71 to 61, the House of Representatives approves the purchase of Jefferson's personal library.

JANUARY 28 - Patrick Magruder resigns his position as clerk of the House and, by inference, the position of Librarian of Congress.

The modern reconstruction of Jefferson's 1815 library is on exhibit in the southeast pavilion of the Library's Thomas Jefferson Building. The reassembly of the approximately 6,500 volumes is arranged according to Jefferson's classification scheme. In Thomas Jefferson's day, most libraries were arranged alphabetically, but Jefferson preferred to arrange his by subject. His books were organized as Memory (History), Reason (Philosophy), and Imagination (Fine Arts) and then filed into subcategories. This system was used at the Library until 1898.

Dear Sir   Monticello May 8. 15.

Our 10th and last waggon load of books goes off to-day
this closes the transaction here, and I cannot permit it to close
without returning my thanks to you who began it. this I sincerely
do for the trouble you have taken in it. when I first proposed
to you to make the overture to the library committee, I thought that
the only trouble you would have had, that they would have
said yea, or nay directly, have appointed valuers, and spared
you all further intermediation: and I saw with great regret this
agency afterwards added to the heavy labors of your office.
it is done however, and an interesting treasure is added to your
city, now become the depository of unquestionably the choicest collec-
-tion of books in the US. and I hope it will not be without some
general effect on the literature of our country.

When will the age of wonders cease in France? the first revolu-
-tion was a wonder. the restitution of the Bourbons a wonder. the
re-enthronement of Bonaparte as great as any. joy seems to have
been manifested with us on this event; inspired I suppose by the
pleasure of seeing the scourge again brandished over the back of
England. but it's effect on us may be doubted. we stood on good
ground before, but now on doubtful. the change cannot improve
our situation, & may make it worse. if they have a general war
we may be involved in it; if peace, we shall have the hostile and
ignorant caprices, of Bonaparte to regulate our commerce with that country, in-
-stead of it's anient and regular course. but these considerations
are for the young; I am done with them. present me affectionately
to mrs Smith, with my wishes that you could make a visit to Monti-
-cello a respite to your labors, and the asseverances of my friendship & respect
                                    Th. Jefferson

mr. Saml. H. Smith.

JANUARY 30 - President Madison approves an act of Congress appropriating $23,950 for the acquisition of Jefferson's library.

MARCH 21 - President Madison appoints George Watterston, a local novelist and journalist, as the new Librarian of Congress, the first Librarian who does not also serve as clerk of the House of Representatives. The Library occupies temporary quarters on the third floor of Blodgett's Hotel at Seventh and E Streets NW.

NOVEMBER - The Library adopts the classification devised by Thomas Jefferson for his library, a modified version of the organization of knowledge created by British philosopher Francis Bacon. The new *Catalogue of the Library of the United States: To Which is Annexed, a Copious Index, Alphabetically Arranged*, prepared by Librarian Watterston, is based on Jefferson's catalog of his library.

1816

APRIL 16 - President Madison approves an act that raises the annual salary of the Librarian of Congress to $1,000, retroactive to March 21, 1815, and extends the use of the Library to the US attorney general and to members of the diplomatic corps.

On May 8, 1815, Thomas Jefferson wrote to Samuel H. Smith, the friend who helped arrange the Library's purchase of his collection, to say that the "10th and last waggon load" of books for the library had been packed. Now that his volumes were on their way to Washington, he told Smith, "an interesting treasure is added to your city, now become the depository of unquestionably the choicest collection of books in the US, and I hope it will not be without some general effect on the literature of our country."

1817

FEBRUARY 18 - Unhappy with the Library's temporary quarters, Joint Library Committee Chairman Senator Eligius Fromentin from Louisiana advocates a separate building for the Library "on Delaware Avenue, north of the Capitol." On February 22, Senator Fromentin's resolution is defeated. In a letter of March 25 to the *National Intelligencer*, under the heading "National Library" and signed "W," Librarian Watterston regrets the failure of Fromentin's "proposal to erect a building for the reception of the Library of the United States."

1818

DECEMBER - The move of the Library from Blodgett's Hotel back into the Capitol is completed.

1822

APRIL 30 - Representative Enoch Lincoln of Maine introduces a resolution that would require the deposit of all government manuscripts in the Library. The resolution is tabled.

1824

MAY 26 - President James Monroe approves an act of Congress that increases the Library's annual book appropriation to $5,000.

AUGUST 17 - The Library is moved from the north wing into a spacious new room in the center of the west front of the Capitol designed by Architect of the Capitol Charles Bulfinch.

1825

DECEMBER 22 - A fire, started by a candle left burning in the gallery, is controlled before it can do serious damage to the Library's 14,000-volume collection.

1827

FEBRUARY 24 - Library Committee Chairman Everett reports a resolution urging that "proper measures be adopted, at the discretion of the President, to procure from the public offices in England copies of documents illustrative of the history of America." The resolution fails.

1828

MAY 24 - President John Quincy Adams approves an act of Congress that authorizes the Librarian of Congress to employ an assistant at an annual salary of $800.

1829

MAY 28 - Newly elected President Andrew Jackson, a Democrat, replaces Librarian of Congress George Watterston, a Whig, with John Silva Meehan. Meehan is a local printer and publisher and, of course, a Democrat.

1830

JANUARY 13 - President Jackson approves a joint resolution that grants the use of the books in the Library to the secretary of state, the secretary of the treasury, the secretary of war, the secretary of the navy, the postmaster general, the secretary of the Senate, the clerk of the House of Representatives, the chaplains of Congress, and "ex-Presidents (when in the District of Columbia)."

MAY 21 - Obadiah Rich, 12 Red Lion Square, London, is designated to purchase the English books on a list prepared by the Joint Library Committee, along with "valuable books not contained in the Library nor in said list, to an amount not exceeding £100 sterling."

1831

MARCH 1 - The Joint Library Committee agrees "that each member of the committee is authorized, during the recess, to make purchases for the Library on his own selection and judgment to any amount not exceeding $50."

1832

MARCH 31 - The Joint Library Committee instructs Librarian of Congress Meehan to "strictly enforce" the rule that all visitors to the Library should be introduced by a member of Congress.

JUNE 23 - Librarian Meehan is authorized "to visit the public libraries at Baltimore, New York, West Point, and Boston to instruct himself in their modes of managing libraries for preservation, exhibition, use, etc."

JULY 14 - President Jackson approves an act of Congress "to increase and improve" the Library's law department, including creation of a separate "apartment" for the law collection.

1836

MARCH 15 – The Joint Library Committee recommends the purchase of the 25,000-volume library of the "late Count Bourtoulin" of Florence, a noted collection of early Italian, Greek, and Latin works. Joint Library Committee Chairman William Preston of South Carolina strongly urges its purchase, citing Jefferson's very wide and pointed statement that there was "no subject to which a member of Congress may not have occasion to refer." On June 4, by a vote of 17 to 16, the Senate rejects the purchase of the Bourtoulin collection, continuing to see the Library primarily as a tool for legislative activities. On the motion of Senator Henry Clay, who voted with the majority, it is "laid on the table."

1837

JANUARY 10 – The Joint Library Committee authorizes the first exchange of official publications with foreign nations. Three years later, President Martin Van Buren approves a joint congressional resolution that authorizes the exchange of duplicate documents and books for their equivalents in foreign countries.

1842

MARCH 11 – Joint Library Committee Chairman William Preston asks historian George Bancroft to recommend book purchases for the Library because "we have a very scant bibliographical store of knowledge on the committee."

Senator Rufus Choate, chairman of the Joint Library Committee, argued in favor of establishing the projected Smithsonian Institution, not the Library of Congress, as the national library.

By 1834, the date of this view of the US Capitol, the Library was located in the center of the west front, overlooking the National Mall.

The Capitol, seen in a
painting from ca. 1846–55 by
Augustus Köllner, dominated
the still rural capital city.

President James
Polk signed a bill in
1846 creating the
Smithsonian Institution.

1843

JANUARY 20 - President John Tyler approves an act of Congress authorizing
the distribution of the Library's printed catalog "to each of the colleges and
universities of the United States that
has not already been furnished with
the same and to each person entitled
to the use of the Library."

1844

JUNE 7 - The Joint Library Committee
rejects the proposed purchase of the
10,000-volume library of the Durazzo
family of Genoa, one of the choicest
private libraries in Europe. Senator
George P. Marsh of Vermont explains
that although "it would be a highly de-
sirable acquisition to a well-endowed
literary institution, it is not suited to
the purposes of Congress."

1845

JANUARY 8 - Senator Rufus Choate,
chairman of the Joint Library Committee, argues in favor of establishing
the projected Smithsonian Institution
as the national library since the small
appropriation allowed the Library
of Congress could never enable it "to
fulfill the functions of a truly great
and general public library of science,
literature, and art."

1846

AUGUST 10 - President James Polk approves an act of Congress that establishes the Smithsonian Institution "for
the increase and diffusion of knowledge among men." Funding is provided
for the gradual formation of a library
"composed of valuable works pertaining to all departments of human
knowledge." One section of the act authorizes the Library of Congress, along
with the Smithsonian, to receive as a
deposit one copy of every copyrighted
"book, map, chart, musical composition, print, cut, or engraving."

American physicist Joseph Henry became the first secretary of the Smithsonian Institution in 1846. He felt the Smithsonian bequest should be used to promote science and opposed the national library idea proposed by members of Congress.

On December 29, 1851, five days after the disastrous fire in the Capitol, Librarian of Congress John Silva Meehan reported to Joint Library Committee Chair Pearce that the Library's copy of Audubon's *Birds of America*, containing this *Hooping Crane*, was "saved and uninjured."

1848

JUNE 26   President Polk approves an act authorizing the Joint Library Committee to establish exchange agencies for participation in a large-scale system for the exchange of public documents. On July 25, the committee appoints Alexandre Vattemare to be its agent in this new international exchange system, which will have its headquarters in Paris.

AUGUST 12 - President Polk approves an act that authorizes the Joint Library Committee to "print and publish" the papers and manuscripts of Thomas Jefferson and Alexander Hamilton.

1849

MAY 8 - Testifying in London before a House of Commons committee seeking information about public libraries in the United States and other countries, American book dealer Henry Stevens assures the committee that the Library of Congress "is free to all the world," that any "stranger" or "native of the United States of any class" may walk right in.

1851

DECEMBER 24 - A fire in the Library of Congress destroys approximately 35,000 of the Library's 55,000 volumes, including nearly two-thirds of Jefferson's library. The next day, after changing the document's wording from "the National Library" to "the Library of Congress," the House of Representatives approves a joint resolution authorizing an investigation.

INTERIOR VIEW,
LIBRARY OF CONGRESS

Architect of the Capitol
Thomas U. Walter
successfully proposed and
designed an elegant new
fireproof expansion of the
Library on the west front of
the Capitol following the fire
in 1851. Widely admired as
"the largest room made of
iron in the world," it opened
on August 23, 1853.

1852

JANUARY 27 - Architect of the Capitol
Thomas U. Walter presents a plan for
the repair and enlargement of the
Library. The cost for the new, fireproof
room, which will "embrace the entire
western projection" of the Capitol is
estimated to be $72,500. In August,
President Franklin Pierce approves
an appropriation of $72,000 for the
purchase of books and furniture. The
same measure repeals the Foreign Exchange Act of June 26, 1848. Late in the
year, Architect Walter reports that his
construction estimate was too low and
a deficiency appropriation of $20,500
is necessary.

AUGUST 20 - In his 1851 annual report,
Joseph Henry, the secretary of the
Smithsonian Institution, warns that
the limited income of the Smithsonian
fund can never support a library "suf-
ficient to meet the needs of the American scholar." Instead, he looks to the
Library of Congress—once it has been
restored after the recent fire—as the
appropriate foundation "for a collection of books worthy of a Government
whose perpetuity principally depends
upon the intelligence of the people."

1853

JUNE 15 - Librarian Meehan explains to Alexandre Vattemare that
Congress rescinded the law of 1848,
which appointed Vattemare the
Library's international exchange
agent, due to his poor performance.

Charles Coffin Jewett was the foremost American librarian in his day and a vigorous proponent of the Smithsonian as the national library. He was the assistant secretary and librarian of the Smithsonian Institution from 1847 until 1854, when Secretary Henry dismissed him.

The conservative Senator James A. Pearce of Maryland served as chairman of the Joint Library Committee from 1846 until his death in 1862. Throughout his committee chairmanship the Library of Congress stringently focused on its legislative role.

1854

MAY 20 – A special committee of the Smithsonian Board of Regents decides that the Smithsonian Institution should not spend its funds on the accumulation of a great library. In July the board itself affirmed the power of Secretary Henry "to remove" his assistants, and on July 10, Henry dismisses Smithsonian Librarian Charles Coffin Jewett, the chief advocate of a large national library.

1857

JANUARY 18 – The Library loses two national functions when President Pierce approves a joint resolution that transfers responsibility for the international exchange of books and documents and for the distribution of public documents, until then functions of the Library of Congress, to the Departments of State and the Interior, respectively.

1859

FEBRUARY 5 – President James Buchanan approves an act of Congress that repeals the copyright provision of the act of Congress of August 10, 1846. The Smithsonian Institution and the Library of Congress no longer receive copyright deposits.

1861

MARCH 8 – Senator James A. Pearce of Maryland, chairman of the Joint Library Committee, informs newly elected President Abraham Lincoln that the president "has always deferred to the wishes of Congress regarding the appointment of a Librarian of Congress and that the present committee wished to retain Librarian Meehan." Lincoln ignores Pearce, and on May 24, appoints a physician and political supporter, John G. Stephenson from Terre Haute, Indiana, to become the fifth Librarian of Congress.

SEPTEMBER – After dismissing Assistant Librarian Edward B. Stelle, Librarian Stephenson hires Ainsworth Rand Spofford, a Cincinnati newspaperman and former bookseller, to be the new assistant. The Library has six employees.

1862

JANUARY 31 – Assistant Librarian Spofford tells his friend, visitor Ralph Waldo Emerson, that the institution's modern literature collections are "very imperfect" because the Library has "been under Southern domination and as under dead men."

1863

MAY–JULY – Leaving the Library in the hands of Assistant Librarian Spofford, Librarian of Congress Stephenson serves as a volunteer aide-de-camp at the battles of Chancellorsville and Gettysburg during the Civil War.

NOVEMBER – In an almanac article, Assistant Librarian Spofford asserts: "The United States will never possess a public library which can be called national, until Congress shall take a more liberal view of the value and importance of such a collection."

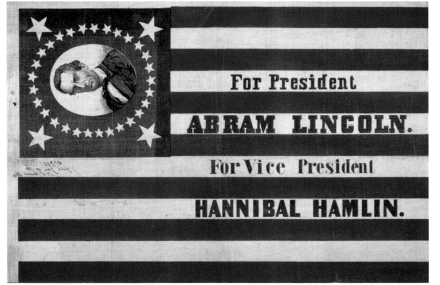

Abraham Lincoln, elected in 1861, appointed John G. Stephenson to be fifth Librarian of Congress. On the last day of 1864, Lincoln appointed Ainsworth Rand Spofford as Stephenson's successor.

1864

OCTOBER 22 - In justifying a budget request for the expansion of the Library, Spofford informs the secretary of the treasury that "the sum of $160,000, although large in itself, is not so in comparison with the great object of providing safe and permanent room for this rich historical collection."

DECEMBER 22 - Librarian of Congress Stephenson submits his resignation, effective December 31, 1864. The same day, Assistant Librarian Spofford forwards to President Lincoln eight letters and a petition signed by members of Congress endorsing his application for Librarian, explaining that thus far 22 senators and 87 representatives have provided such endorsements.

DECEMBER 31 - President Lincoln appoints Ainsworth Rand Spofford to be the sixth Librarian of Congress. The Library has a staff of seven, including assistant librarians, laborers, and a messenger. It now has an annual appropriation of approximately $20,000.

1865

MARCH 2 - President Lincoln approves the $160,000 appropriation for the expansion of the Library's room. Two new fireproof wings are to be added. The next day, as recommended by Spofford, the copyright law is changed to once again require the deposit of copyrighted materials in the Library of Congress; one printed copy of every copyrighted "book, pamphlet, map, chart, musical composition, print, engraving, or photograph" must be sent to the Library for its use.

1866

APRIL 5 - President Andrew Johnson approves an act of Congress that transfers to the Library the 40,000-volume library of the Smithsonian Institution, based on a joint recommendation of Secretary Henry and Librarian Spofford. The Smithsonian retains the use of the collection, which the general public can also "consult." This "Smithsonian Deposit" is especially strong in science and in publications of learned societies, including those of both public and private scholarly organizations. It fully occupies one of the Library's new fireproof wings.

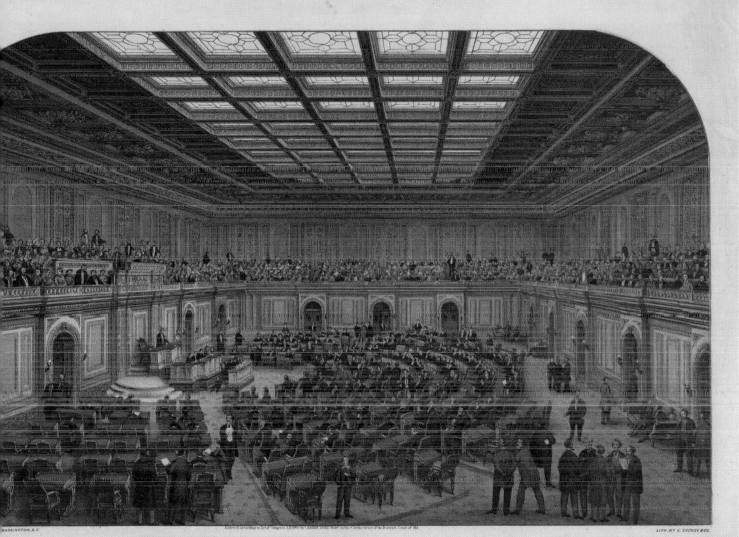

THE HOUSE OF REPRESENTATIVES, U.S. CAPITOL
WASHINGTON, D.C.

This lithograph by E. Sachse & Co. shows the House of Representatives as it looked in 1866, when it was a neighbor to the Library of Congress in the US Capitol.

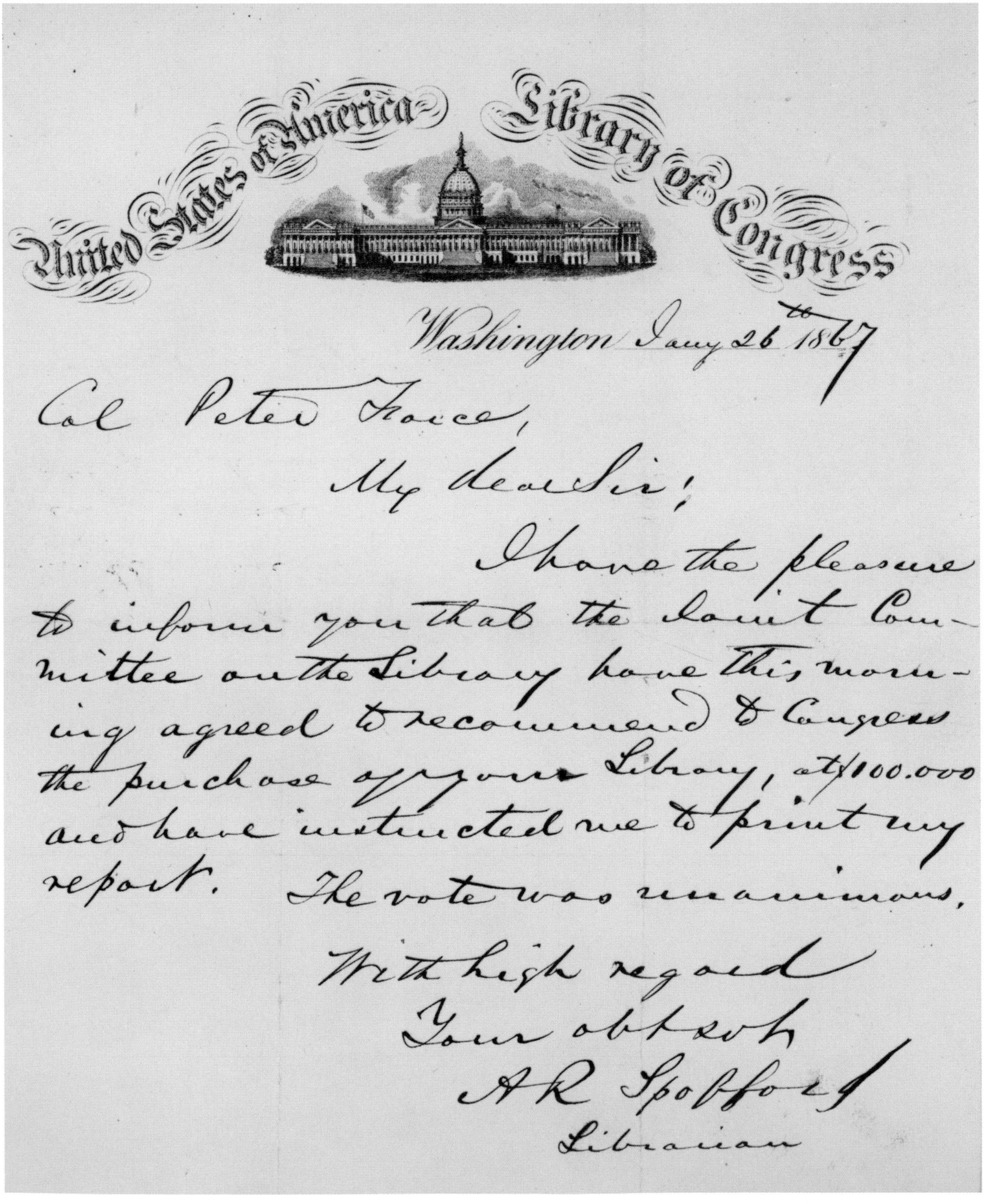

United States of America Library of Congress

Washington Iany 26th 1867

Col Peter Force,

My dear Sir;

I have the pleasure to inform you that the Joint Committee on the Library have this morning agreed to recommend to Congress the purchase of your Library, at $100.000 and have instructed me to print my report. The vote was unanimous.

With high regard

Your obt svt

A R Spofford

Librarian

Collector Peter Force, pictured above, received an official letter in 1867 (opposite page) from Librarian A.R. Spofford confirming the Library's purchase of his collection, which included valuable items from the Revolutionary War period, such as rare pamphlets and broadsides.

The interior of the Library of Congress in the Capitol building, ca. 1866. The orderly Library was poised to receive a flood of copyright submissions, which would fill it to capacity, starting in 1871.

1867

FEBRUARY 18 – Spofford obtains Joint Library Committee approval for an exchange of government documents with foreign governments through a system already established by the Smithsonian Institution: the works obtained in exchange will come to the Library of Congress. By December 1, positive responses have been received from Great Britain, Russia, Denmark, Belgium, the Netherlands, Greece, Switzerland, Chile, and Costa Rica.

MARCH 2 – President Johnson approves an act of Congress that appropriates $100,000 for the purchase of the library and archives of collector Peter Force, considered by Librarian Spofford to be "the largest and best collection of the sources of American history yet brought together in this country." The foundation of the Library's Americana and incunabula collections, it fills the second new fireproof wing.

More than any other individual, Ainsworth Rand Spofford was responsible for transforming the Library of Congress from a legislative library into an institution of national significance. He served as Assistant Librarian from 1861 to 1864, as Librarian of Congress from 1864 to 1897, and as Chief Assistant Librarian of Congress from 1897 until his death in 1908.

1869

JUNE - The emperor of China sends a gift of ten works, consisting of 934 volumes, to the US government, a donation that eventually forms the nucleus of the Library's Chinese collection.

NOVEMBER - In his 1869 annual report, Boston Public Library superintendent Justin Winsor states that his recently completed survey has determined that the Library of Congress, with a collection of 175,000 volumes, has become the largest library in the United States.

1870

APRIL 9 - In a lengthy letter to Representative Thomas A. Jenckes of Rhode Island, chairman of the Committee on Patents, Spofford outlines "some leading reasons why the transfer of the whole copyright business and books to the care of the Library of Congress would promote the public interest." He argues that "we should have one comprehensive library in the country, and that belonging to the nation, whose aim should be to preserve the books which other libraries have not the room nor the means to procure."

MAY 20 - Educator Francis Lieber donates three books to the Library. He inscribes them "To the National Library" and explains to Spofford: "It is not the official name, but I take the liberty. It is the name you have come to. Library of Congress was good enough in Jeffersonian times, but it is not now after the war and for the current age."

JULY 8 - President Ulysses S. Grant approves an act of Congress that centralizes all US copyright registration and copyright activities at the Library of Congress. The Library will receive, for its collections, two copies of all copyrighted items. On December 1, Spofford informs Congress that the "increased receipts will soon compel the provision of room for more books." As one alternative, he suggests a new and separate building to house the Library.

Strong support from two of the Senate's most powerful members, Justin S. Morrill of Vermont (left) and Daniel W. Voorhees of Indiana (right), was essential to the success of Librarian Spofford's 15-year struggle to obtain authorization for the Library's first building.

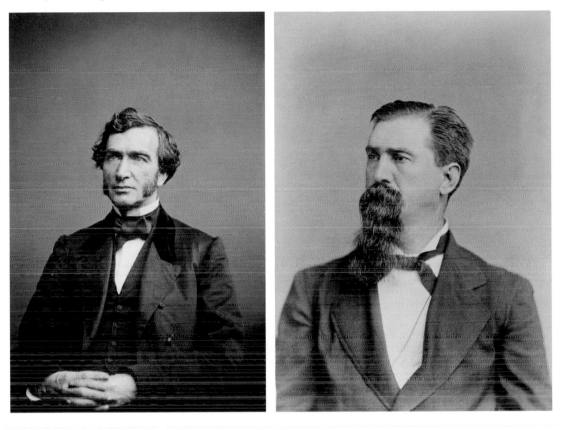

1872

FEBRUARY 14 - In response to a request from John Shaw Billings, librarian of the Surgeon General's Library, Spofford begins transferring copyright deposits in medical subjects to the Surgeon General's Library.

DECEMBER 2 - Spofford points out that severe overcrowding has made the Library "comparatively an unfit place for students." Furthermore, he estimates, "without calculating upon specially large accessions," that the Library will contain 2,500,000 volumes by the year 1975. Now convinced of "the absolute necessity of erecting a separate building for the Library and the copyright department conjoined," he presents an "outline of a plan for such an edifice."

1873

MARCH - For the sum of $1,000, the Library purchases from Andrew Boyd of Albany, New York, a collection of nearly 1,500 books and pamphlets relating to the life and work of Abraham Lincoln.

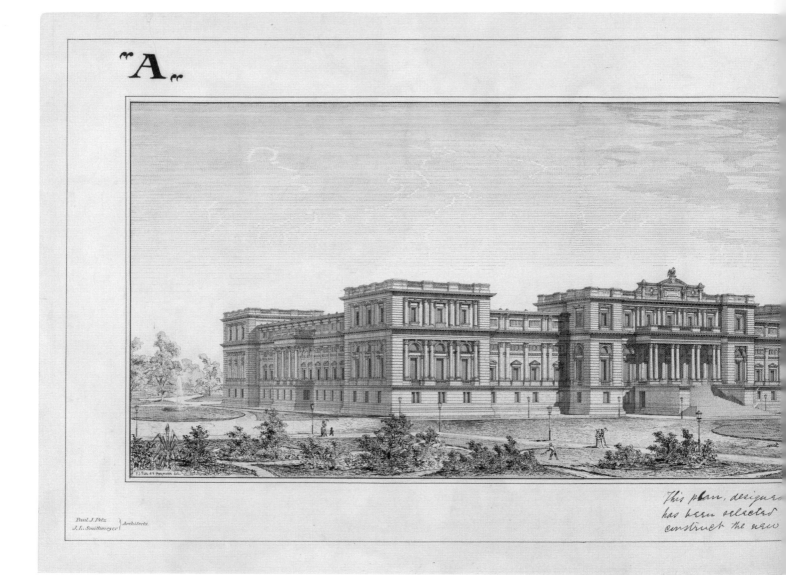

"A"

Paul J. Pelz
J.L. Smithmeyer } Architects.

This plan, designed
has been selected
construct the new

The Washington, DC, architectural firm
of Smithmeyer & Pelz won the 1873
Congress-authorized competition with
this Italian Renaissance design for a
new Library building.

MARCH - President Grant approves an appropriation of $5,000 for a commission that will select a plan and "supervise the location and erection of a building" for the Library of Congress. The same act authorizes a competition to design plans for the structure. Spofford provides general specifications for the building and in December a winner is announced: Smithmeyer & Pelz of Washington, DC, for its Italian Renaissance design. However, Congress, seeking a wider range of plans and possible locations, nullifies the results and reopens the competition in 1874. Various plans and locations are considered until the building is finally authorized in 1886.

1874

MAY 6 - The Joint Library Committee authorizes the Librarian to subscribe to two newspapers from each state. The newspapers are to reflect differing political views.

JUNE 18 - President Grant approves an amendment to the copyright law transferring responsibility for prints and labels for articles of manufacture to the Patent Office.

1875

NOVEMBER - The Japanese government accepts the Smithsonian Institution's proposal for the exchange of documents, which marks the beginning of the Library's Japanese collection.

1876

JANUARY 1 - Spofford reports to Congress that the Library has exhausted all shelf space. In the same annual report, he urges Congress to authorize the Library to employ "a competent historical scholar" since "every manuscript or written paper in the Library which can throw any light on any portion of American history should be systematically arranged and indexed."

Ohio Congressman James Garfield relied heavily on Spofford, noting in his diary on June 25, 1873, "Every day I miss Spofford and our great Library of Congress."

COMES THE FLOOD: THE LIBRARY AND COPYRIGHT DEPOSIT

Books and pamphlets dominated the initial flood of copyright deposits triggered by the 1870 law, but maps, music, prints, engravings, and photographs were included and increasingly important. As demonstrated in this photograph, throughout the twentieth century, both the kinds of items eligible for copyright protection and the creativity of those producing such items surged.

The US copyright system became a primary source of acquisitions for the Library of Congress in 1870, when Librarian Ainsworth Rand Spofford successfully advocated for the Library to be the center for copyright registration and deposit. The concept of copyright deposit for library use was fundamental to Spofford's argument that the Library of Congress not only served Congress, but was also the national library of the United States. Moreover, it was the most practical method of acquiring a comprehensive collection of American publications. In fact, it started a deluge that continues to this day.

The US Constitution gave Congress the power "to promote the Progress of Science and useful Arts by securing for limited times to Authors and Inventors the exclusive Right to their respective Writings and Discoveries." Congress enacted the first federal copyright law in May 1790, specifying that the US Courts handle copyright registration. The first work was registered within two weeks: John Barry's *The Philadelphia Spelling Book*, in the US District of Court of Pennsylvania. Barry received copyright protection, or the right to print, reprint, publish, or vend his work, for a term of 14 years, renewable for another 14. The original copyright act also required a single copy of each registered work to be delivered within six months to the US Secretary of State.

When the Smithsonian Institution was established in 1846, Congress included a copyright deposit provision authorizing the Smithsonian and the

Library of Congress each to receive a copy of every work copyrighted for use. However, the law did not provide for enforcement, and the lack of compliance eventually led Spofford, who became Librarian in 1864, to seek new and stronger legislation that would transfer all copyright business solely to the Library.

On April 9, 1870, he wrote a persuasive 1,600-word letter to Representative Thomas A. Jenckes of Rhode Island, the chairman of the Patent Committee, outlining "some leading reasons why the transfer of the entire copyright business and books to the Library of Congress would promote the public interest." Jenckes agreed, so did Congress, and President Ulysses S. Grant approved the act on July 8, 1870. The new law centralized both the registration and deposit of two copies of each work—one copy for legal record

and one for library use. The Librarian of Congress was named as the responsible official—in effect, the first register of copyright. The US law is unusual; similar statutes in other nations do not combine copyright protection with registration and deposit.

Spofford's success unleashed a flood of material. For the next 26 years, the relatively small Library staff was increasingly preoccupied with copyright matters. In 1874, for the first time, the copyright law brought in more books than were obtained that year through purchase; by 1880 the number of deposits had doubled. Storage space throughout the Capitol was found as Spofford continued to plead with Congress for authorization for a separate Library building. Construction of the building did not begin until 1888, and by 1896, the year before it was

occupied, the administration of the copyright law required more than three-fourths of Spofford's time and the undivided attention of 26 of the Library's 42 employees.

In spite of the overcrowded conditions in the Library, Spofford always placed great value on the comprehensiveness of the collections brought in by copyright, strongly believing that "what is pronounced trash today may have unexpected value hereafter, and the unconsidered trifles of the press of the nineteenth century may prove highly curious and interesting to the twentieth." He never ceased defending the Library against charges that it was filling up with "trash" brought in by the wide net of the law, asserting that "every nation should have, at its capital city, all the books that its authors have

43

produced, in perpetual evidence of its literary history and progress—or retrogression, as the case may be." He carefully ensured the complete representation in the Library of all editions of works from authors well known in his day, frequently querying established writers directly concerning the dates of new or revised editions of their works.

In 1897, when the Library finally moved from its crowded rooms in the Capitol into its spacious new building, nearly 40 percent of the approximately 800,000 items in the collection had been acquired through copyright. With the move came a long-awaited administrative reorganization. Separate map, music, graphic arts, and copyright departments were established. Thorvald Solberg, who had worked at the Library from 1876 to 1889 and was by then a nationally known copyright authority, was appointed the first official Register of Copyrights. The creation of a separate copyright department in the Library of Congress officially recognized, for the first time, the value of the copyright function to the national library.

Through the years, because of the widening diversity of formats in materials eligible for copyright, the deposit provision has turned out to be more important than Spofford could have ever imagined. Maps, music, prints, engravings, and photographs were included in the 1865 and 1870 laws. Subsequent changes of copyright laws and regulations have included motion pictures (1912); choreography, in the form of dance motion (1952), which stimulated the deposit of television scripts; sound recordings (1972); computer programs (1980); architectural works (1990); works in CD-ROM format; and electronic works published in the United States and available online only (2010).

JUNE 8 - The Joint Library Committee, chaired by Senator Timothy Howe of Wisconsin, reports that the congressional failure to provide "additional accommodations for the National Library" is "absurd . . . almost insane, if not wicked." The committee recommends a Library building on the grounds of the Botanic Garden, at the foot of Capitol Hill.

1877

DECEMBER 3 - In his first annual message, President Rutherford B. Hayes recommends that Congress approve construction of a fireproof Library building since "the question of providing for the preservation and growth of the Library of Congress is . . . one of national importance."

1878

JANUARY 2 - Librarian Spofford is politely indignant regarding the congressional delay, asserting that unless there is action soon, "Congress will hardly be held to have discharged the trust reposed in it as the custodian of what President Jefferson called with prophetic wisdom the Library of the United States."

1879

MARCH 31 - Senator Justin S. Morrill of Vermont strongly supports a separate library building east of the Capitol and Spofford's national library concept in his speech, "The Library of Congress, the Capitol and its Grounds," asserting that "the higher education of our common country demands that this institution shall not be crippled for lack of room."

OCTOBER 22 - The Library purchases more than 2,500 Chinese and Manchu works assembled by Caleb Cushing, the first American minister to China.

As American Minister to China, Caleb Cushing negotiated the Treaty of Wanghia (1844), the first bilateral agreement between the United States and China. This *View of Green Island, Macau*, 1844, from the Library's Caleb Cushing Collection, is by George West, the official artist attached to Cushing's delegation.

PUCKOGRAPHS—NEW SERIES, NO. I.

"MARK TWAIN,"
America's Best Humorist.

On March 11, 1880, Samuel L. Clemens, a.k.a. Mark Twain, pictured here in an 1885 lithograph in *Punch* magazine, told Spofford that he was sending his nephew "to burrow a little" in Spofford's "grand literary warehouse."

1880

MAY 5 - Concluding a lengthy speech in which he strongly urges a new Library building, Senator Daniel W. Voorhees of Indiana declares: "Let us therefore give this great national library our love and our care. Nothing can surpass it in importance."

SEPTEMBER 25 - The Joint Select Committee on Additional Accommodations for the Library, consisting of three architects, rejects the idea of enlarging the Capitol to accommodate the Library. As requested, each submits a separate design of a new building for consideration.

1881

DECEMBER 6 - In his first annual message, President Chester A. Arthur urges approval of a new Library building.

1882

MAY 19 - President Arthur approves a joint resolution of Congress that authorizes the Library to accept a sizable gift of medical books, early imprints, and personal papers from the medical research library of Dr. Joseph Meredith Toner, described by Joint Library Committee member Senator John Sherman of Ohio as the "first instance in the history of this government of the free gift of a large and valuable library to the nation."

OCTOBER - The Joint Select Committee on Additional Accommodations sends architect John L. Smithmeyer to Europe to examine the buildings of the British Museum and the "national libraries at Paris, Berlin, Munich, and Vienna, and the new library at Rome."

"Let us therefore give this great national library our love and our care. Nothing can surpass it in importance."

— Senator Daniel W. Voorhees, 1880

حكىنتاحنة هاذسك حذة فعوش

Intérieur de la Salle des Tuberculeuses
Hôpital des femmes Hasschi

1884

A gift of more than 400 volumes from the Sultan Abdul-Hamid II of Turkey establishes the nucleus of the Library's Turkish collection. Acquired through the efforts of Representative Abram S. Hewitt of New York, each volume has the same cover inscription in English, French, and Ottoman Turkish: "Gift made by H.I.M. the Sultan Abdul-Hamid to the national library of the United States of America through the Honorable A.S. Hewitt, Member of the House of Representatives in Washington A.H. 1302 – 1884 A.D."

FEBRUARY 7 – Senator Morrill, characterizing the Library as "the property of the nation, open to all the people without any ticket of admission," pleads for a new building, informing the Senate, "Our duty is obvious, and neglect cannot escape reproach."

This albumen print of the *Tuberculosis Ward of the Hasköy Hospital for Women,* taken between 1880 and 1893, is from the Abdul-Hamid II Collection.

Engineer Bernard Green was put in charge of the building's construction after the death of General Casey in 1896. Challenged by Librarian Spofford's insistence on rapid book service from the stack area, Green designed new steel bookstacks, nine floors high, which were serviced by the first efficient library pneumatic tube and conveyer system in America.

After Smithmeyer's dismissal as architect, Paul J. Pelz assumed the job. His ebullient rendering of the Library's new Great Hall is from 1888.

MAY 23 – The Joint Library Committee recommends the purchases, through the secretary of state, of copies of documents in European archives relating to the Paris Peace Treaty of 1783. The project of "obtaining copies of all documents in the European archives illustrative of the early history of the United States" will be carried out by B.F. Stevens, dispatch agent in London for the United States.

1885

DECEMBER 8 – In his first annual message, President Grover Cleveland asks Congress to take prompt action in providing a new Library building.

1886

APRIL 15 – President Cleveland approves the authorization of the construction of a new building for the Library, to be located directly across the east plaza from the Capitol. A building commission consisting of the secretary of the interior, the Architect of the Capitol, and the Librarian of Congress is placed in charge. The structure will be in the Italian Renaissance style, in accordance with a design prepared by the Washington architectural firm of Smithmeyer & Pelz. A sum of $5,000 is appropriated to begin construction.

1887

AUGUST – Work on the construction of the building stops while the cement for the foundation is tested.

1888

FEBRUARY 15 – The cement issue is resolved and work begins on laying the building's foundation.

MARCH – Engineer Bernard R. Green is named superintendent of construction.

JUNE 19 – In a House of Representatives debate about the new Library, Congressman Newton W. Nutting of New York advocates a monumental building; "The structure which emphasizes the value that we set upon the education of our people, upon the means which can put our people in a position to understand the principles upon which our Government is founded, ought to be our largest and best building." Representative Thomas Holman of Indiana protests: "The movement now on foot is the first attempt to create a national library in imitation of European monarchies." The House of Representatives halts work on the structure.

SEPTEMBER 12 - Architect of the Capitol Edward Clark testifies before a special House of Representatives Committee to Investigate Contracts for Construction of the New Library Building that architect Smithmeyer was responsible for the placement of the new Library's foundation and for the grading which "set the building on a mound." Clark personally would have preferred a plan prepared by landscape architect Frederick Law Olmsted, which provided for grading "in a manner corresponding" to the Capitol grounds.

OCTOBER 2 - The building commission is dissolved and Congress places Brigadier General Thomas Lincoln Casey, chief, US Army Corps of Engineers, in charge of construction, to be assisted by Bernard Green. The next day, architect Smithmeyer is dismissed and replaced by his former assistant, Paul J. Pelz.

1889

MARCH 2 - President Cleveland approves a Sundry Appropriations Act that provides for a new Library building costing approximately $6 million.

1890

AUGUST 28 - At 3 p.m. and without a formal ceremony, the cornerstone for the new building is laid. It is placed in the northeast corner. The construction pace quickens.

1891

FEBRUARY 28 - Spofford reports to Congress that "the great portion of the Library now unprovided with shelf room renders the embarrassment of producing books with promptitude extreme." He estimates that the Library now contains about 650,000 books and about 207,000 pamphlets.

On August 28, 1890, at 3 p.m., workers laid the cornerstone for the new building.

MARCH 3 – President Benjamin Harrison approves an amendment to the copyright law that affords protection to works of foreign origin under certain conditions and requires deposit of those works in the Library of Congress.

DECEMBER 3 – General Casey reports that the first story of the new building has been completed and that the walls of the courtyard stacks and the Main Reading Room have reached the second story. The iron stacks, devised by Green, have been installed.

1892

MAY 19 – Spofford asks the House of Representatives Committee on Appropriations for more positions to help "the necessities of public service in my office as register of copyrights." He points out that the Library has a maximum force of only "28 assistants, three of whom are employed in the law library, while the Boston Public Library, with half the number of books, has 89 assistants, and the British Museum Library, with twice as many books, but no copyright business, has 95 assistants."

JUNE 28 – The keystone is placed in the southwest clerestory arch of the new building's rotunda.

AUGUST 12 – President Harrison approves a joint resolution of Congress authorizing access to the "scientific and literary" collections of government institutions, including the Library of Congress, to higher education students in the District of Columbia.

The construction team installed the keystone at the apex of the new building's rotunda on June 28, 1892.

1893

JANUARY 31 – A "List of Books, Pamphlets, and Periodicals Relating to Banking and Finance in the United States," prepared by Spofford for Secretary of the Treasury Charles Foster, is published as part of a Senate document.

OCTOBER 28 – Spofford reports to Congress that any count of the books and other publications in the Library's collections is now impossible because the collections "are now scattered in sixteen separate halls and storage rooms in the Capitol."

THE BOOK PALACE OF THE AMERICAN PEOPLE

When its doors opened on November 1, 1897, the Thomas Jefferson Building was seen as an unparalleled national achievement: its 23-carat-gold-plated dome capped the "largest, costliest, and safest" library building in the world. Its elaborately decorated façade and interior, for which more than 40 American painters and sculptors produced commissioned works of art, were designed to show that the United States could surpass Europe in grandeur and devotion to classical culture. A contemporary guidebook boasted: "America is justly proud of this gorgeous and palatial monument to its National sympathy and appreciation of Literature, Science, and Art. It has been designed and executed solely by American art and American labor and is a fitting tribute for the great thoughts of generations past, present, and to be."

Situated directly across the east plaza from the Capitol, it was known as the Library of Congress (or Main) Building until June 13, 1980, when it was named for Thomas Jefferson, the Library's principal founder. The structure was built specifically to serve as the American national library, and its architecture and decoration express and enhance that ambitious purpose. The elaborate Entrance Pavilion and Great Hall lead to the inspiring Main Reading Room, where members of the public can take full advantage of the Library's vast, multimedia resources of knowledge and information. A national library for the United

The paintings in the four lunettes in the second floor northeast pavilion in the Jefferson Building illustrate the seals of eight departments of the US government. In this north lunette, the Department of Justice is featured on the left side of the circular tablet in the center, the Post Office Department on the right. The paintings are by William Brantley Van Ingen. The inscription on the circular tablet, chosen by Librarian Spofford, is from Thomas Jefferson: "Equal and exact justice to all men, of whatever state or persuasion, religious or political: peace, commerce, and honest friendship with all nations—entangling alliance with none."

This 1894 photograph shows men creating decorations for the new building in impromptu studios. The large eagle at the right of center and one of the two matching eagles at the left flank the marble tablet above the Great Hall's commemorative arch.

States was the dream and goal of Librarian of Congress Ainsworth Rand Spofford, and the new building was a crucial step in this direction.

The early years of planning and construction of the building were filled with delays and controversies. After two competitions and differing suggestions about design and location, in 1886 Congress finally chose a plan in the Italian Renaissance style submitted by Washington architects John L. Smithmeyer and Paul J. Pelz. The architects had followed a plan from Librarian Spofford, which was inspired by the British Museum Library's reading room: a circular, domed reading room at the center, surrounded by ample space for the Library's various collections and departments. In the final Smithmeyer & Pelz plan, the reading room was enclosed by rectangular exterior walls, which divided the open space into four courtyards. The corner pavilions were devoted to major departments and exhibits.

However, the disputes and inaction continued after the building was authorized. On August 8, 1887, Senator Justin Morrill of Vermont, one of Spofford's principal supporters, complained to Secretary of the Interior L.Q.C. Lamar, "I really had hoped to see the building completed in my lifetime, but I now fear that I shall never see it done." Responsibility for clearing the site was debated. Capitol landscape architect Frederick Law Olmsted protested in vain architect Smithmeyer's decision about the building's location, pointing out that it shut out the "whole view of the Capitol building from Pennsylvania Avenue—the main approach from Capitol Hill."

A controversy about the selection of the cement for the building's foundation proved to be Smithmeyer's undoing, and he was dismissed in 1888. On October 22, 1888, Congress placed the construction of the building under the direction of Brigadier General Thomas Lincoln Casey, chief of the US Army Corps of Engineers. Casey and his superintendent of construction, Bernard R. Green, had completed the construction of the State, War, and Navy Building (now the Old Executive Office Building) and the Washington Monument, and members of Congress trusted them and their work. The cornerstone was laid with no more ceremony than a photograph on August 28, 1890.

Paul J. Pelz, who had replaced Smithmeyer as architect, was also dismissed in March 1892 as construction neared completion. His successor as architect, named in December 1892, was Edward Pearce Casey, a 28-year-old engineer and architect who had worked at the architectural firm of McKim, Mead & White before graduating from the École des Beaux Arts in Paris. Casey, the son of General Casey, continued to live in New York, developing a private practice while supervising the interior design and decoration of the new Library building. General Casey died on March 25, 1896. On April 2, President Grover Cleveland approved a joint resolution of Congress "authorizing and directing" Bernard R. Green to assume General Casey's duties and powers "in relation to the construction and completion of the Library of Congress."

The Jefferson Building's striking and elaborate decoration, which combines sculpture, painting, and architecture on a scale unsurpassed in any American public building, was possible only because General Casey and Bernard Green lived up to their reputations as efficient construction engineers, completing the building for a sum less than that appropriated by Congress. When it became apparent in 1892 that funds might be available for "artistic enrichment," the two seized the opportunity and turned an already remarkable building into a cultural monument that indeed, as many hoped, would "out-Europe" Europe—with an American flair.

In reports to Congress in 1896 and 1897, Bernard Green stated that the cost of the mural and decorative painting, the interior sculpture, and the three massive bronze doors at the main entrance symbolizing Tradition, Writing, and Printing was $364,000. Even with the additional cost of the gilded dome, including the Torch of Learning at its apex, and the construction of the Court of Neptune Fountain in front, the total construction cost of the entire building was approximately $6,300,000—$200,000 less than the sum authorized for the structure.

This new national "Temple of the Arts" met with overwhelming approval from the American people. Especially grateful for the space it provided for the national collections he had been developing for more than three decades, Ainsworth Rand Spofford called it the "The Book Palace of the American People." The Jefferson Building also is an inspirational setting for a national institution that simultaneously celebrates learning and American optimism. Few structures represent human aspiration in such dramatic fashion.

The Edison Kinetoscopic Record of a Sneeze is one of a series of short films made by W.K.L. Dickson, an assistant to Thomas Edison. The "star" is Fred Ott, an Edison employee. Copyrighted in 1894, it is the earliest surviving copyrighted motion picture.

Edison Kinetoscopic Record of a Sneeze
Taken & Copyrighted by W.K.L.Dickson
Orange N.J. — Jan. 7th 94

DECEMBER 4 – General Casey reports to Congress on the completion of the new building's 195-foot-high dome, including the Torch of Learning at its apex, which has been coated with 23-carat-gold leaf.

1894

JANUARY 9 – As a copyright deposit, the Library acquires a paper print of Thomas Edison's *Kinetoscopic Record of a Sneeze*, January 7, 1894, the earliest motion picture in the Library's collections. Prior to 1912, films were deposited as photographs, in paper print form.

JANUARY 26 – General Casey and Superintendent of Construction Green meet with a committee from the National Sculpture Society, which includes John Q.A. Ward, Augustus Saint-Gaudens, and Olin L. Warner, to plan the sculpture in the interior of the new building.

JUNE – Librarian Spofford announces his choice of nine famous writers to be honored with granite busts across the west facade of the building (Dante, Demosthenes, Scott, Emerson, Hawthorne, Irving, Franklin, Goethe, and Maccauley) and their sculptors (Herbert Adams, J. Scott Hartley, and F. Wellington Ruckstuhl).

JULY 7 – The last stone in the superstructure is set in place.

AUGUST – The subjects of the eight symbolic statues inside the dome of the Main Reading Room and the two bronze portrait statues representing each subject are announced. All were chosen by Spofford. They are: Poetry, Homer and Shakespeare; Art, Michelangelo and Beethoven; Science, Newton and Henry; History, Herodotus and Gibbon; Philosophy, Plato and Bacon; Commerce, Columbus and Fulton; Religion, St. Paul and Moses; Law, Solon and Kent.

1895

MARCH 29 – Green and Spofford agree on the interior arrangement of the Main Reading Room.

A city's worth of builders and craftsmen employed their talents in the construction of America's new "Book Palace." Workers' sheds were erected outside.

Sculpted by J. Scott Hartley, this granite portrait bust of American writer Nathaniel Hawthorne is on the west portico of the new building, directly across First Street from the Capitol Building. Hawthorne was one of nine writers chosen by Librarian Spofford for this place of honor. Four other American writers are commemorated on the portico: Ralph Waldo Emerson, Washington Irving, and—in the center—Benjamin Franklin.

APRIL. 11, 1895.

DESIGN FOR MINERVA CONGRESSIONAL LIBRARY

APRIL - The painters who will decorate the building are chosen.

SEPTEMBER 13 - A workman is killed when he falls 70 feet from the scaffolding constructed in the Main Reading Room.

OCTOBER - Approximately 70 tons of unclassified copyright deposits are transferred from the southern crypt under the Capitol to the basement of the new Library building.

DECEMBER 2 - In a special report addressing the reorganization of the Library once it has moved into its own separate building, Spofford recommends the expansion of the institution into nine separate departments (called divisions after 1900): printed books, periodicals, manuscripts, maps and charts, works of art, cataloging, binding, copyright, and superintendence of the buildings and grounds. He feels the functions of the register of copyrights should be separated from those of Librarian of Congress and that the Law Library should remain in the Capitol "so long as the Supreme Court continues its sessions in the Capitol."

1896
MARCH 25 - General Casey dies.

APRIL 2 - President Grover Cleveland approves a joint resolution of Congress placing Bernard Green in charge of construction of the new Library building.

MELVIL DEWEY,
Secretary University State of New York and Director State Library.

In his 1896 testimony before Congress regarding the future national role of the Library, Melvil Dewey, the director of the New York State Library, emphasized the importance of the National Library in Washington as a "center to which the libraries of the whole nation can turn to for inspiration, guidance, and practical help." Another witness, Herbert Putnam, head of the Boston Public Library and a future Librarian of Congress (1899-1939), fully agreed.

APRIL 7 - Artist Edwin Howland Blashfield completes his mural *The Evolution of Civilization* in the collar and the lantern of the dome of the Main Reading Room.

MAY 28 - President Cleveland approves the Appropriations Act for fiscal year 1896, which includes funds for 30 "assistants" for the general library and 12 copyright clerks who will work "under the direction of the Librarian of Congress."

This marble mosaic of Minerva, protector of civilization, is by Elihu Vedder and dominates the staircase landing that leads to the Visitors' Gallery overlooking the Main Reading Room. Her armor partially laid aside, this Minerva of Peace is a vigilant guardian of all civilization.

NOVEMBER 16 – As authorized by a Senate resolution approved on May 5, the Joint Library Committee, chaired by Senator George Peabody Wetmore of Rhode Island, begins hearings about the "condition" of the Library on the eve of its move into the new building, focusing on its future organization and management. Librarian Spofford is the principal witness, testifying for four full days before the hearings conclude on December 7. Spofford expanded upon his reorganization plan of December 2, 1895, which provided for nine separate departments and his request of February 7 for 97 new positions—58 for the Library and the remainder for the proposed copyright department. The Joint Library Committee also invited and listened to advice from six prominent library directors, all members of the American Library Association.

DECEMBER 2 – Herbert Putnam, librarian of the Boston Public Library, states his view that the Library of Congress, as the national library, should stand "first and foremost as a model and example of assisting forward the work of scholarship in the United States." Supplementing his testimony the next day, he emphasizes that "an endeavor should now be made to introduce into the Library the mechanical aids which will render the Library more independent of the physical limitations of any one man or set of men."

DECEMBER 7 – Superintendent Green presents a detailed report to Congress about the construction of the building, pointing out that the structure "is a product of American talent and skill in architecture and art and practically so in workmanship." He includes a list of 22 sculptors and 20 artists, "all of whom are citizens of the United States," who furnished the special sculptures and mural paintings necessary "to fully and consistently carry out the monumental design and purpose of the building."

The Library was bursting at the seams before its move into the new building. An 1897 illustration, which appeared in *Harper's Weekly,* shows the Library of Congress when it was located in the US Capitol, with Librarian Ainsworth R. Spofford standing at the extreme right, looking at a paper. The man on the left holding a lamp is David Hutcheson, Assistant Librarian.

This detail is from *The Evolution of Civilization*, a large mural by Edwin Howland Blashfield in the collar of the Main Reading Room dome. Twelve figures represent countries, or epochs, which Blashfield felt contributed most to American civilization. On the left, the figure resembling Abraham Lincoln represents America, a nation associated with science. Egypt, on the right, represents the written record.

1897

JANUARY - An editorial in *Library Journal*, the official ALA organ, contends that "the future of the national library in its new home is really *the* library question of the year." An anonymous article, "A Congressional or a National Library?" concludes by calling on Congress to "renounce the right, now 96 years old, which it holds in the Library of Congress," and to constitute the institution as an executive establishment governed by a board of regents, "as the Smithsonian Institution is organized."

FEBRUARY - The new building is completed and ready for occupancy. Plans are made for the move into the structure as soon as Congress adjourns in early March.

FEBRUARY 19 - President Cleveland approves the reorganization and expansion of the Library as part of the Legislative, Executive, and Judicial Appropriations Act for fiscal year 1898, which will become effective on July 1, 1897. For the first time, the president's appointment of a Librarian of Congress must be approved by the Senate; the Librarian is given sole authority and responsibility for making "the rules and regulations for the government" of the Library, including the selection of the staff; and all appointments will be made "by reason of special aptitude for the work of the Library." The annual salary of the Librarian is established at

$5,000 and the size of the Library staff is increased from 42 to 108. Effective July 1, separate "departments" or offices are established for copyright, law, cataloging, periodicals, manuscripts, music, graphic arts, and maps and charts. Provision is made for a congressional reference library in the Capitol, and for reading room attendants in the Main Reading Room and in the separate reading rooms in the new building for the House of Representatives and the Senate. A separate position of register of copyrights is created; the register will serve under the "direction and supervision" of the Librarian. The superintendent of building and grounds, a presidential appointment with an annual salary of $5,000, is authorized to hire a separate staff. Bernard Green is designated as the first superintendent, effective March 4, 1897.

APRIL 22 - Superintendent Green reports to Congress that the net cost of the new building was $6,032,124.54, a sum $200,000 less than the total construction appropriation.

JUNE 30 - President William McKinley nominates journalist and former diplomat John Russell Young to be Librarian of Congress and asks Bernard Green to continue to serve as superintendent of the Library building and grounds. The Senate approves both nominations.

JULY 1 - John Russell Young takes office as the new Librarian of Congress. He immediately appoints Ainsworth Rand Spofford, now 72 years old, to be Chief Assistant Librarian.

When the new Library building opened to widespread acclaim in 1897, John White Alexander's *The Evolution of the Book*, a series of six lunettes in the Great Hall, was among the most popular attractions. This final lunette, *The Printing Press*, is above the Library's unique copy of the Gutenburg Bible near the west entrance to the Main Reading Room.

JULY 22 - Thorvald Solberg, a Boston book dealer and acknowledged copyright expert, takes office as the first register of copyrights.

JULY 31 - Except for the copyright department, the Library is closed and preparation for the move into the new building—delayed because of an unforeseen extra session of Congress in the spring—begins. On August 2, the ten-week transport of the books and other collections across the east plaza of the Capitol by horse-drawn wagons begins.

NOVEMBER 1 - At 9 a.m. the monumental new Library building officially opens for service to the public. Its 23-carat-gold-plated dome caps the "largest, costliest, and safest" library building in the world and its elaborate interior decoration, painting, and sculpture are widely praised. The south gallery on the second floor has been set aside for "a series of graphic-art exhibitions."

NOVEMBER 8 - A reading room for the blind is opened and readings for the blind are inaugurated. One of the first programs features poet Paul Laurence Dunbar, a Library of Congress staff member.

NOVEMBER 20 - The transfer of Library materials into the new building is completed. Superintendent Green estimates that a total of 800 tons of material was moved and that at least two-fifths of it was not in the Library proper, but scattered in various locations throughout the Capitol.

NOVEMBER 25 - On this Thanksgiving Day holiday, more than 4,700 visitors tour the new Library building.

DECEMBER 6 - In his first annual report, Librarian Young advocates the transfer of historical manuscripts from the State Department to the Library of Congress and decries the use of cheap, nondurable paper by publishers, warning that many of the works coming into the Library "threaten in a few years to crumble into a waste heap, with no value as record."

DECEMBER 14 - In response to a request from Senator Henry Cabot Lodge of Massachusetts, the Library's chief clerk reports that the Library received 2,872 applications for positions, from which Librarian Young made 65 probationary appointments.

This 1898 photo is labeled "Congressional Library, The Entrance Pavilion." Congressional Library was the name by which the Library of Congress was still popularly known when the new building first opened.

CONGRESSIONAL
LIBRARY
THE ENTRANCE
PAVILION

PART TWO

★

FOR THE NATION
1898–1959

This 1901 photograph of the Main Reading Room includes three of the massive semicircular stained-glass windows in which the seals of the states and territories of the Union at the time the building was constructed are reproduced. At the top, in the middle of each of the windows, is the Great Seal of the United States. To the right and the left, following the curve of each window, are the seals of states and territories, three on a side, six in each window. The name of the state or territory is inscribed above each seal, along with the date of the year in which it was admitted to the Union or organized under a territorial form of government. The series begins chronologically in the west window.

INTRODUCTION

The Library's struggles in the nineteenth century—for identity, space, and funds—were rewarded with a grand, new building. The twentieth century would see that magnificent structure welcome new staff, diverse collections, and a steady stream of patrons. Much of this progress was shaped by Herbert Putnam, who was appointed Librarian of Congress in 1899, just as the country entered the Progressive Era.

An experienced librarian, Putnam came to his post with a comprehensive plan for the Library of Congress as the national library, which he presented to President Theodore Roosevelt. He explained how the Library could become a bureau of information for the entire country, efficiently serving other libraries and promoting research. The president supported Putnam's efforts for the next several years, beginning with a 1903 executive order that transferred the records of the Continental Congress and the personal papers of many of the founding fathers to the Library to be "preserved and made accessible."

With President Roosevelt's endorsement, a vote of confidence through an increased budget from Congress, and the space provided by the new building, Putnam pursued his plan with what others described as "energetic nationalism." The result, between 1901 and 1928, was a series of new national library services, research publications and catalogs, cultural functions, and new offices. The most important development was the approval by Congress in 1925 of the Library of Congress Trust Fund Board, enabling the Library to accept private gifts or bequests for the benefit of the institution, its collections, or its services. Some of the fruits of this ruling were a series of chamber music concerts in an auditorium built for that purpose, the commissioning of new musical works, and the creation of the Archive of American Folk Song.

The Progressive Era saw the rise in academic disciplines and the scientific application of knowledge. This climate gave rise to a new legislative reference service at the Library of Congress. Specialized library units for legislative research were established in several states, notably Wisconsin, in the early 1900s. Wisconsin Senator Robert M. LaFollette promoted this idea, and a separate Legislative Reference Service with specialists in diverse fields was created in the Library of Congress in 1914. By 1915, the Librarian reported that the new service was receiving a wide range of questions regarding conservation, immigration, railroad securities, federal aid for road construction, and campaign contributions.

The Library played important roles during times of war and peace in the early part of the century. In 1917, the American Library Association asked Putnam to become the general director of its Library War Service, which supplied books and other reading matter to American troops training or engaged in the fighting in World War I. He immediately accepted, feeling this was a duty of the Library of Congress to American libraries and librarians. He was equally committed to the Library's role as a protector of democracy. When President Harding transferred the original copies of the Declaration of Independence and the US Constitution from the State Department to the Library in 1921, Putnam was honored to display and protect the founding documents.

The Library's symbolic role as a repository and promoter of the American democratic tradition also was of special appeal to Putnam's successor, Archibald MacLeish, who served as Librarian of Congress during most of World War II. MacLeish relished the Library's role as the custodian of the Declaration of Independence and the US Constitution and helped plan the shipment in late 1940 of these two documents and other Library treasures to Fort Knox, Kentucky, for safekeeping during the war. He also helped the ever-expanding Library move into its second building, and brought in government-sponsored art collections from agencies such as the Works Progress Administration.

Luther Evans, who became Librarian in 1954, helped usher the Library from the post–World War II era toward the information age. Again, the Library needed to adapt to the times while preserving its

treasures, acquiring new collections, and providing knowledge and information to researchers and scholars. The challenge was how to embrace technology and growth without losing its greatest asset—the printed book—and unsettling its most important and longtime patron: the United States Congress.

Family and Education are the major themes in this richly decorated corridor, located behind the north staircase on the first floor of the Great Hall. The corridor is dominated by paintings by Charles Sprague Pearce. The largest, *The Family,* is at the east end. Smaller paintings along the north side depict *Religion, Labor, Study, Recreation,* and *Rest.* The surnames of distinguished men of education from throughout the world are inscribed in the ceiling

1898

JANUARY - Newly hired catalogers J.C.M. Hanson and Charles Martel begin reclassifying the Library's collections according to a new classification scheme.

FEBRUARY - The Court of Neptune Fountain by Roland Hinton Perry, located in front of the new Library building, is completed.

FEBRUARY 16 - Librarian John Russell Young invites diplomatic representatives throughout the world to send research materials that "would add to the sum of human knowledge" to the new national library. Approving the text of the message, Assistant Librarian Spofford reminds the Librarian: "I fought to bring us oceans of books and rivers of information."

JUNE 12 - Librarian Young writes in his diary: "I am trying to build the library far into the future, to make it a true library of research."

JULY 7 - President McKinley approves a joint resolution authorizing the Librarian of Congress to accept the Gardiner Greene Hubbard collection of European and American prints, one of the finest private collections in the United States. A 1912 bequest from Hubbard's widow, Gertrude M. Hubbard, supports the future growth of the collection.

The Court of Neptune Fountain in front of the Jefferson Building was the creation of sculptor Roland Hinton Perry. It was completed in 1898 and immediately introduced classical culture as the structure's basic theme. At the time it was celebrated as the most lavishly ornamental fountain in the country. The colossal figure of Neptune, the Roman god of the seas, presides over an infusion of other bronze, allegorical inhabitants of the oceans. The fountain was restored during the 1986–94 renovation and restoration of the Jefferson and Adams Buildings.

The new building immediately began to attract gifts to the Library's collection. In 1898, Mrs. Gardiner Greene Hubbard donated an extraordinary collection of 2,700 European and American prints. One was Albrecht Dürer's *The Expulsion from Paradise, or The Fall of Man.*

More than 800 tons of books, pamphlets, maps, manuscripts, pieces of music, and other materials were moved from the Library and its 16 storage rooms throughout the US Capitol to the new building. These copyright deposits would be sorted, counted, and classified before being added to the collections.

JULY 8 - Thousands of visitors come to view the building when it is illuminated at night on an experimental basis. The new Library is the first public building in Washington planned and constructed to take full advantage of new technologies available through the use of electricity.

AUGUST 18 - Librarian Young alerts the staff to a new development: since "the Government has taken possession of Manila under circumstances that look to its permanent retention," he asks that additional books about the Philippines be purchased immediately.

OCTOBER 1 - Already open at 9 a.m., six days a week, the Library extends its closing hour to 10 p.m.

DECEMBER 12 - Librarian Young points out, in his second annual report, that the bibliographic bulletins issued during the past year about Cuba and Hawaii were printed "in the belief that Congress might value the information presented." Moreover, while the Library, through its collections, should be "American in the highest sense," he feels there is no reason why it should not "seek out and gather in the learning and piety of every age."

1899

JANUARY 8 - Herbert Friedenwald, superintendent of the Manuscripts Department, departs for Puerto Rico for the purpose of collecting "rare manuscripts, books, and maps pertaining to that Island."

JANUARY 17 - Librarian Young succumbs to a lingering illness and dies. The next day Spofford becomes Acting Librarian of Congress.

MARCH 13 - During the congressional recess, President McKinley appoints Herbert Putnam, librarian of the Boston Public Library, to be Librarian of Congress.

APRIL 5 - Herbert Putnam takes the oath of office as the eighth Librarian of Congress. The Library has a book collection of approximately 900,000 volumes, a staff of 134, and an appropriation in fiscal year 1898 of $280,000. Bernard Green, the superintendent of building and grounds, has a staff of 99.

OCTOBER 10 - Putnam submits his estimated budget for the next fiscal year. He asks for five new departments of work, an increase in staff from 134 to 230, and a substantial increase in the allotment for collections. He notes that the entire collection must be reclassified and includes funds to purchase an electric automobile to replace the Library's one wagon and two horses.

Librarian of Congress Herbert Putnam at his desk in the early years of his 40-year administration, which extended from 1899 to 1939. Under his "responsible eye" (his expression), the Library of Congress expanded and flourished into a national institution that served Congress, other libraries, scholars, and the general public. He also began development of the Library's international collections.

DECEMBER 6 - President McKinley sends the Senate the nomination of Herbert Putnam as Librarian of Congress, "to which he was appointed during the last recess of Congress." The Senate confirms the nomination, without debate, on December 12.

1900

JANUARY - The Library publishes the *Preliminary List of Books and Pamphlets by Negro Authors for the Paris Exposition and Library of Congress*. Its compiler is Daniel Murray, an African American who was hired as an assistant librarian by Librarian of Congress Spofford in 1871.

APRIL 7 - Librarian Putnam informs Melvil Dewey that if there had been any way he could have justified the use of the Dewey Decimal Classification system for the Library of Congress, he would have done so. However, the arguments against using it at the Library seemed "insuperable," in particular its need for an expansive system suitable for a large research library. In November 1953, the Library and the Lake Placid Club Foundation, holder of the copyright for the *Dewey Decimal Classification*, agree that the Library will prepare the next edition, the 16th, of the *Classification*. To perform the work, the Library establishes a Dewey Classification Office in November 1958.

At the turn of the new century, local teachers brought their curious students to see the Library, its exhibits, and collections. In the Main Reading Room, Librarian Putnam maintained a watchful eye.

This 1898 view of the new
Library building encompasses
the dome on top of the Main
Reading Room, including
the Torch of Learning at its
apex, all coated in 1893
with 23-carat gold leaf; a
partial view of several of
the portrait busts of famous
authors across the building's
front portico; and visitors
viewing the Court of Neptune
Fountain on the right. Beyond
the fountain and across
Independence Avenue on
the far right are buildings
that were replaced when the
Library's Madison Building
was constructed between
1975 and 1980.

77

DANIEL MURRAY — A COLLECTOR'S LEGACY

A pioneering African American bibliographer and historian, Daniel Alexander Payne Murray spent 51 years (1871–1922) working at the Library of Congress, leaving a legacy of rare and important literary materials that document the lives and accomplishments of African Americans. He believed that "the true test of the progress of a people is to be found in their literature." An agent of change in a period when many African Americans were plagued by racial discrimination, unemployment, and poverty, he eventually bequeathed to the Library a unique collection of pamphlets and books about the contributions of African American writers and organizations working for political and social advancement. This collection, now in the Library's Rare Book and Special Collections Division, is available online. In 1979, the Daniel A.P. Murray Association was formed at the Library to honor Murray for his exceptional service.

Daniel Murray was born in Baltimore, Maryland, on March 3, 1853, the youngest son of freed slave parents. As a young man, he moved to Washington to work for his brother who managed the Senate restaurant in the US Capitol, which was also then the site of the Library of Congress. The restaurant was located on the ground floor near the Senate committee rooms, and in due course the 19-year-old Murray came to the attention of Senator Timothy Howe of Wisconsin, a member of the Joint Library Committee, and Librarian of Congress Ainsworth Rand Spofford.

Murray impressed both Howe and Spofford, and they arranged a part-time, minor position for him in the Library. His first day of work was January 1, 1871. In the crowded Library, which stretched across the entire projection of the west side of the Capitol's central section, he joined Spofford and a staff of eight assistant librarians, one messenger, and three laborers. The Library was open to Congress and the public daily, except Sundays, from 9 a.m. to 4 p.m. At the time, only members of Congress and the Supreme Court, the president, the vice president, cabinet secretaries, and certain other privileged officials could borrow material. Books were delivered to their offices and sometimes even directly to their homes.

Murray was not the only African American on the Library's staff. John F.N. Wilkinson, a native Washingtonian, was two decades Murray's senior. Wilkinson began working in the Law Library in 1857, and was rewarded with the Assistant Librarian title in 1872. He served as Murray's immediate model. The two of them made themselves proficient at what really mattered to Spofford: finding and delivering books rapidly. Urged by Spofford, whose own memory was legendary, Wilkinson and Murray each developed an infallible recall for books, titles, and locations, which made them indispensable as employees.

The 49-year-old Spofford, largely self-educated, was a bookseller, editorial writer, and abolitionist in his younger days in Cincinnati, Ohio. He also was a founder of the Cincinnati Literary Society. Enthusiasm, especially in one's work, was the quality he valued above all others. He decided to become Murray's mentor and made him his full-time personal assistant in 1874. He trained Murray in how to help congressmen in their research and encouraged his interest in reading, history, and the study of foreign languages. As an Assistant Librarian, Murray's annual salary was $1,000. Murray appreciated Spofford's patronage and friendship, describing him as "a man singularly free from the blight of color prejudice." Spofford's influence helped shape Murray's lifelong interest in "putting scholarship to the service of Negro protest and advancement."

In 1879, Daniel Murray married Anna Jane Evans, a Washington, DC, schoolteacher and graduate of Oberlin College and Howard University. During the course of their 46-year marriage, Daniel and Anna Murray raised seven children and aided each other in their careers as they became one of the wealthiest and most socially prominent African American families in Washington.

Widely recognized as an authority on African American culture and history, Daniel Murray also excelled in business as the owner and developer of

EXHIBIT OF AMERICAN NEGROES AT THE PARIS EXPOSITION.

several buildings in the city. In 1894, the Washington Board of Trade inducted him as its first African American member in recognition of his skillful drafting of a legislative proposal that secured federal expenditure and support for the municipal government of the District of Columbia. He and Anna also worked to advance educational opportunities for African Americans in District of Columbia public schools.

In the violent 1890s, African American leaders such as Booker T. Washington, W.E.B. DuBois, and Murray spearheaded projects designed to counter what they considered dangerous theories of black racial inferiority. While Booker T. Washington emphasized black advancements in the physical and social sciences and W.E.B. DuBois gained an international reputation as the intellectual leader of the African American community, Daniel Murray focused on black literary achievements.

A prolific writer and researcher, Murray authored numerous articles on black history and culture, published several reference bibliographies on black literature, and amassed thousands of biographi-

cal sketches, hundreds of books, pamphlets, and musical compositions, and even plot synopses of 500 novels, all for his planned, but never published, grand work, "Murray's Historical and Biographical Encyclopedia of the Colored Race." Drawing on his bibliographic efforts directed toward the Encyclopedia, in 1900—on behalf of the Library of Congress—he made a major contribution to the success of the American Negro Exhibit in the Hall of Social Economy at the Exposition Universelle held in Paris. In 1900, the Library of Congress published the eight-page *Preliminary List of Books and Pamphlets by Negro Authors for Paris Exposition and Library of Congress* by Daniel Murray. It was the Library's first bibliography of African American literature.

A self-educated, self-made man, Daniel Murray pursued his work with zeal and grace, ever mindful of his mission to dispel disparaging myths about black people and to stimulate greater public awareness and appreciation of African American culture and history.

APRIL 17 - President McKinley approves the Appropriations Act for fiscal year 1901, which includes funds to enact Librarian Putnam's recent proposals. An increase in the annual salary of the Librarian to $6,000 also is included.

JUNE - Librarian Putnam departs for a European trip to "stimulate" the Library's exchange agreements and reorganize its overseas purchase methods.

OCTOBER 19 - Putnam tells William I. Fletcher, librarian of Amherst College, Massachusetts, that after intensive study he has reached the reluctant conclusion the Library cannot use any classification system in current use—its collection is too vast and varied in its formats. Therefore, it is resuming the development of its own classification system.

OCTOBER 20 - Putnam informs the chairman of the Joint Library Committee that the Library's specialty is Americana and that it is a "bureau of information" for Americana that serves the entire nation and the world. Moreover, it will sustain active relations directly with libraries abroad and, through the Smithsonian, with all learned societies abroad.

Large coal furnaces in the cellar kept the monumental building heated.

Philip Lee Phillips was the first superintendent of maps when the Hall of Maps and Charts was established in the new Library building in 1897. During his tenure Phillips acquired maps and atlases from the wealth of material sent to the Library for copyright deposit. He traveled abroad to add to those collections. Called the "King of Maps" by the *Washington Post* in 1905, he developed a classification system that became the standard for cartographic libraries and is still in use by some today.

DECEMBER - A branch of the Government Printing Office is established within the Library to print and bind publications, continue the repair of historical manuscripts, and print catalog cards.

DECEMBER 4 - In his annual report, Putnam notes that the Library has expanded its foreign newspaper collection "to include those which would exhibit most accurately the current political, industrial, and commercial intelligence of the various countries in whose activities Congress and the public might be interested."

1901

JANUARY - The Library publishes its first new classification schedule, *Class E and F: American History and Geography*. During the same month, it begins printing catalog cards for all books being cataloged or recataloged.

MARCH - The Library publishes its first finding aid for a manuscript collection: *A Calendar of Washington Manuscripts in the Library of Congress*.

MARCH 3 - The president approves the Appropriations Act for fiscal year 1902, which further extends access to government libraries for "scientific investigators and duly qualified individuals." Putnam interprets the law as authority for the Library to inaugurate an interlibrary loan service.

APRIL - The Library replaces its wagon and two horses with an electrical automobile at the cost of $2,000. Putnam points out that the automobile can be charged at the Library's electric plant without expense.

Librarian Putnam called the Library's
new 1901 card service "the most
significant of our undertakings of this
first year of the new century." Cards
being prepared for distribution to
libraries throughout the US filled this
entire room.

JULY 4 – At the annual meeting of the American Library Association, Putnam addresses the subject "what may be done for libraries": "If there is any way in which our National Library may 'reach out' from Washington, it should reach out," he says. One proposal he discusses is centralized cataloging through the national distribution of Library of Congress printed cards.

OCTOBER 15 – Putnam explains to President Theodore Roosevelt why "a national library for the United States should mean in some respects more than a national library in any other country has hitherto meant." The Librarian points out that other American libraries must "look to the National Library" for standards and leadership in uniformity of methods, cooperation in processing, interchange of bibliographic service, and, in general, the promotion of efficiency in services.

OCTOBER 28 – The Library issues a circular announcing the sale and distribution of Library of Congress printed catalog cards to more than 500 American libraries. Putnam calls the new card service "the most significant of our undertakings of this first year of the new century."

DECEMBER 2 – The Library publishes its annual report for 1901, a 380-page volume featuring a "manual" that describes its history, organization, facilities, collections, and operations. Putnam reports an increase in the Library's total appropriation to more than $500,000 and announces that it has become the first American library to contain more than one million volumes. The purpose of the administration, he states, is "the freest possible use of the books consistent with their safety; and the widest possible use consistent with the convenience of Congress."

DECEMBER 3 – In his first State of the Union message, President Roosevelt calls the Library of Congress "the one national library of the United States" and a library that "has a unique opportunity to render to the libraries of this country—to American scholarship—service of the highest importance."

1902

JUNE 28 – President Roosevelt approves an act of Congress authorizing the Library to sell copies of its "card indexes" and other publications "to such institutions and individuals that may desire to buy them." All proceeds shall be deposited in the US Treasury.

OF CARDS, CATALOGS, AND COMPUTERS

In 1877, librarian Melvil Dewey asked a hypothetical question: Could the Library of Congress catalog for the entire country? Decades later, in 1901, he received an answer. Librarian of Congress Herbert Putnam, speaking from the impressive new Library building and confident about the Library's new national mission, replied "yes." In October of that year Putnam told President Theodore Roosevelt, "American instinct and habit revolt against multiplication of brain effort and outlay where a multiplication of results can be achieved by machinery." The machinery in this case was authoritative Library of Congress cataloging information and the delivery means was the new technology of the day, the 3 x 5 inch catalog card.

With moral support from Dewey and Richard Rogers Bowker, editor and publisher of *Library Journal*, Putnam made up his mind. On October 28, 1901, he mailed a circular to more than 500 libraries announcing the sale and distribution of the Library's printed catalog cards. Libraries immediately showed interest. A separate Card Division, under the direction of the energetic Charles H. Hastings, was established.

The Library had already started printing cards in 1898, using the recently invented linotype machine. In the fall of 1900, it established a branch of the Government Printing Office in the basement to do the printing. In 1902, Roosevelt signed a law authorizing the Library to sell such cards at a price covering their cost plus 10 percent, with all proceeds deposited in the US Treasury. And so the Library of Congress entered into the mail-order business, selling and distributing its cataloging to all who might want it. The librarian's long-held dream of laborsaving centralized library cataloging, articulated by librarian Charles Coffin Jewett at the Smithsonian in the early 1850s, had come true. Furthermore, the Library of Congress found it had a growing national audience on its hands, especially among the more than 2,500 public libraries established by Andrew Carnegie and his foundation between 1890 and 1917.

The card distribution service became self-supporting in 1905 and soon boomed. By 1914, nearly 2,000 subscribers received cards and 41 staff members worked to fill orders. Within the Library the growth in the inventory of cards soon became a problem as tens of thousands of books were cataloged or recataloged each year. Second and third tiers were added to the steel card-storage stacks, with a fourth needed in 1921 when the stock ballooned to 63,625,000 cards. *The Washington Herald* for June 30, 1933, featured an article titled "Card Catalog Division of Library Recognized as Model of World." When Charles Hastings retired in 1938, the number of subscribers stood at 6,311; the number of cards sold that year totaled 13,939,565.

The Library of Congress cataloging and classification systems were helping to shape the American library movement and having a positive influence not only on libraries but also on scholarship. In 1942, "in order to further the progress of scholarly research," the Library and the Association of Research Libraries reached an agreement to print a complete set of the Library's printed catalog cards in book form. In his December 1942 preface to the 167-volume *A Catalog of Books Represented by Library of Congress Printed Cards*, Librarian of Congress Archibald MacLeish lauded five "very great Americans"—Charles Coffin Jewett, Ainsworth Rand Spofford, Richard Rogers Bowker, Melvil Dewey, and Herbert Putnam—whose names, he noted, were not well known, "but have done far more for the enduring life of their country than many whose first names and photographs are familiar around every wood-burning stove in the forty-eight states."

The Library of Congress soon began a successful program of publishing, on a regular basis, different book catalogs, which contained the newly issued catalog cards in different physical arrangements. In the meantime, in the 1950s, the Library's own card catalog bulged with more than nine million cards crammed into more than 10,000 catalog trays. About the same time, computer companies were making major innovations and new possibilities were on the horizon for cataloging and storing data.

In January 1958, Librarian of Congress L. Quincy Mumford established a Mechanical Information Re-

trieval Committee to study "the problem of applying machine methods to the control of the Library's general collections," and the possible automation of the Library's main catalog. Under the leadership of Henriette D. Avram, the Library devised in January 1966 the first automated cataloging system in the world, known as Machine-Readable Cataloging (MARC). Through MARC, cataloging information could be searched on a computer terminal. In March 1969, the MARC Distribution Service began sending out magnetic computer tapes containing cataloging data.

It was just in the nick of time. The number of subscribers to the overloaded but still operating Card Distribution Service peaked in 1968, when the total number of subscribers reached 25,000—and the size of the staff was nearing 600. MARC was recognized as an international standard and as its automated distribution system grew, the demand for paper catalog cards produced by the Card Division fell. In 1972, for the first time in the history of the Card Division, the dollar sales of cards dropped below the sales of cataloging in other physical forms. The end was in sight. In 1975, the Card Division was changed to the Cataloging Distribution Division, which soon became the Cataloging Distribution Service. The first computer terminals soon were installed in the Main Reading Room. On December 31, 1980, the last new cards were filed in the Main Reading Room's card catalog and the Library launched a new catalog of its collections online.

DECEMBER 1 - In his annual report, Putnam announces the appointments of several subject specialists, including two new division chiefs: Oscar George Theodore Sonneck of the Music Division and Worthington Chauncey Ford of the Manuscript Division. He also reports that the Library's Orientalia collection of more than 10,000 volumes is now "believed to be the largest representation in this country of the literature of the Far East."

1903

JANUARY 27 - Putnam informs the Joint Library Committee that to make the Library a general circulating library for the public would "tend rather to the injury of serious research in this Library, including its use by Congress." He points out that this function "can be more effectively dealt with by the Public Library of the District of Columbia."

FEBRUARY 23 - President Roosevelt approves the Appropriations Act for fiscal year 1904. The new law authorizes US government agencies to transfer to the Library of Congress "any books, maps, or other material no longer needed for its use and in the judgment of the Librarian of Congress appropriate for the uses of the Library."

MARCH 9 - An executive order issued by President Roosevelt directs the transfer of the records and papers of the Continental Congress and the personal papers of George Washington, James Madison, Thomas Jefferson, Alexander Hamilton, James Monroe, and Benjamin Franklin from the Department of State to the Library of Congress, "to be there preserved and rendered accessible" for historical and "other legitimate" uses.

JULY - The Johann Georg Kohl Collection of manuscript copies of maps significant in the history of cartography is transferred from the Department of State to the Library of Congress.

1904

JANUARY 24 - A cylinder recording of the voice of Kaiser Wilhelm II is made. The recording, presented to the Library shortly thereafter, is the first phonograph record acquired by the Library of Congress.

APRIL 20 - The Louisiana Purchase Exposition at St. Louis opens. Putnam proudly notes in his annual report that the Library of Congress exhibition, which emphasized the "National Library as a function of our Government," was "the first direct participation of the Library in any of the great international expositions."

Visitors took in the Great Hall in 1904.

(16w) Decorative splendors of the Entrance Hall of the great Congressional Library, Washington, U.S.A.   Copyright 1904 by Underwood & Underwood.

DECEMBER 5 - Putnam explains that his annual reports are lengthier than those of the British Museum or the Bibliothèque nationale de France only because the Library of Congress is pursuing activities "of which their operations offer no example." One new activity is highlighted: the publication of historical texts from the Library's collections, beginning with the Journals of the Continental Congress and the Records of the Virginia Company, which describe the settlement of Virginia.

1905

JULY 5 - The Librarian justifies the liberal interlibrary loan policy of the Library of Congress, explaining that if a volume be lost in the process, "I know of but one answer: that a book used, after all, is fulfilling a higher mission than a book which is merely being preserved for possible future use."

DECEMBER - The Library's program for copying manuscripts in foreign archives that relate to American history officially begins.

"A book used, after all, is fulfilling a higher mission than a book which is merely being preserved for possible future use."

— Librarian of Congress Herbert Putnam, 1905

1906

MAY 17 - Writer H.G. Wells is among the luncheon guests hosted by Librarian Putnam at his "Round Table," an informal dining room on the top floor of the Library. A few months later, Wells describes the event in his book *The Future in America*: "I found at last a little group of men who could talk. It was like a small raft upon a limitless empty sea. I lunched with them at their Round Table, and afterwards Mr. Putnam showed me the Rotunda."

OCTOBER - President Roosevelt congratulates Putnam on the purchase of the 80,000-volume private library of G.V. Yudin of Siberia. The acquisition will give the Library preeminence in Russian literature, not only in the United States but also, as far as Roosevelt knows, "in the world generally outside of Russia."

1907

APRIL - The last shipment of the Yudin library arrives from Siberia. Since the sum paid for the collection "scarcely exceeded a third of what the owner himself had expended," Putnam considers the acquisition "primarily a gift."

NOVEMBER 4 - Putnam receives approval from the attorney general to use the following wording for gifts or bequests to the Library: "To the United States of America, to be placed in the Library of Congress and administered therein by the authorities thereof."

DECEMBER 20 - Responding to an inquiry from the president regarding a proposal from J. Franklin Jameson of the Carnegie Institution about the desirability of a Hall of Records for governmental departmental papers, Putnam approves, as long as the records themselves "are not appropriate for the collections of the Library." On December 24, on learning of Putnam's endorsement of an archives building, Jameson thanks the Librarian and restates his understanding of the position held by both: "that there is no conflict at all between the desirability of gathering into the Library of Congress as much as it cares to house of those manuscript materials which are primarily historical and the necessity (and utility to historical scholars incidentally) of providing a better storehouse for the main masses of administrative papers."

G.V. Yudin, the wealthy Siberian distiller and amateur bibliographer, whose collection of Russian literature came to the Library in 1906, is pictured (opposite page) along with sample slips from his handwritten inventory (above).

1908

MAY 22 - Congress approves $320,000 to construct a bookstack in the southeast courtyard.

JULY - The American Library Association publishes the American edition of the Anglo-American cataloging rules, which represent a compromise between cataloging rules developed by the Library of Congress and other libraries. The editor is J.C.M. Hanson, chief of the Library's Cataloging Division.

NOVEMBER - The Library purchases, from Albert Schatz of Rostock, Germany, Mr. Schatz's renowned collection of more than 12,000 early opera librettos.

NOVEMBER 12 - In the Library's Senate Reading Room, Putnam presides over a memorial meeting for Ainsworth Rand Spofford, who died on August 11. In his annual report, Putnam eloquently notes that Spofford's title of Chief Assistant Librarian during the past eleven years "did not obscure his greatest office, that of Librarian Emeritus, nor the distinction to the Library or the honor to himself of the service which for thirty-two years he has rendered as Librarian-in-Chief."

DECEMBER 29 - The Librarian accepts a complete set of the world's largest printed encyclopedia, the 5,041-volume *Tu Shu Tsi Cheng*, presented by the Chinese government "with the acknowledgements of China to the United States for the remission of the 'Boxer indemnity.'"

1909

MARCH 4 - President Roosevelt approves the Appropriations Act for fiscal year 1910. The new law authorizes the Librarian of Congress to transfer surplus materials to other governmental agencies within the District of Columbia as well as to other public libraries and also "to dispose of or destroy such material as has become useless."

MARCH 4 - The President approves an act of Congress that amends and consolidates the copyright law. The revision is based primarily on a bill prepared by the Copyright Office.

JUNE 30 - Oscar G.T. Sonneck, chief of the Music Division, reports to Putnam on his "gratifying" success in soliciting gifts of original music manuscripts for the Library.

AUGUST - The Library publishes the first volume of *A List of Geographical Atlases of America in the Library of Congress*, which contains analytical descriptions of more than 3,200 atlases. The compiler, Philip Lee Phillips, chief of the Division of Maps and Charts, notes that atlases have not received the bibliographic attention they deserve.

In 1906, a large crowd gathered
to hear President Theodore
Roosevelt speak at the
cornerstone-laying ceremony for
the House of Representatives
Cannon House Office
Building. The Library, located
across the street, loomed in
the background.

FOUNDING—AND
LOST—DOCUMENTS

Librarian of Congress Herbert Putnam was a happy man on September 29, 1921. President Warren G. Harding had just issued an executive order directing the transfer of the original copies of the Declaration of Independence and the US Constitution from the State Department to the Library. Part of Putnam's argument for the transfer was that the Library could take better care of the documents than the State Department. There were no National Archives in those days, so the transfer seemed logical. President Harding declared his intention "to satisfy the wish of patriotic Americans to have an opportunity to see the original fundamental documents upon which rests their independence and their government." Putnam picked up the treasures the next day in the Model-T Ford truck that served as the Library's mail wagon and deposited them in the wall safe in the Librarian's office.

On March 22, 1922, President Harding approved the Library's appropriation for fiscal year 1923, which included $12,000 for a "safe, permanent repository of appropriate design" for what turned out to be a "shrine" for the display of the Declaration and the Constitution in the Library. The appropriation language made it clear that Putnam had more than preservation in mind when he acquired the documents: while fully "safe-guarded," they also "should be open to inspection by the public at large."

Francis H. Bacon, brother of Henry Bacon, the architect of the Lincoln Memorial, designed the shrine. It was located on the west side of the second floor of the Jefferson Building's Great Hall, directly in front of a blocked center window that faced the Capitol. The dedication took place on February 28, 1924, in the presence of President Calvin Coolidge and Mrs. Coolidge. From today's perspective, it is hard to believe that there were no speeches, the ceremony taking place "without a single utterance, save the singing of two stanzas of 'America.'"

The shrine display also included two dozen auxiliary documents about the Revolutionary Era from the Library's Manuscript Division, along with portraits of the signers of the Declaration and the Constitution, and their biographies. In all likelihood this material was inspired at least in part by the list of the names of all the signers of the Declaration in the stained glass ceiling panels on the second floor of the Jefferson Building's south gallery.

From the 1920s into the 1950s, the Library relished and took full advantage of its role as the possessor and protector of the nation's sacred founding documents. Two weeks after the Japanese attacked Pearl Harbor in late 1941, the Declaration, Constitution, and other top Library treasures were sent by train to Fort Knox, Kentucky—the precise location being kept secret at the time—for safekeeping. Armed Secret Service agents and Verner Clapp, who had recently been promoted to Chief Assistant Librarian of Congress, acted as couriers for the documents. When the documents were returned with great fanfare to public display at the Library on October 1, 1944, a Marine Guard of Honor stood beside the shrine in the Great Hall.

Given the heavy symbolic importance the Library placed on its custody of the Declaration of Independence and the Constitution, it is not surprising that the eventual transfer of the documents to the National Archives, which were established in 1934, would be a painful—and drawn out—experience. At the laying of the cornerstone for the new National Archives building in 1933, President Herbert Hoover announced that the Archives, as home of official government records, would house the Declaration and the Constitution in the great exhibition space then being planned. Later that year, Architect John Russell Pope commissioned two huge murals for the new exhibition hall. One depicts Jefferson presenting the Declaration to the Continental Congress; the other shows James Madison presenting the final draft of the Constitution to George Washington.

But the emotional wrench of giving up the documents was too much for longtime Librarian Putnam. He refused to surrender them, and all concerned decided to wait patiently until he retired, which did not happen until 1939. His successor, Archibald Mac-Leish, Librarian of Congress from 1939 to 1944, was preoccupied with the safety of the documents during the World War II years. So, the eventual transfer fell to Luther H. Evans, Librarian of Congress from 1945 to 1953, who had worked at the newly opened National Archives from 1935 to 1939 before Librarian MacLeish hired him for a senior position at the Library of Congress.

Aware of the opposition to the transfer among the Library's senior managers, Evans asked the Joint Library Committee to "instruct" him to surrender the documents, and it did so on April 30, 1952. On sunny December 13, 1952, Chief Assistant Librarian of Congress Verner Clapp and Senator Theodore Green of Rhode Island, chairman of the Joint Library Committee, placed the two "sacred parchments"—carefully encased and crated—on mattresses inside an armored Marine personnel carrier and accompanied them on the trip down Constitution Avenue to their new home. The next day, President Harry Truman delivered the principal address at their enshrinement in the central exhibition hall of the National Archives.

DECEMBER – Superintendent of the Reading Room William Warner Bishop informs an audience of academic librarians that the Library of Congress already is "on the way toward becoming a national lending library and bureau of information."

1910
MARCH – The Librarian's catalog card program is expanded to include the printing of cards from copy prepared by librarians outside the District of Columbia.

MARCH – The much-needed new bookstack in the southeast courtyard is completed. It contains 44 miles of shelving. The total size of the Library's book collection is now approximately 1,800,000 volumes.

APRIL 27 – Mrs. John Boyd Thacher places her husband's 840-volume collection of fifteenth-century books, manuscripts, and related materials on American exploration and the French Revolution on deposit at the Library. On her death on February 18, 1927, the collection is bequeathed to the Library.

On February 28, 1924, President Calvin Coolidge and his wife Grace attended the dedication of the "shrine" in the Library's Great Hall.

MAY 13 - Bibliographer and historian Henry Harrisse dies, bequeathing to the Library of Congress his personal library of maps, manuscripts, and rare books and a complete file of his own writings about the early exploration of America. The collection comes to the Library in 1915.

NOVEMBER 29 - Putnam requests a salary increase for the office of Librarian of Congress: "The position justifies the increase and really, in its own interest, permanently requires it." He adds: "Librarians in general are not people given to luxuries: they are content to live modestly; but they ought not have to live penuriously."

1911

MARCH 4 - The Librarian announces that he has arranged for the continuation of service to Congress whenever the House of Representatives is sitting, including all-night sessions, holidays, and "Sunday mornings when Congress is sitting, even when eulogies are being delivered."

APRIL 6 - In response to the introduction in Congress of several bills on the subject, Putnam submits a special report aimed at improving legislation through the establishment of a legislative reference bureau. Included are materials describing legislative reference bureaus in several states, particularly New York and Wisconsin. He concludes by emphasizing "that for the work to be scientific (i.e. having only truth as its object) it must be strictly nonpartisan."

DECEMBER 4 - Putnam notes that the Library recently declined to accept custody, from another government agency, of the records of the American military occupation of Cuba from 1898 to 1902. The reason was that "such papers should go to a national archives repository."

The Government Printing Office truck, parked at the Library's loading dock in 1912.

> "Librarians in general are not people given to luxuries: they are content to live modestly; but they ought not have to live penuriously."

— Librarian of Congress Herbert Putnam, 1910

שפך

חמתך על הגוים אשר לא ידעוך
ועל הממלכות אשר בשמך לא
קראו"

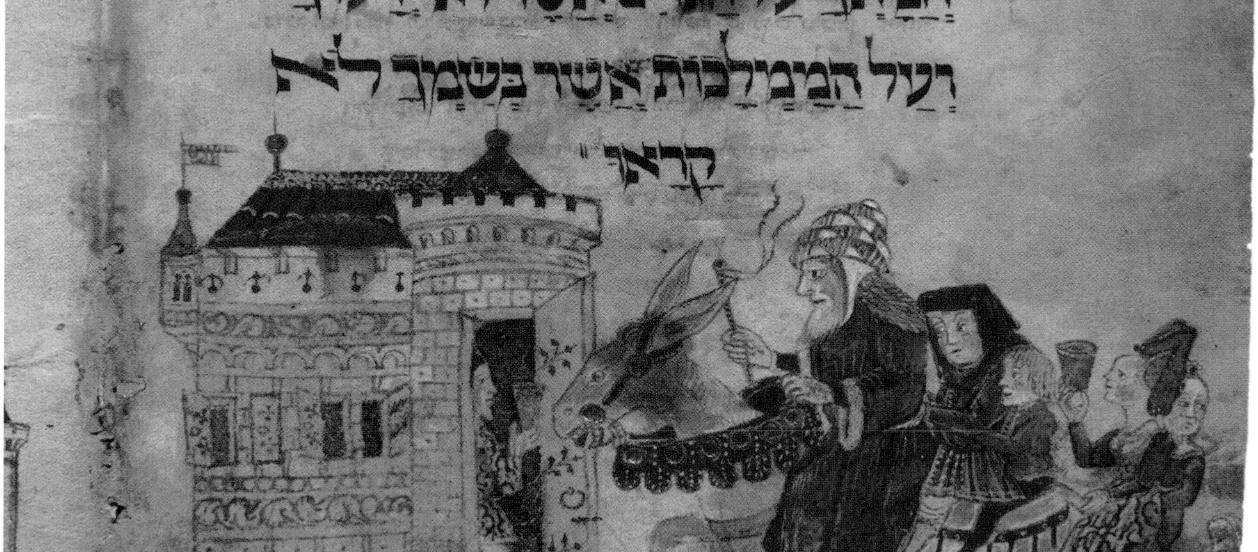

1912

JANUARY - In a handbook describing the Library's organization, collections, and services, William Warner Bishop, superintendent of the Main Reading Room, emphasizes that since 1897 the institution, "while rendering greatly increased service to Congress, has begun a career of service to the whole nation."

JANUARY 25 - Appearing before the House of Representatives Appropriations Subcommittee, Putnam proudly displays copies of maps, prints, and newspaper pages made by the Library's new Photostat and Flexotype machines and asks the subcommittee to approve a small appropriation for the salary of the machine operator.

FEBRUARY 26 - The House Library Committee (part of the Joint Library Committee) holds hearings to consider a bill that would establish a congressional reference bureau. Witness James Bryce, British ambassador to the United States, testifies in favor, but only after he is satisfied that the subject "was one of entirely non-partisan character." Charles A. McCarthy of the Wisconsin legislative reference department emphasizes the need for close supervision so such an office "will not go to sleep and become a great big bureau of red tape and checked so that it cannot be made a football of politics."

MARCH 16 - President William H. Taft issues an executive order directing the Librarian to review documents not wanted by the executive agencies in order to preserve "such of the papers as he may deem to be of historical interest."

APRIL - A collection of nearly 10,000 volumes and pamphlets of Hebraica, gathered by Ephraim Deinard, is donated to the Library by Jacob H. Schiff of New York City. Putnam states that the collection is a notable foundation that will be expanded "into a significant department embracing all Semitica."

MAY - The Library publishes the *Guide to the Law and Literature of Germany* by law librarian Edwin M. Borchard, the first in a series of guides to the laws of foreign countries.

MAY 20 - Putnam notifies American universities of a new plan that will result, with their cooperation, in the collection and cataloging by the Library of doctoral dissertations sent to their institutions and the publication by the Library, beginning in 1912, of an annual list of American doctoral dissertations.

The Library's most important illuminated Hebrew manuscript is called the *Washington Haggadah* because of its presence in the Library of Congress. It was completed in Central Europe on January 29, 1478. It is part of a major collection of Hebraica donated to the Library in 1912.

AUGUST 24 - The president approves an act of Congress extending copyright protection to motion pictures as a distinct form; previously motion pictures were deposited as photographs in paper print form.

OCTOBER 9 - Librarian Putnam speaks at the funeral service for John F.N. Wilkinson, an African American staff member who had worked in the Library's Law Division since 1857. In his remarks at the A.E. Israel Church, Putnam notes that Wilkinson, in fact, "was at his post, and performing his duties even on the day of his death." At the time, Wilkinson's 55 years of employment was a record for the number of continuous years of service at the Library.

NOVEMBER 19 - J. Pierpont Morgan informs President Taft that he is donating a complete bound set of letters and documents from the signers of the Declaration of Independence to the Library, a gift "more fittingly preserved in the National Library than in that of any individual."

NOVEMBER 20 - Putnam directs employees to announce the name of their division first when answering telephone calls: "the exclamations, 'Hello!' 'What is it' etc., now much in use are unnecessary."

1913

MARCH 14 - President Woodrow Wilson approves the Appropriations Act for fiscal year 1914. The new law directs the American Printing House for the Blind in Louisville, Kentucky, to deposit in the Library of Congress one copy of each embossed book that it manufactures with federal financial assistance.

JULY 10 - Because of the "great changes to be made in the laws of the Nation" under President Wilson's New Freedom program, the Senate Library Committee (part of the Joint Library Committee) urges that a legislative reference bureau be established in the Library "as quickly as possible."

Librarian of Congress Herbert Putnam (bottom row, fifth from left) and his executive staff posed on the steps of the Library building in 1914.

1914

JULY 1 - Putnam establishes the Library's Division of Semitica and Oriental Literature.

JULY 16 - President Wilson approves the Appropriations Act for fiscal year 1915, which—after a year of legislative debate—includes $25,000 for "legislative reference" for the Library. Senator Robert M. La Follette, Sr., of Wisconsin played a major role in formulating the final compromise. On July 18, by administrative order, Putnam establishes the Library's Legislative Reference Service.

1915

MARCH 4 - President Wilson approves the Appropriations Act for fiscal year 1916, which broadens the range of the kinds of information the new Legislative Reference Service can provide to Congress.

AUGUST - Putnam reports that the new Legislative Reference Service is anticipating questions from Congress concerning conservation, immigration, railroad securities, federal aid in roadmaking, publicity in campaign contributions, and a national budget system.

1916

APRIL 13 - Two drafts of President Abraham Lincoln's Gettysburg Address, believed to be the original and second drafts, are presented to the United States government by the descendants of Lincoln's private secretary John Hay and placed in the custody of the Library of Congress.

1917

JANUARY - The Library receives the first installment of the gift of the Theodore Roosevelt Papers, the first group of presidential papers to be received directly from a former president.

Between 1913 and 1915, Senator Robert M. La Follette, Sr., of Wisconsin helped shape the Library's Legislative Reference Service—today known as the Congressional Research Service (CRS). One of the major research arms of the United States Congress, CRS provides independent, nonpartisan research and analysis for Congress and its committees. The La Follette Reading Room in the Madison Building is an important CRS center of activity.

MAY 24 - Mr. and Mrs. Joseph Pennell, the authorized biographers of artist James McNeill Whistler, present a valuable collection of prints and sketches by Whistler to the Library, along with a collection of books and research materials about the artist and his era.

OCTOBER - Putnam becomes the director of the American Library Association War Service, which supplies reading matter to American troops training for or engaged in the World War. Its headquarters is at the Library of Congress.

1918

FEBRUARY - The Library publishes a *Guide to the Cataloging of Periodicals*, prepared by Mary Wilson MacNair of the Catalog Division, to provide guidance to catalogers "without entrenching on the exercise of good judgment on their part."

APRIL - The Library publishes a 750-page *Handbook of the Manuscripts of the Library of Congress*, which describes the Manuscript Division's resources "in a comprehensive way for the practical use of the writer, reader, scholar, and student."

This 1919 photograph of the Library's Card Division shows the three-tier steel card-storage stack from which an attendant is pulling printed catalog cards that have been sold to libraries around the world.

Robert Todd Lincoln, the only surviving son of Abraham Lincoln, deposited a major collection of his father's papers in the Library. In this 1922 photo he was attending dedication ceremonies at the Lincoln Memorial. The Lincoln papers, sealed until 1947, were opened with much fanfare by Librarian Luther H. Evans. They were immediately reviewed by a panel of distinguished Lincoln scholars.

"You have much to discourage you in the present situation. Your expenses are increasing; your salaries are not. . . . But don't for a moment believe that—outside of the fighting ranks themselves—there is any 'war work' more necessary or more patriotic than that you are doing here."

— Librarian of Congress Herbert Putnam, 1918

JULY 25 - Librarian Putnam distributes a letter addressed to the loyal staff of the Library of Congress: "You have much to discourage you in the present situation. Your expenses are increasing; your salaries are not. . . . But don't for a moment believe that—outside of the fighting ranks themselves—there is any 'war work' more necessary or more patriotic than that you are doing here."

NOVEMBER - The Library publishes *Dramatic Compositions Copyrighted in the United States, 1870 to the Present*, prepared by the Copyright Office.

1919

MAY 7 - Robert Todd Lincoln, the son of former president Abraham Lincoln, deposits a major collection of his father's papers in the Library. He donates them formally on January 23, 1923, on the condition that they are kept sealed until 21 years after his own death. He dies in 1926, and accordingly the papers are opened to the public on July 26, 1947.

A scene in the bookbinding
department at the Library,
photographed in 1919–1920.

1920

DECEMBER 7 – Librarian Putnam presides over ceremonies marking the planting of the first memorial tree on Library grounds. The tree honors four Library of Congress servicemen who died in World War I. Subsequent memorial trees have recognized not only Library of Congress employees who fought in World War II, but also staff who have made outstanding administrative contributions to the institution.

DECEMBER 20 – The Prints Division reports the acquisition of more than 300 original daguerreotype portraits of prominent Americans made between 1845 and 1853 by the studio of photographer Mathew B. Brady of Washington, DC, and New York. The collection was transferred to the Library from the US Army War College.

On December 7, 1920, Librarian Putnam planted a tree in front of the Library as a memorial to Library of Congress staff members who died in World War I

Photographer Mathew B. Brady opened a daguerreotype studio in New York City in 1844. He went on to become one of America's greatest documentary photographers. As he once said, "From the first, I regarded myself as under obligation to my country to preserve the faces of its historic men and mothers."

Harriet DeKraft Woods, the Library's first woman
superintendent of buildings and grounds, in
1922. The superintendent's responsibilities were
transferred to the Architect of the Capitol for
budget reasons that year, but Woods remained at
the Library until her retirement in 1928.

Under the supervision of Librarian Putnam, the Declaration of Independence and the US Constitution were loaded into the Library's Model-T Ford mail wagon, for transfer from the State Department to the Library of Congress.

1921

SEPTEMBER 29 – President Warren G. Harding issues an executive order directing the transfer of the original copies of the Declaration of Independence and the US Constitution from the Department of State to the Library of Congress. The documents are transferred the next day.

1922

MARCH 22 – The president approves the Appropriations Act for fiscal year 1923, which includes $12,000 for a "shrine" within the Library for the public display of the Declaration of Independence and the US Constitution.

MAY 9 – Representative Robert Luce of Massachusetts, on behalf of the Joint Library Committee, reports in favor of a bill that would abolish the office of the Library's superintendent of buildings and grounds and transfer its responsibilities to the Architect of the Capitol and the Librarian of Congress. The Architect of the Capitol would be responsible for the building's structural work, repairs, physical equipment, and operation of the physical plant. On June 29, President Harding approves an act of Congress making these changes, which become effective on July 1, 1922.

1923

DECEMBER 3 – In his 1923 annual report, Putnam emphasizes the "imperative need" for a new bookstack, which will fill the Library's northeast courtyard, and the need to improve the salaries of the Library's staff, upon whom "the future of the Library as a learned institution must rest."

1924

FEBRUARY 7-9 - The Library sponsors three chamber music recitals, which are held at the Freer Gallery in Washington, DC, and supported by Elizabeth Sprague Coolidge of Pittsfield, Massachusetts, in connection with her gift to the Library of the original scores of several musical compositions. Putnam hails the event as an especially "notable recognition by our Government . . . of music as one of the finer arts—entitled to its concern and encouragement."

FEBRUARY 28 - In the presence of President Calvin Coolidge, Secretary of State Charles Evans Hughes and a representative group of congressmen, Putnam places the Declaration of Independence and the US Constitution in a specially designed "shrine" for protection and public exhibition. The ceremony takes place "without a single utterance save the singing of two stanzas of 'America.'"

1925

JANUARY 19 - With approvals from Congress and President Coolidge, Elizabeth Sprague Coolidge (no relation) makes a $60,000 gift to support construction of an auditorium within the Library for the performance of chamber music. Through a deed executed by the Northern Trust Company of Chicago, Mrs. Coolidge establishes an endowment, to be paid annually to the Librarian of Congress, to aid the Music Division "in the development of the study, composition, and appreciation of music." The division will be able to hold concerts,

conduct music festivals, and award prizes for original compositions. In addition, the division chief will receive an honorarium recognizing the "special labor and responsibilities" imposed by such activities. The first Library of Congress chamber music concerts take place in the new Coolidge Auditorium, located in the northwest courtyard, on October 28–30, 1925.

MARCH 3 - President Coolidge approves an act of Congress creating a Library of Congress Trust Fund Board, enabling the Library to accept and administer gifts or bequests of personal property for the benefit of the Library, its collections, or its services.

MARCH 4 - Congress approves funding for the construction of a new bookstack in the northeast courtyard.

V. Valta Parma (left), who served as the Library's first rare book curator from 1926 until 1940, sharing a volume with a patron. Parma's major interest was building the collections of American popular culture, including dime novels and children's literature. However, he also pursued acquisitions in more traditional areas; during this period the Library's holdings of early printed books increased markedly, most notably through the 1930 purchase of the Vollbehr collection of incunabula, which included one of the three perfect copies of the Gutenberg Bible.

AUGUST 10 - In a letter to Andrew W. Mellon, secretary of the treasury and chairman of the Library of Congress Trust Fund Board, James B. Wilbur establishes an endowment for the acquisition, in photocopy, of "manuscript material on American history in European archives." In 1933, Mr. Wilbur endows a chair of geography and provides funds for the development of additional source materials in American history.

DECEMBER 7 - The Victor Talking Machine Company of Camden, New Jersey, donates a Victrola and a collection of 412 recordings.

DECEMBER 7 - In his annual report for 1925, Putnam describes Mrs. Coolidge's gift and endowment as "absolutely consistent with the scheme and policy of the Library as the National Library and an agency of the Federal Government, which is, not to duplicate local or ordinary effort, nor supplant it where the project is within its proper fields or abilities, but to do for American scholarship and cultivation what is not likely to be done by other agencies." He asserts that the Coolidge gift and the Wilbur and Coolidge endowments have initiated a "new era" for the Library.

1926

JANUARY - William Dawson Johnston begins his duties as a Library of Congress acquisitions representative in Europe. His headquarters are in Paris.

APRIL 23 - Joseph Pennell dies, bequeathing most of his estate to the Division of Prints in the Library of Congress, to be used to promote its collections and services. He chooses the US government as beneficiary "because the United States is spending money on prints and encouraging art and artists."

OCTOBER-NOVEMBER - James B. Childs, chief of the Documents Division, visits Russia, Latvia, and Lithuania "to form new connections" for the acquisition of government publications.

1927

MARCH - The new bookstack in the northeast courtyard is completed. The book collection now totals more than 3.5 million volumes. The first separate custodial unit for the Library's rare books is located on the top floor of the new bookstack; Putnam assigns V. Valta Parma to be keeper of the Rare Book Room.

APRIL - Putnam announces two new endowments: one for a chair in American history, the other for a chair in fine arts. The Librarian explains that a "chair" takes the form of an honorarium paid directly to a division chief for work in "interpreting" the collections to the inquiring public.

JUNE - The recent endowment for a chair for American history enables Putnam to appoint the well-known historian J. Franklin Jameson of the Carnegie Institution as the chief of the Library's Manuscript Division.

SEPTEMBER 1 - The Library initiates two large projects, each funded for a five-year period by John D. Rockefeller. Project A will enable the Library to acquire, on a greatly expanded scale, copies of source materials in foreign archives relating to American history. Project B provides for the further development of the Library's bibliographical apparatus, in particular the National Union Catalog.

NOVEMBER 18 - Archer M. Huntington of New York City establishes an endowment for the purchase of books relating "to Spanish, Portuguese, and South American arts, crafts, literature, and history." On April 24, 1928, he donates funds to establish a chair of Spanish and Portuguese literature. On November 17, 1936, he donates funds to the Library of Congress Trust Fund Board "to equip and maintain" in the Library a room to be known as the Hispanic Society Room of Spanish and Portuguese Arts and Letters and to establish and maintain a chair of poetry of the English language.

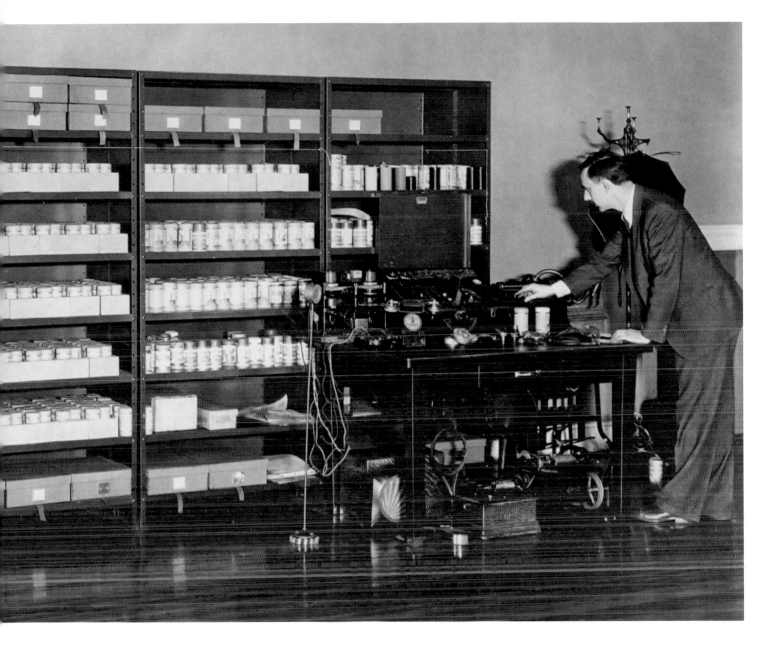

1928

FEBRUARY-APRIL - Charles Martel, chief of the Catalog Division, joins two former Library of Congress colleagues—William Warner Bishop and J.C.M. Hanson—in Rome to install in the Vatican Library "the methods of cataloguing in vogue in American libraries." The Carnegie Corporation pays for the project.

MAY - Using funds donated by "public-spirited citizens," Putnam establishes the Archive of American Folk Song in the Music Division. The project will protect and preserve the folk songs and ballads now "endangered by the spread of the radio and the phonograph, which are diverting the attention of the people from their old heritage."

Robert Winslow Gordon, the first head of the Archive of American Folk Song, in the Library's new recording studio in 1930.

MAY 21 - President Coolidge approves an act of Congress authorizing the purchase of land, at a cost not to exceed $600,000, directly east of the Library to be used as a site for a second Library of Congress building.

JULY 1 - Putnam establishes a division of Chinese literature, which he plans to make into "the center on this hemisphere for the pursuit of oriental studies." Sinologist Arthur W. Hummel is placed in charge.

DECEMBER 11 - More than 100 private citizens meet and organize the Friends of Music in the Library of Congress; the first president is Nicholas Longworth of Ohio, the Speaker of the House of Representatives.

1929

APRIL 5 - On the occasion of his thirtieth anniversary as Librarian of Congress, Putnam is honored by a festschrift edited by William Warner Bishop, director, University of Michigan Libraries and superintendent of Reading Rooms, Library of Congress, 1905–15, and Andrew Keogh, director, University of Yale Libraries. The Library now has an annual appropriation of more than $1 million, a book collection of more than three million volumes, and a staff of nearly 800.

Speaker of the House of Representatives Nicholas Longworth, the first president of the Friends of Music in the Library of Congress, in the mid-1920s.

In 1930, in the midst of an increasing financial crisis, Congress approved the $1.5 million purchase of the Vollbehr collection of incunabula for the Library. Among its treasures is this Gutenberg Bible, printed by Johann Gutenberg in Mainz, Germany in 1455. It was the first great book printed in Western Europe from moveable metal type, and therefore marked a turning point, not only in technology, but also in the transition from the Middle Ages to the modern world

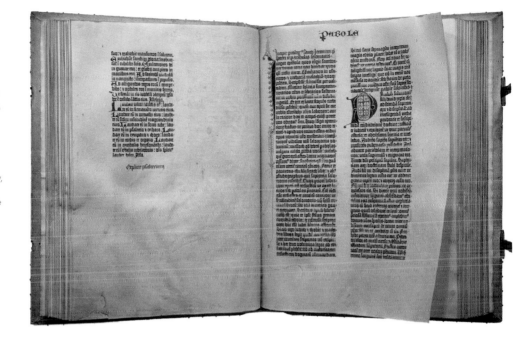

SEPTEMBER 10 - Through the Library of Congress Trust Fund, the Beethoven Association of New York establishes the Sonneck Memorial Fund, to be used by the Music Division for the advancement of musical research. The fund is named for Oscar G.T. Sonneck, a former officer of the association and chief of the Music Division.

OCTOBER 29 - Harry F. Guggenheim, president of the Daniel Guggenheim Fund for the Promotion of Aeronautics, provides funds for the endowment of a chair of aeronautics and for the purchase of aeronautical material. On January 1, 1930, the Library establishes a new Aeronautics Division.

1930

FEBRUARY 7 - Congressman Ross A. Collins of Mississippi makes a one-hour speech in the House of Representatives advocating the purchase of the Otto H.F. Vollbehr collection of incunabula, which includes one of the three perfect vellum copies of the Gutenberg Bible. The cost would be $1.5 million.

APRIL 1 - As a result of a cooperative project with the American Library Association, the Library begins supplying Dewey Decimal Classification numbers on its printed catalog cards.

APRIL 16 - The Carnegie Corporation gives the Library $5,000 to organize a collection of pictorial archives of early American architecture.

JUNE 4 - In reporting in favor of the purchase of the Vollbehr collection to the House of Representatives, Library Committee Chairman Robert Luce of Massachusetts points out that the purchase would set a new precedent, because the US government has not previously "to any significant degree engaged in aiding the arts from the Public Treasury, in other words, subsidizing culture." On June 16, testifying in favor of the Vollbehr purchase, Putnam reminds the Senate Library Committee of the 1815 purchase by the government of the library of Thomas Jefferson for $24,000, "in proportion to the resources of the country a sum not much short of the million and a half" asked for the Vollbehr collection. Moreover, "what is true of that purchase is certainly true of the one before you." It would form "a most admirable substratum for a (greater) national library, such as yours is not yet, but should develop into." President Hoover approves a Supplemental Appropriations Act, which includes $1.5 million for the Vollbehr collection, on July 3.

JUNE 13 - President Herbert Hoover approves an act of Congress that authorizes the extension and remodeling of the east front of the Library, to include a new Rare Book Room, and an appropriation of up to $6 million for the construction of an annex building, to be located on the land east of the Library, which was acquired by the act of May 21, 1928.

1931

MARCH 3 - The president approves the Pratt-Smoot Act, which appropriates $100,000 annually to the Library to "provide books for the use of the adult blind readers of the United States" and its territories.

SEPTEMBER - In his new book *The Epic of America*, historian James Truslow Adams pays tribute to the Library "as a symbol of what democracy can accomplish on its own behalf. . . . Anyone who has used the great collections of Europe, with their restrictions and red tape and difficulty of access, praises God for American democracy when he enters the stacks of the Library of Congress."

"Anyone who has used the great collections of Europe, with their restrictions and red tape and difficulty of access, praises God for American democracy when he enters the stacks of the Library of Congress."

— Historian James Truslow Adams, 1930

1933

FEBRUARY 10 - Because he "knows of no greater contribution this government has made to the public than the Library of Congress," Representative Simon Fess of Ohio, chairman of the Joint Library Committee, urges his fellow members of Congress to appropriate funds to construct the Library's annex.

1934

FEBRUARY 15 - At a meeting of the House of Representatives Appropriations Subcommittee, Putnam states that the Library's collection is now the largest in the world, but he cautions that the methods of counting used by the British Museum and the Bibliothèque nationale de France "are somewhat different than ours and it is not safe to undertake comparisons."

MARCH - The extension of the east front of the Library building is completed, providing new, specially designed quarters for the Rare Book Room, which are modeled after Independence Hall in Philadelphia.

MAY 9 - President Franklin D. Roosevelt approves an act adding sound reproductions for the use of the blind to the Library's service for the blind program.

JUNE 19 - President Roosevelt approves an act of Congress establishing the National Archives of the United States. It stipulates that "all archives or records belonging to the Government of the United States (legislative, executive, judicial, and other) shall be under the charge and superintendence of the Archivist." The Librarian of Congress and the secretary of the Smithsonian Institution are included as members of the advisory council for the new organization.

1935

JANUARY 21 - In a letter to Carl H. Milam, secretary of the American Library Association, Putnam rejects the idea of locating a federal library bureau, which would coordinate the activities of federal libraries, at the Library of Congress, asserting that the functions of such an agency "would tend to confuse and impede the service to learning which should be the primary duty of our National Library." Instead, the Librarian feels the bureau "should be associated with one of the executive departments of the government."

MARCH 6 - Former Supreme Court Justice Oliver Wendell Holmes, Jr., dies, bequeathing his private library to the Library of Congress.

APRIL 8 - Radio station WMAL in Washington, DC, broadcasts part of a concert by the Kolisch Quartet from the Coolidge Auditorium—the first radio broadcast of a Library chamber music concert.

JUNE - The Library provides approximately 25,000 duplicate volumes from its law collections to the newly established Supreme Court Library, located directly across from the Library at First Street on Capitol Hill.

JUNE 6 - President Roosevelt approves an act increasing by $2,866,340 the limit on funds to be appropriated for the construction of the Library's new annex.

JUNE 12 - The Architect of the Capitol awards the contract to construct the Library of Congress Annex.

NOVEMBER - The Library publishes the *Guide to the Diplomatic History of the United States, 1775–1921*, by historian Samuel F. Bemis and bibliographer Grace Gardner Griffin; they dedicate their volume to Herbert Putnam, "that organizer of opportunity." Bemis, chairman of the George Washington University History Department from 1924 to 1934, also headed a Library of Congress project funded by John D. Rockefeller, Jr., from 1927 to 1932, which enabled the institution to acquire, on a greatly expanded scale, resource materials from foreign archives for the study of American history.

Gertrude Clarke Whittall, who between 1935 and 1938 donated five Stradivari instruments to the Library, established a foundation to support concerts in which the instruments were to be used, and donated funds to build a pavilion in which they were to be housed.

DECEMBER - Philanthropist Gertrude Clarke Whittall donates four stringed instruments made by Antonio Stradivari to the Library. On March 2, 1936, she establishes a foundation to support the maintenance of the instruments as well as concerts in the Coolidge Auditorium in which those instruments will be played. In January 1937, she adds a fifth Stradivari instrument to her gift. In 1938 she donates funds to build an elegant pavilion in which the instruments are to be housed and displayed. The Whittall Pavilion, adjacent to the Coolidge Auditorium, opens on March 6, 1939.

1936

JANUARY - The Library publishes the first issue of the *Digest of Public Bills*, prepared by the Legislative Reference Service at the direction of Congress. The *Digest* was a description and status report concerning legislative bills currently being considered by Congress that were not of a private or local nature. On November 1, 1967, the Library installs two leased computer terminals to be used in the preparation of the *Digest of Public General Bills and Resolutions*, the first use of computer terminals in the Library.

In 1935, Mrs. Gertrude Clarke Whittall donated the "Castelbarco" cello, made by Antonio Stradivari in Cremona, Italy, in 1699 and originally owned by Count Cesare Castelbarco of Milan. Whittall was passionate about the instrument, declaring, "As for the 'Castelbarco' 'cello, any artist who has once drawn his bow across its strings will be haunted forever by its unforgettable tone. When all the strings are playing together the ensemble is like a heavenly choir, for they all speak the same language."

RARE BOOK COLLECTION

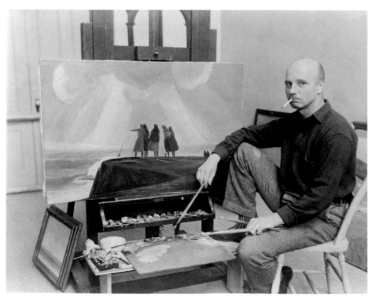

In 1937, designer Rockwell Kent (bottom) presented the Library with a new bookplate (top) for its rare book collection. Its design, emphasizing the institution's "national character," was described by Mr. Kent: "The central part of my design, the book and the American eagle, towering as it does monumentally over a background suggestive of our cities and mountains and a foreground dotted by little figures that may be taken to be the publica, is as all-embracing a graphic expression as I could contrive of the importance that the Library of Congress should be to America."

JANUARY 3 - Herman H.B. Meyer, director of the Books for the Adult Blind Project, reports on the rapid development of "talking books" and announces the inauguration of a new annual publication, *Talking Book Titles*.

MARCH 1 - At the suggestion of the Association of Research Libraries, the Library establishes an interlibrary loan clearinghouse.

1937
JUNE 23 - Describing the new Library Annex at an American Library Association meeting, Martin S. Roberts, the superintendent of the Main Reading Room, points out that with its 249 miles of shelves, it will hold about 10 million volumes—or about twice as many as the main Library building.

1938
JANUARY 3 - Putnam reports that Joseph Auslander, lecturer on poetry at Columbia University and poetry editor of the *North American Review*, has been hired for the present year to serve as the Library's first consultant in poetry.

MARCH – A five-year juvenilia bibliographic project is inaugurated, using funds donated by J.K. Lilly, Jr.

MARCH 1 – Using funds from the Rockefeller Foundation, the Library establishes a Photoduplication Service to supply "distant investigators with microfilm and other photoduplicates of materials otherwise not available for use outside of Washington."

JUNE 20 – President Roosevelt approves an act of Congress providing that "upon separation from the service, by resignation or otherwise, on July 1, Herbert Putnam, the present Librarian of Congress . . . shall become Librarian Emeritus." Putnam's annual salary as Librarian Emeritus will be $5,000.

NOVEMBER 1 – The Carnegie Corporation gives the Library a three-year grant totaling $13,500 for the development of its Indica collection and "for the promotion of greater interest at large in the study of India.

DECEMBER – The Library begins to move staff and materials into its newly completed Annex Building.

1939
Actor Jimmy Stewart stars in director Frank Capra's classic political film *Mr. Smith Goes to Washington*. In one scene, he admires the Great Hall in the Library's Jefferson Building; the "shrine" displaying the Declaration of Independence and the US Constitution, then on public view at the Library, can be seen in the background.

JANUARY 3 – The Annex Building is opened to the general public with the exception of the two sixth-floor reading rooms, which are not ready until the spring.

JANUARY 27 – In a special tribute addressed to Putnam, the American Council of Learned Societies informs the Librarian that he, and the collaborators and associates whom he has chosen, have made the Library of Congress "an indispensable instrument on the American continent for the promotion of learning and the increase of knowledge."

JANUARY 30 – In its request for funds for fiscal year 1940, the Library asks for $1,000 to initiate a program of "microfilming the more important newspaper files in the Library to preserve them from complete loss through disintegration."

APRIL 5 – On the 40th anniversary of Putnam's taking the oath of office as Librarian of Congress, the reading rooms of the new Annex open to the public.

MAY 11 – In a letter to President Roosevelt, Supreme Court Justice Felix Frankfurter endorses the president's suggestion that poet and writer Archibald MacLeish would make a good Librarian of Congress, primarily because "only a scholarly man of letters can make a great national library a general place of habitation for scholars." On June 7, President Roosevelt nominates MacLeish to be Librarian

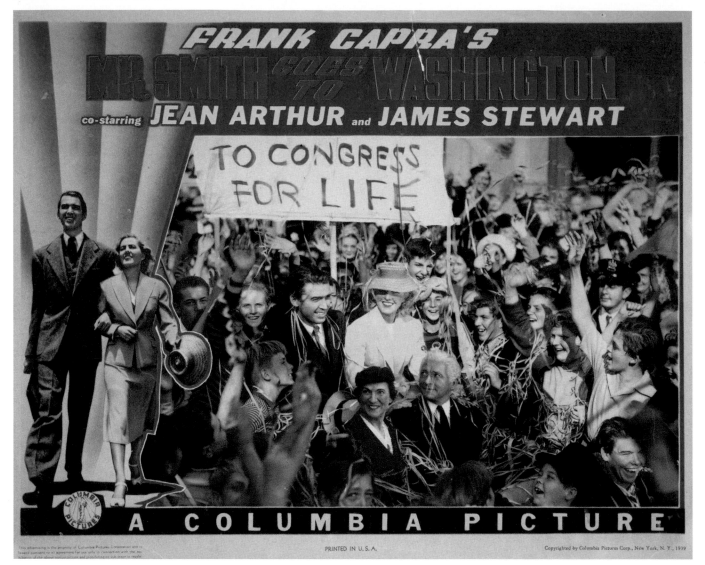

FRANK CAPRA'S
MR. SMITH GOES TO WASHINGTON
co-starring JEAN ARTHUR and JAMES STEWART

TO CONGRESS
FOR LIFE

COLUMBIA PICTURES

A COLUMBIA PICTURE

PRINTED IN U.S.A.   Copyrighted by Columbia Pictures Corp., New York, N. Y., 1939

of Congress. The Senate Library Committee, chaired by Senator Alben W. Barkley of Kentucky, holds hearings on the MacLeish nomination on June 13. MacLeish is the only nominee. The Senate committee continues its hearings on June 19. Representatives of the American Library Association testify against the nomination, reiterating the resolution adopted the previous day by the association at its annual conference in San Francisco: "the Congress and the American people should have a Librarian . . . one who is not only a gentleman and a scholar but who is also the ablest library administrator available."

Senator Barkley presents an executive report favoring MacLeish's confirmation on June 20, and on June 29, after a two-hour debate, the Senate confirms MacLeish's nomination by a vote of 63 to 8.

Mr. Smith Goes to Washington, starring Jimmy Stewart, was one of the first popular films to feature a scene at the Library of Congress.

MAY 24 - Under the terms in the will of the composer's mother, Mrs. Rose Gershwin, the Library receives its first manuscripts by George Gershwin. The group includes the original scores of *Rhapsody in Blue*, *An American in Paris*, and *Porgy and Bess*. Through the years, the continually expanding Gershwin collection comes to include other musical manuscripts, correspondence, documentation, and pictorial materials, such as photographs and both paintings and drawings by George and Ira Gershwin. The Ira and Leonore S. Gershwin Fund is established in 1992. On March 17, 1998, the George and Ira Gershwin Room near the Coolidge Auditorium opens to the public.

The Gershwin family presented a series of gifts to the Library, including this original score of *Porgy and Bess* (left), and a self-portrait painted by George Gershwin (right).

FROM ANNEX TO ADAMS

Artist Ezra Winter's rendering of *The Canterbury Tales,* a mural on the walls of the north reading room in the Adams Building.

Called the Annex Building when it opened to the public in 1939, the Library's handsome John Adams Building was officially named for the nation's second president in 1980. John Adams was a book-loving and -collecting president; he also signed the Library's founding legislation in 1800.

The simple classical structure of the Adams Building was intended, essentially, to function as an efficient bookstack "encircled with work spaces." The Washington architectural firm of Pierson & Wilson designed the structure, with Alexander Buel Trowbridge as consulting architect. The contract stipulated completion by June 24, 1938, but the building was not ready for occupancy until December 2, 1938. The move of the Card Division began on December 12 and the building opened to the general public on January 3, 1939. The two reading rooms on the top floor, however, were not ready for use by researchers until early April.

The Adams Building's somewhat understated decorative style contains striking elements of Art Deco inspired by the Exposition Internationale des Arts Décoratifs held in Paris in 1925. In recent times it has been recognized as one of the few distinguished Art Deco buildings in Washington, DC. The building's dignified exterior is faced with white Georgia marble and pink granite from North Carolina. The history of the written word is depicted in bas-relief figures by designer Lee Lawrie on the bronze doors at both the west and east entrances. Reflecting the Library's increasing international role and collecting interests, emphasized by Librarian Putnam, the figures on the doors represent cultures that, since ancient times, have influenced the art of writing.

When it opened the Annex contained 180 miles of shelving (compared with 104 miles in the Jefferson Building when it opened in 1897) and was designed to hold 10 million volumes. It has entrances and decorative doors at both the west and east entrances. At its heart are 12 tiers of stacks, extending from the cellar to the fourth floor. A sculpted stairway with stylized owls and ornate lamps leads to the southern entrance on Independence Avenue. This entrance, which has never been used, was intended for the US Copyright Office.

Murals by artist Ezra Winter are the "hidden treasures" of the two public reading rooms on the top floor of the Adams Building. In *The Canterbury Pilgrims*, composed for the walls of the north reading room, Winter presents the Pilgrims in very nearly the order in which Chaucer introduced them in the Prologue to *The Canterbury Tales*. The mural topic in the south reading room presents less of a surprise but is worthy of attention: inscriptions of Thomas Jefferson's carefully crafted thoughts on freedom, labor, the living generation, education, and democratic government.

The owl as a symbol of learning is an especially prominent motif in the Library's Adams Building. This stunning art deco depiction is seen throughout the building.

The Library's John Adams Building, originally known as the Annex.

Soon after he became Librarian of Congress on November 12, 1975, Daniel J. Boorstin declared that he "had never met anyone named Mr. Annex," and announced his intent to change the building's name. He did so on April 13, 1976, in a ceremony that also marked the birthday of Thomas Jefferson. President Gerald Ford signed into law an act of Congress that changed the name of the Annex Building to the Thomas Jefferson Building. But the change only lasted four years. With the James Madison Memorial Building due to open in 1980, the Architect of the Capitol asked the Library to consider a greater uniformity in the names of the Library's buildings. Why not name each for a Founding Father who indeed had a strong connection to the Library? Fortunately, John Adams was available. Therefore, on June 10, 1980, the grand 1897 structure known for so many years as "The Library," rightfully became the Thomas Jefferson Building and the structure called the Annex, but briefly renamed for Jefferson, became, permanently, the John Adams Building.

JULY 1 - As provided in the Appropriations Act for fiscal year 1939, the Library establishes the Hispanic Foundation.

JULY 10 - Knowing he was not expected to take office until the fall and wanting to stay in his hometown of Conway, Massachusetts, during the summer to finish his poem *America Was Promises*, "on the spur of the moment" Archibald MacLeish persuades the local postmaster to swear him in as the 9th Librarian of Congress. The only witness was another postal employee.

OCTOBER 1 - Herbert Putnam becomes the first Librarian of Congress Emeritus.

OCTOBER 2 - Librarian of Congress Archibald MacLeish assumes his duties.

OCTOBER 12 - MacLeish dedicates the new Hispanic Room "to the preservation and study and the honor of the literature and scholarship of those other republics which share with ours the word American."

OCTOBER 17 - With approval from President Roosevelt and cooperation from the District of Columbia Work Projects Administration, Librarian MacLeish creates a special Library of Congress WPA project. Its primary purpose is to edit, index, and make available for use research materials from WPA cultural projects and to continue the national editorial functions of the Federal Writers' Project and the Historical Records Survey.

On November 28, 1939, Librarian MacLeish (left) accepted from the British ambassador the temporary deposit of the Lincoln Cathedral copy of the Magna Carta for safekeeping during World War II. The charter had previously been on display at the 1939 New York World's Fair.

OCTOBER 28 - Southeast Asian specialist Horace I. Poleman leaves on an acquisitions trip to Southeast Asia. He takes with him a "portable microfilming apparatus" furnished by the American Council of Learned Societies.

NOVEMBER 19 - Speaking on the occasion of the laying of the cornerstone of the new Franklin D. Roosevelt Library in Hyde Park, New York, Librarian MacLeish urges greater cooperation among libraries: "The unit for scholarly purposes is no longer the individual library, but libraries as a whole."

NOVEMBER 28 – With war raging in Europe, the British ambassador to the United States deposits the Lincoln Cathedral copy of the Magna Carta in the Library for temporary safekeeping. In accepting its wartime custody, MacLeish emphasizes that, "the institutions of representative government are the protectors, and the only possible protectors, of the charters of the people's rights."

DECEMBER 19 – The Library's new Committee on Acquisitions, appointed by MacLeish and supplemented by specialists from the academic community, documents how, in its view, the Library "is not maintaining its proper position in respect to the quality of its holdings." It recommends that the annual appropriation for general book purchases be increased dramatically.

1940

JANUARY 3 – Alan Lomax, assistant in charge of the Archive of American Folk Song, reports a dramatic increase in acquisitions, which he feels has been stimulated by a "developing consciousness of the significance of a native culture." He cites the expansion of the archive's collections to include recordings of Finnish, Serbian, Russian, Polish, Portuguese, Cuban, and Mexican songs and dances.

FEBRUARY – As the federal arts projects started in the 1930s begin to wane across the country, MacLeish gives the Library of Congress WPA project a new purpose: to "collect, preserve, and organize" the research materi-

Folklorist Alan Lomax joined the Library staff in 1936, and from 1937 until 1942 was assistant in charge of the Archive of American Folk Song. In 2004, the Library acquired his ethnological collection, supplementing his earlier folklife contributions. Here he performs at a North Carolina festival in the late 1930s.

als gathered and produced by Federal Project Number One (divided into the Federal Art, Music, Theatre, and Writers' Projects and the Historical Records Survey) in order to add the material to the Library's collections. Arts projects across the nation are instructed to accelerate their efforts to send research materials to the Library. More than 5,000 cubic feet of materials from the five original divisions of Federal Project Number One are forwarded between 1939 and 1941.

FEBRUARY 28 - MacLeish explains his $4.2 million budget request for fiscal year 1941 to Congress, describing the staff and outside advisory committees he has appointed, but emphasizing that his first priority is to improve the Library's "salary situation."

MARCH 13 - The House of Representatives Committee on Appropriations, while not allowing all of the requests submitted by the new Librarian, feels it "should frankly express its pleasure at the industrious and intelligent manner in which Mr. MacLeish has entered upon his duties." The committee approves 130 of the 287 new positions requested.

APRIL - At the request of the Librarian, the Civil Service Commission agrees to conduct a survey "in order to adjust existing inequalities" in the job grade classifications of Library employees.

APRIL - With support from the Carnegie Corporation, MacLeish appoints a Librarian's Committee of three distinguished librarians from outside the Library of Congress to analyze and make recommendations for improving the operations of the Library, especially its cataloging and processing activities. Three additional specialists from libraries around the country will assist them.

APRIL 19 - The Librarian announces a grant from the Carnegie Corporation to establish a complete sound laboratory in the Music Division for duplicating phonograph recordings, making master recordings, originating broadcasts, and making transcriptions for radio broadcast. In addition, the Library will purchase a sound truck with six portable receivers to make recordings in the field.

MAY 31 - With the war in Europe as context, MacLeish addresses a meeting of the American Library Association and asserts that librarians "must become active and not passive agents of the democratic process."

JUNE 15 - The Librarian's Committee submits a detailed, 300-page report to MacLeish. The major conclusion is that "the Library cannot be an efficient operating agency until its organic structure has been thoroughly overhauled," and the report outlines a reorganization plan that reduces the span of administrative control "at all levels of the hierarchy." It calls for a restatement of the Library's objectives,

focuses on cataloging arrearages as a special concern, and presents dozens of specific recommendations.

SEPTEMBER 1 - The Library establishes a program of resident fellowships for young scholars "who will spend a year in the Library on leave from their institutions." In making the funds available, the Carnegie Corporation acts from the conviction "that American cultural institutions can be greatly strengthened if scholars will accept a responsibility for the collections of the national library and if the national library will accept a responsibility for the instruction of scholars in the services it is expected to render." The first fellows are appointed in the subjects of modern European history, population, romance languages, library science, geology, and Slavic languages and literature.

This display featured instruments from the notable flute collection donated to the Library in 1941 by physicist Dayton C. Miller.

OCTOBER 14 - The Budapest String Quartet presents its first concert as the Library's "resident" ensemble. For two periods of three months each during 1940 and 1941, the quartet will reside in Washington and use the Library's Stradivari instruments for frequent public performances in the Coolidge Auditorium. The Gertrude Clarke Whittall Foundation supports this new endeavor.

NOVEMBER 15 - In his 555-page annual report for 1940, MacLeish summarizes the condition of the Library, its needs, and "the action taken and plans prepared to meet those needs." He identifies the special strengths and weaknesses of the collections, presents a comprehensive statement of its acquisitions policies ("The Canons of Selection") and research objectives ("The Canons of Service") and emphasizes the institution's role as "a people's library."

1941

JANUARY 1 - The Library of Congress Radio Research Project begins operation. Funded for one year by the Rockefeller Foundation, its purpose is "to find, through experiment and research, radio forms by which pertinent parts of the record of American culture maintained in the Library of Congress may be made available to the American people."

FEBRUARY 22 - Physicist Dayton C. Miller dies, bequeathing to the Library his collection of more than 1,600 flutes and related instruments and music, along with his 3,000-volume library containing virtually every publication about the flute up to 1940. He also provides funds to support and expand the collection.

FEBRUARY 27 - Poet Robinson Jeffers reads his poems for the first time at the Library, inaugurating The Poet in a Democracy, a series of readings and talks by distinguished American poets. A one-month exhibit devoted to Jeffers is open to the public.

Members of the Budapest String Quartet, the Library's "resident" ensemble in 1940–41, performing at the Coolidge Auditorium.

Mexican men and boys surround Charles Todd of the American Folklife Center, who, in 1941, used the equipment pictured to make field recordings.

JUNE – Through the efforts of more than 700 staff members, who volunteered their time outside of normal duty hours, the Library completes a four-month project of selecting and preparing unique and irreplaceable books and manuscripts from the collections for possible evacuation in the event of wartime emergency.

JULY 3 – The Library of Congress WPA project is terminated because of a sharp reduction in funds supporting all WPA projects in the District of Columbia.

AUGUST – Artist Ezra Winter's four large murals illustrating "the basic idea of the Jefferson creed" are placed on the walls of the Jefferson Reading Room on the south side of the top floor of the Annex (now the John Adams Building). The four panels, which form a continuous frieze completely surrounding the room, depict quotations that reflect Jefferson's thoughts on freedom, labor, the living generation, education, and democratic government. On December 15, Attorney General Francis Biddle dedicates the murals in a ceremony that also commemorates the sesquicentennial anniversary of the adoption of the Bill of Rights.

AUGUST 5 - Librarian MacLeish announces the creation of the Gertrude Clarke Whittall Foundation Collection of Musical Autographs in the Music Division. The first purchase is a collection of original manuscripts by Beethoven, Brahms, Haydn, Mozart, Schubert, Wagner, and Weber.

SEPTEMBER 10 - The Library creates a "democracy alcove" for readers in the Main Reading Room, which offers books and writings about American democracy.

DECEMBER 15 - Because of the new wartime emergency, instituted after the Japanese attack on Pearl Harbor on December 7, the Library begins providing a 24-hour service to the government, which requires temporary curtailment of the hours of service to the general public.

The first purchase by the new Gertrude Clarke Whittall Foundation Collection of Musical Autographs included this manuscript, Sonate für das Hammerklavier, holograph score, 1820, by Ludwig van Beethoven.

DECEMBER 23 - The Declaration of Independence, the US Constitution, and the Gutenberg Bible are removed from the Library Great Hall exhibit area "to places of greater security." On December 29, they, along with four other Library of Congress "top treasures," are sent to a secret location outside of Washington, DC, for safekeeping during World War II. The four other treasures are the Articles of Confederation, the Gettysburg Address, Lincoln's Second Inaugural Address, and the Lincoln Cathedral copy of the Magna Carta, which was entrusted to the Library for temporary safekeeping by the British ambassador on November 28, 1939. In addition to these "top treasures," more than 4,000 packing cases of other unique and irreplaceable books, documents, and research materials selected by the staff between February and June are sent to several other distant locations.

1942

JANUARY 12 - The Library dedicates four large paintings by Brazilian muralist Cândido Portinari. Installed at the entrance to the Hispanic Room, they depict people and events over a succession of time periods, beginning with the Spanish and Portuguese contact in America. The remarks of the Brazilian ambassador, Lewis Hanke, director of the Library's Hispanic Foundation, and Nelson Rockefeller, US coordinator of Inter-American Affairs, are broadcast by shortwave radio to Brazil.

Brazilian artist Cândido Portinari executed four large murals about the Spanish and Portuguese presence in America, which hang at the entrance to the Library's Hispanic Room, established in 1939. This, the second painting in the cycle, is called *Entry into the Forest* and depicts the conquest and domination of the land. The paintings were dedicated in 1942.

MAY 18 - Librarian MacLeish announces a new program for selecting motion pictures for preservation in the Library's collections. He expects the new arrangement, which has been made possible by the Rockefeller Foundation and the Museum of Modern Art in New York, to "gradually build up in the national library a collection of the most important films produced by the American motion picture industry." Another new plan is soon developed for handling motion pictures deposited for copyright.

JUNE 26 - At the annual meeting of the American Library Association, MacLeish is introduced as "a man of whom we librarians are very proud" and delivers an address calling on writers, scholars, and librarians to take "an intellectual offensive" in World War II.

OCTOBER 9 - The executive committee of the Librarian's Council, MacLeish's internal governing board, begins to formulate plans for a cooperative acquisitions project among American research libraries. The meeting, held at the home of Council Chairman Wilmarth S. Lewis in Farmington, Connecticut, includes representatives from many major institutions.

DECEMBER - In his preface to *A Catalog of Books Represented by Library of Congress Printed Cards Issued to July 31, 1942*, published by Edwards Brothers of Ann Arbor, Michigan, MacLeish places the projected 160-volume series in historical perspective: "What will touch the imaginations of imaginative users

(readers there will be none) is the fact that this enormous work is not merely a catalog of books, but a source book for the study of catalogs." He pays tribute to its major formulators, citing men unknown to most Americans but who "have done far more for the enduring life of their country" than many more familiar figures: Charles Coffin Jewett, Ainsworth Rand Spofford, Richard Rogers Bowker, Melvil Dewey, and Herbert Putnam, "the" Librarian of Congress.

1943

MARCH 17 - The Library announces the gift of a magnificent collection of rare books and manuscripts from Lessing J. Rosenwald of Jenkintown, Pennsylvania. With the illustrated book as its central theme, it includes more than 200 incunabula. In July 1964, Mr. Rosenwald donates an additional 700 rare books to the Library. The gifts, which continue until Mr. Rosenwald's death in 1979, result in a collection of 2,653 titles, including 588 incunabula.

APRIL 12 - To celebrate the bicentennial of Thomas Jefferson's birth, the Library opens a major exhibition in its two buildings to honor the man whom Librarian MacLeish, in his introduction to the exhibition catalog, calls "the founder" of the Library of Congress. On April 13, Jefferson's birthday, Supreme Court Justice Felix Frankfurter presents a public address, "The Permanence of Jefferson," at the Library. Also on April 13, on the occasion of the dedication of the Jefferson Memorial at the Tidal Basin, Librarian MacLeish hosts a two-

This beautifully illustrated Book of Hours from 1524 is from the magnificent collection of rare books and manuscripts of Lessing J. Rosenwald of Jenkintown, Pennsylvania. Rosenwald began donating his collection to the Library in 1943.

This 1943 photograph shows students studying in the South Reading Room of the Adams Building under a mural with the words of Thomas Jefferson: "The Earth belongs always to the living generation."

In October 1944, the collections and documents sent outside of the Library for safekeeping during World War II were returned. In this photograph, Librarian of Congress Archibald MacLeish (center) examines the Declaration of Independence, along with senior officials David C. Mearns (left) and Verner W. Clapp (right).

hour symposium in his office to discuss "the application of the Jeffersonian experience to our experience." Participants include scholars Dumas Malone, Gilbert Chinard, Howard Mumford Jones, and Alan Nevins; author Van Wyck Brooks; columnist Walter Lippman; editors Malcolm Cowley and Henry Seidal Canby; Fiske Kimball, director of the Philadelphia Museum of Art; and former presidential candidate Wendell Willkie.

JULY 1 - Poet and literary critic Allen Tate begins a one-year term as the Library's consultant in poetry. He also will advise the Library regarding "its program of acquisition in English letters generally." In addition, he will edit a new Library publication, the *Quarterly Journal of Current Acquisitions*. On July 23, 1944, MacLeish appoints Robert Penn Warren to be poetry consultant and editor of the journal.

Among the approximately 175,000 photographs from the Library's Farm Security Administration archive is *Migrant Mother*, the iconic and often reproduced photograph of the Great Depression by Dorothea Lange.

OCTOBER - The Library begins microfilming the Thomas Jefferson Papers.

1944

JANUARY 1 - The Library assumes custody of the Office of War Information (OWI) collection of about 175,000 photographs, which includes the vast archive organized by Roy E. Stryker from 1936 to 1942 for the Farm Security Administration's "photo-documentation of America." The collection includes many now iconic images by such photographers as Dorothea Lange, Walker Evans, Arthur Rothstein, and Gordon Parks.

MAY 26-27 - The Fellows in American Letters of the Library of Congress hold their organizational meeting. The members are Van Wyck Brooks, Katherine Garrison Chapin, Paul Green, Katherine Anne Porter, Carl Sandburg, Allen Tate, Willard Thorp, and Mark Van Doren.

OCTOBER - MacLeish describes the Library's reorganization in a lengthy article in the journal *Library Quarterly*. He concludes by expressing his hope and belief that the extensive reorganization has given "an increasing number of men and women the sense of participating creatively and responsibly in a work which all of them may well feel proud to share."

This is a scene from the world premier of *Appalachian Spring,* choreographed by Martha Graham with music by Aaron Copland, performed in the Coolidge Auditorium on October 30, 1944 (left). As a tribute to their founder and the Library, the Martha Graham Dance Company recreated the work in the Coolidge Auditorium in 2016 (right).

OCTOBER 1 - After officials determine that there is no longer a wartime threat to Washington, DC, the Declaration of Independence and the US Constitution are placed back in the "shrine" for public display.

OCTOBER 30 - The ballet *Appalachian Spring*, commissioned by the Library's Elizabeth Sprague Coolidge Fund, premiers in the Library's Coolidge Auditorium, with a performance by the Martha Graham Dance Company. Graham choreographed the work to music by Aaron Copland.

NOVEMBER 13 - MacLeish announces that a recent grant from the Rockefeller Foundation will enable the Library to take the initial steps toward the establishment of a Slavic center.

Composer Aaron Copland in his studio in 1946.

NOVEMBER 29 - The Library announces the creation, with a $100,000 grant from the Rockefeller Foundation, of the Library of Congress Grants-in-Aid for Studies in American History and Civilization.

DECEMBER 19 - MacLeish resigns to become US assistant secretary of state.

DECEMBER 20 - Luther H. Evans, Chief Assistant Librarian of Congress, becomes the Acting Librarian of Congress.

1945

FEBRUARY 1 - The Library completes microfilming its unique collection of slave narratives, which includes 17 volumes of transcripts based on Federal Writers' Project interviews with former slaves.

FEBRUARY 4 - The Library discloses what previously was a military secret—that Fort Knox, Kentucky, was the wartime repository for the Declaration of Independence and the US Constitution.

FEBRUARY 21 - Barney Balaban, president of Paramount Pictures, gives the Library a contemporary manuscript copy of the original enrolled copy of the Bill of Rights.

MARCH 3 - Senator Claude Pepper of Florida opens an exhibition commemorating the centennial of Florida's admission to the Union, the first in a series of Library exhibits honoring significant anniversaries in the histories of the American states and territories. In his introduction to the illustrated 36-page catalog, Acting Librarian Evans expresses his hope that by featuring state treasures from the book, manuscript, and pictorial materials of the Library of Congress, the catalog series will help Americans "come to know what is ours, and what we may become." The series ends in 1972 with the exhibition and catalog marking the sesquicentennial of the statehood of Missouri.

APRIL 23 - The first meeting of the United Nations Conference on International Organization—organized and assembled by the Library of Congress in cooperation with the State Department and other American libraries—opens in San Francisco.

JUNE 18 - President Harry S. Truman nominates Acting Librarian Luther H. Evans to be Librarian of Congress.

JUNE 28 - The Senate Library Committee, chaired by Alben W. Barkley of Kentucky, holds hearings on the Evans nomination and listens to testimony from the nominee. On behalf of the committee, Senator Barkley submits an executive report to the Senate favoring the nomination. Without objection, the Senate confirms the nomination on June 29.

JUNE 30 - Luther H. Evans takes the oath of office to become the tenth Librarian of Congress. The Library has a book collection of more than seven million volumes, a staff of 1,200, and an appropriation in fiscal year 1945 of over $4 million.

JULY - With the approval of the War Department, a special Library of Congress "Mission to Europe" begins acquiring "multiple copies of European publications for the war period" for distribution to American libraries and research institutions.

JULY - In a report to President Truman titled *Science, the Endless Frontier*, Vannevar Bush, director of the Office of Scientific Research and Development, suggests that new federal aid for the library system of the country "might well have as its central object the strengthening of the Library of Congress so that it could foster programs of cooperation."

JULY 21 - In a radio address, Evans defines a new national task: building up the library resources of the nation, "at the head of which stands the Library of Congress," so that "this Nation possesses the printed, the pictorial, the cartographic and the other material which will be needed by the Government and its people."

JULY 22 - The Librarian announces a further expansion of the Library's collecting activities for motion pictures.

AUGUST 20 - The Library establishes a Near East section in the Orientalia Division.

AUGUST 27 - The Library's work week is shortened from six days a week, 13 hours a day, to five days a week, eight hours a day.

SEPTEMBER 19 - The War Department and the Library formulate plans for a cooperative overseas acquisitions program that will focus on "locating and forwarding the bookstocks believed to be in Germany (especially in the Russian Zone) as a result of prewar orders placed by American libraries." The Library of Congress Mission to Europe will serve as the "procuring arm" of the project.

OCTOBER - The Library publishes *Sixty American Poets, 1896–1944*, with selection and critical notes by Allen Tate, consultant in poetry, 1943–44, and a bibliography of the writings of each poet.

1946

JANUARY 11 - In a ceremony at the Library, the Lincoln Cathedral copy of the Magna Carta is entrusted to John Balfour, British ambassador to the United States, for safe return to England now that the war is over.

MARCH 4 - The Joint Committee on the Organization of Congress recommends that the Legislative Reference Service immediately be increased in size and scope to more adequately serve the needs of Congress.

MARCH 28 - In a speech before the National Board of Review of Motion Pictures, Evans outlines his plans to develop a national motion picture collection at the Library.

APRIL 20 - British novelist W. Somerset Maugham presents the original manuscript of his classic novel *Of Human Bondage* to the Library of Congress to acknowledge the "kindness and generosity" with which the United States "received the women and children of my country when in fear of a German invasion they came to America."

APRIL 22 - Librarian Evans submits a lengthy fiscal year 1947 budget request, which calls for a rapid and comprehensive expansion of the Library's national services and a budget increase from $5,104,568 to more than $9 million. He explains that the request was "conceived in the light of what we believe to be the Congressional conception of the role and work of the Library."

MAY 14 - The House of Representatives Committee on Appropriations recommends an appropriation of $5,859,900 for the Library. It explains that a principal reason for rejecting the substantial increase requested by Librarian Evans was "to give attention to the need for a determination as to what the policy of the Library of Congress is going to be in the way of expansion and service to the public and to the Congress."

JULY 1 - President Truman approves the Legislative Branch Appropriations Act for fiscal year 1947, which grants the Library $6,069,967.

As a silent film actress and cofounder of United Artists, Mary Pickford amassed an important private film collection. She personally held domestic and foreign camera negatives, work prints, and early generation and reissue prints of much of her work, all of which were donated to the Library in 1946.

AUGUST 2 - President Truman approves the Legislative Reorganization Act of 1946, which expands the responsibilities of the Library's Legislative Reference Service (LRS) in assisting Congress and its committees and gives the service permanent status as a separate department. The act authorizes increased appropriations to enable LRS to employ nationally eminent specialists in 19 broad subject fields.

AUGUST 8 - The Librarian announces that Edith Bolling Wilson, widow of the former president, has donated Woodrow Wilson's 9,000-volume personal library to the Library of Congress. It contains books associated with every period of Wilson's life, including volumes he read as a child; texts used from preparatory through law school; works in the fields of economics, political science, history, and literature, that Wilson acquired during his years as an educator; and inscribed volumes that were presented to him during and after his presidency.

AUGUST 22 - In recognition of "the development of folklore as a field of scholarly inquiry," the Library establishes a Folklore Section, which incorporates the Archive of American Folk Song, in the Music Division.

SEPTEMBER - Secretary of State James F. Byrnes appoints Librarian Evans to the US National Commission on the United Nations Educational, Scientific and Cultural Organization (UNESCO).

OCTOBER - Librarian Evans strengthens the Library's motion picture project, expands its services to the blind, consolidates its processing department, and establishes regularly scheduled tours of the Library for the general public.

OCTOBER 15 - The Librarian submits a 538-page annual report for fiscal year 1947 to Congress. In his introduction, he points to the May 14 report of the House of Representatives Appropriations Committee as a glaring example of "how guilty the Library has been of failure to provide essential information on itself" to Congress and the public. As one corrective, the report includes a 214-page history of the Library, "The Story Up to Now," by the director of the Reference Department. The budget justification for the fiscal year also is reprinted. Moreover, the Librarian announces the recent appointment of a Library of Congress Planning Committee of eminent persons representing categories of the Library's users to examine and report on what role the Library "ought to play in the national life."

DECEMBER 26 - Actress Mary Pickford donates her personal collection of motion pictures "for preservation and research use." With support from the Mary Pickford Foundation, the Library opens the small Mary Pickford Theater in the Madison Building on May 10, 1983.

[handwritten manuscript page]

1947

MARCH 12 - The Library of Congress Planning Committee, chaired by Keyes D. Metcalf, director of libraries at Harvard University, submits its report, which strongly urges an expansion of the Library's national functions, maintaining that "if the Library fails to provide the services outlined in this report . . . it will be necessary to build elsewhere in the Government and throughout the nation the services which it is recommended that the Library of Congress should provide." The committee recommends that "the actual status of the Library as the National Library should be officially recognized in its name and that it should be designated 'The Library of Congress, the National Library of the United States of America.'"

MAY 12-JUNE 16 - Delegates from 22 nations attend the first Assembly of Librarians from the Americas, held at the Library with support from the Department of State.

JUNE 3 - With a transfer of funds from the US Office of Naval Research, the Library establishes a Science and Technology Project to provide selective bibliographic and library services for the office.

JUNE 9 - The Library announces a cooperative project with the General Education Board and the American Council of Learned Societies to locate and microfilm files of African American newspapers from their earliest dates to 1900.

JULY 31 - In accordance with the Legislative Branch Appropriations Act for fiscal year 1948, the Motion Picture Division is liquidated.

DECEMBER 15 - The US Mission to Japan, which consists of Chief Assistant Librarian Verner W. Clapp and Iowa State College Librarian Charles H. Brown, begins work in Tokyo to plan Japan's new National Diet Library. At the request of the Japanese legislature,

This page is from W. Somerset Maugham's literary masterpiece *Of Human Bondage*. The British novelist donated the manuscript to the Library in 1946 as a thank you to America for assisting his countrymen during World War II.

Members of the Fellows in American Letters of the Library of Congress in the Whittall Pavilion in 1948. Left to right: Allen Tate, Léonie Adams, T.S. Eliot, Theodore Spencer, and Robert Penn Warren.

the institution will be patterned after the Library of Congress.

1948

MARCH 4 - A grant from the Bollingen Foundation enables the Library to establish the Bollingen Prize in Poetry, to be awarded each year "for the best book of verse by an American author published during the preceding year." The selection jury will be the Fellows in American Letters of the Library of Congress, the group of 13 poets and writers serving the Library as honorary consultants.

JULY 1 - The Librarian reports that the Library's Photoduplication Service, established in 1939 with a grant from the Rockefeller Foundation to provide photostat or microfilm copies, has grown from its original staff of two to 62 employees and taken on functions previously performed by the library of the Department of Agriculture, the Army Medical Library, and the Office of Technical Services in the Department of Commerce.

AUGUST - The Cooperative Acquisitions Project for European wartime publications, inaugurated in 1945, is completed.

DECEMBER 10 - The first Juilliard String Quartet concert in the Coolidge Auditorium is also the first Library concert to be broadcast on FM radio.

DECEMBER 20 - Evans announces the Library's sponsorship, with support from the Rockefeller Foundation, of a new 16-volume series of "extended essays" on American civilization, edited by Yale professor Ralph H. Gabriel.

1949

JANUARY 17 - Writing in *The New Republic*, former congressman Maury Maverick of Texas offers advice to new members of Congress: "Go over to the Library of Congress. It has the most beautiful interior in the world. Also, the greatest and richest treasury of knowledge. Work those people to death. They like it. They will do research for you over the phone, and deliver books to you marked right where you want them."

FEBRUARY 18 - Poetry recordings, prepared with funds from the Bollingen Foundation, are offered for sale for the first time. Included among the five-album series is a

"Go over to the Library of Congress. It has the most beautiful interior in the world. Also, the greatest and richest treasury of knowledge. Work those people to death. They like it. They will do research for you over the phone, and deliver books to you marked right where you want them."

— Former US Congressman Maury Maverick, 1949

This image, made from a glass-plate negative, is from the Wright Brothers Collection, which came to the Library in 1949. Titled *First Flight, 120 Feet in 12 Seconds, 10:35 a.m.; Kitty Hawk, North Carolina,* it was taken on December 17, 1903. Orville Wright is at the controls of the flyer, lying prone on the lower wing with hips in the cradle. Wilbur Wright is running alongside to balance the machine. He has just released his hold on the forward upright of the right wing. This photo proved that the Wright brothers had built a machine that could successfully fly.

set recorded for the Library by T.S. Eliot, winner of the 1948 Nobel Prize for Literature.

FEBRUARY 20 - The Library announces that its Fellows in American Letters have awarded the first Bollingen Prize in Poetry to Ezra Pound for his book *The Pisan Cantos*. The Fellows take cognizance of public knowledge that Pound is under indictment for treason and committed to an institution for the insane, stating that they "are aware that objections may be made to awarding a prize to a man situated as is Mr. Pound." On August 19, the Joint Library Committee recommends that the Library "cancel all arrangements for the giving of prizes and the making

of awards." Librarian Evans announces the Library's immediate compliance.

MARCH 21 - Because "recruiting qualified librarians during the past few years has been a formidable task," Evans announces the inauguration of a "special recruiting program" to select and train outstanding library school graduates for the Library's staff.

JUNE 5 - The Library announces a major gift: the papers of Orville and Wilbur Wright, a 30,000-item collection that includes 303 glass-plate negatives documenting their groundbreaking flights

Three of the ancient Hebrew scrolls
discovered on the shores of the
Dead Sea in the summer of 1949
were displayed in the United States
for the first time at the Library of
Congress. In this photo, the Isaiah
Scroll is unrolled in the Library's
Whittall Pavilion prior to being
displayed with the other scrolls.

OCTOBER – The Dead Sea Scrolls are displayed for the first time in the United States at the Library of Congress. Three of the ancient Hebrew scrolls discovered in the summer of 1949 on the northwest shores of the Dead Sea were lent to the Library by the Reverend Athanasius Yeshue Samuel, the Archbishop of Jerusalem.

1950

In director George Cukor's award-winning movie *Born Yesterday*, actors Judy Holliday and William Holden look at the Declaration of Independence, the US Constitution, and other documents on display in the Library's Great Hall. They also appear in a scene at the Court of Neptune Fountain in front of the Library.

APRIL 13 – As the 150th anniversary of the founding of the Library approaches, President Harry S. Truman sends Librarian Evans a congratulatory letter, noting that neither the Library's collections nor its services "could ever have been fashioned without the power of the principle of free inquiry and the support of that principle by the people and the Congress."

MAY 17 – President Truman delivers an address in the Coolidge Auditorium as part of a program marking the publication by the Princeton University Press of the first volume of *The Papers of Thomas Jefferson*.

JULY 24 – The Library publishes a 107-page preliminary bibliography about Korea, a publication which "is suitable for the emergency requirements of the early stages of the Korea conflict."

OCTOBER 29 – The Library announces the completion of the state legislative journals microfilming project, begun in 1941 in cooperation with the University of North Carolina but delayed during the war years. More than 1,700 reels of microfilm are produced; the contents of the reels are described in an 800-page guide published by the Library.

Librarian of Congress Emeritus Herbert Putnam (left), Librarian Evans (middle), and others greeted visitors at the Library's sesquicentennial reception, April 24, 1950.

The Main Reading Room in 1950, the Library's sesquicentennial year.

NOVEMBER 19 - Chicago businessman Alfred Whital Stern begins donating to the Library "the most extensive collection" of material about Abraham Lincoln "ever assembled by a private individual." The entire collection is donated on September 29, 1953. It includes more than 11,000 items, including manuscripts, Lincoln's law papers, sheet music, maps, books, pamphlets, and ephemeral items.

DECEMBER 12 - Librarian of Congress Emeritus Herbert Putnam, now 89 years old, receives a standing ovation at a banquet given by the American Library Association to honor the Library in its sesquicentennial year. In his remarks he notes: "Very few executives have had the fortune to live with their posterity and to be welcomed with a eulogy instead of an elegy. But if you are summoning shades of the past, you must not fail to summon one shade and keep *him* contemporary—the valiant, persistent . . . forecasting, foretelling, prophesying shade . . . Ainsworth Spofford."

DECEMBER 25 - Gertrude Clarke Whittall creates the Whittall Poetry Fund, which will be used to support public poetry readings and programming and a Poetry Room. The literary series begins in 1951, and the Poetry Room, located on the top floor of the Library building with an inspirational view of the entire city, opens in the same year on Shakespeare's birthday, April 23. Mrs. Whittall donates additional funds to support literary programming in 1952 and 1954.

W. H. SEWARD

GEN. U.S. GRANT

Emancipation Proclamation

WHEREAS on the Twenty-second day of September, in the year of our Lord one thousand eight hundred and sixty-two, a Proclamation was issued by the President of the United States, containing among other things the following, to-wit:

"That on the first day of January, in the year of our Lord one thousand eight hundred and sixty-three, all persons held as slaves within any State, or designated part of a State, the people whereof shall then be in rebellion against the United States, shall be then, thenceforward and forever free, and the executive government of the United States, including the military and naval authority thereof, will recognize and maintain the freedom of such persons, and will do no act or acts to repress such persons, or any of them, in any efforts they may make for their actual freedom.

"That the executive will, on the first day of January aforesaid, by proclamation, designate the States and parts of States, if any, in which the people thereof respectively shall then be in rebellion against the United States, and the fact that any State, or the people thereof, shall on that day be in good faith represented in the Congress of the United States by members chosen thereto at elections wherein a majority of the qualified voters of such State shall have participated, shall, in the absence of strong countervailing testimony, be deemed conclusive evidence that such State and the people thereof are not then in rebellion against the United States."

Now, therefore, I, ABRAHAM LINCOLN, President of the United States, by virtue of the power in me vested as Commander-in-Chief of the Army and Navy of the United States in time of actual armed rebellion against the authority and government of the United States, and as a fit and necessary war measure for suppressing said rebellion, do, on this first day of January, in the year of our Lord one thousand eight hundred and sixty-three, and in accordance with my purpose so to do, publicly proclaim for the full period of one hundred days from the day the first above mentioned order, and designate as the States and parts of States wherein the people thereof respectively are this day in rebellion against the United States, the following, to-wit:

ARKANSAS, TEXAS, LOUISIANA (except the parishes of St. Bernard, Plaquemines, Jefferson, St. John, St. Charles, St. James, Ascension, Assumption, Terre Bonne, Lafourche, St. Mary, St. Martin, and Orleans, including the city of New Orleans), MISSISSIPPI, ALABAMA, FLORIDA, GEORGIA, SOUTH CAROLINA, NORTH CAROLINA and VIRGINIA (except the forty-eight counties designated as West Virginia, and also the counties of Berkley, Accomac, Northampton, Elizabeth City, York, Princess Ann and Norfolk, including the cities of Norfolk and Portsmouth), and which excepted parts are, for the present, left precisely as if this Proclamation were not issued.

And by virtue of the power and for the purpose aforesaid, I do order and declare that all persons held as slaves within said designated States and parts of States are and henceforward shall be free; and that the executive government of the United States, including the military and naval authorities thereof, will recognize and maintain the freedom of said persons.

And I hereby enjoin upon the people so declared to be free, to abstain from all violence, unless in necessary self-defence, and I recommend to them that in all cases, when allowed, they labor faithfully for reasonable wages.

And I further declare and make known that such persons of suitable condition, will be received into the armed service of the United States to garrison forts, positions, stations and other places, and to man vessels of all sorts in said service.

And upon this act, sincerely believed to be an act of justice, warranted by the Constitution, upon military necessity, I invoke the considerate judgment of mankind, and the gracious favor of Almighty God.

In testimony whereof, I have hereunto set my name, and caused the seal of the United States to be affixed.

Done at the City of Washington, this first day of January, in the year of our Lord one thousand eight hundred and sixty-three, and of the Independence of the United States the eighty-seventh.

William H. Seward
Secretary of State.

By the President:

A. Lincoln

1951

MAY 1 - Burgess Meredith and Cleanth Brooks present a program about poet Edward Arlington Robinson in the Coolidge Auditorium, the first public program held under the auspices of the Whittall Poetry Fund.

NOVEMBER 19-20 - The Library sponsors the first National Conference on Library Services to the Blind.

1952

JANUARY 12 - Librarian Evans outlines new procedures and policies for the loan of Library materials, which "shall be available for loan in order to promote knowledge in the United States and abroad when such materials are not otherwise reasonably available."

APRIL 1 - Frances Clarke Sayers of the New York Public Library begins a special assignment at the Library of Congress "to make a study looking toward the development of an effective children's literature program in the Library." A joint committee of the American Association of University Women and the Association for Childhood Education International funds her appointment. Sayers recommends establishment of a reference and bibliographic center for children's literature.

APRIL 3 - The Joint Library Committee orders the transfer of the two most important official documents of the US government—the Declaration of Independence and the US Constitution—to the National Archives. The documents had originally come to the Library in 1921, 13 years before the National Archives were established. Evans writes in the Library's *Information Bulletin*: "It is naturally an emotional wrench to surrender the custody of the principal documents of American liberty. Logic and Law require it, however, and we can only join Dr. Wayne C. Grover, the Archivist of the United States, and his staff in celebrating the occasion."

The Declaration of Independence and the US Constitution were packed up for transfer to the National Archives on December 13, 1952.

Among the more than 11,000 items in the Alfred Whital Stern Collection is this lavishly illustrated print of the Emancipation Proclamation, with an image of Abraham Lincoln freeing a man from the shackles of slavery.

APRIL 4 - Philanthropist and rare book collector Lessing J. Rosenwald formally presents to the Library, as a gift to the nation, the Giant Bible of Mainz—a magnificent illuminated manuscript Bible made in Mainz, Germany, between April 4, 1452, and July 9, 1453.

MAY 23 - Gertrude Clarke Whittall donates additional funds to the Library, to be used "to sponsor presentations of general literature" as well as poetry.

JULY 3 - President Truman approves an act of Congress that extends the services of the Library's Division for the Blind to include children as well as adults.

JULY 23 - The Library receives the first installment of a collection of materials related to Sigmund Freud, collected and deposited by the Sigmund Freud Archives of New York.

AUGUST - In response to a request from the acting prime minister of Canada, the Library sends an advisor to Ottawa to assist in the salvaging of more than 200,000 water-soaked volumes, damaged as the result of a fire in the parliamentary building.

SEPTEMBER 12 - The Library publishes the first of five volumes of a definitive catalog of Thomas Jefferson's personal library that was sold to Congress in 1815, the culmination of a Jefferson cataloging project begun in 1942 with support from private funds. The compiler is a staff bibliographer, Millicent Sowerby.

1953

FEBRUARY - The Library initiates the "All-the-Books" plan, whereby publishers supply the Library with advance copies of their books and then print the card number preassigned by the Library in the volume itself.

JUNE 15 - The executive board of UNESCO nominates Librarian of Congress Luther H. Evans to be its director.

JULY 1 - The UNESCO General Council confirms the selection of Librarian Evans to be the organization's new director general. Evans submits his resignation as Librarian to President Dwight D. Eisenhower, effective July 5, 1953.

JULY 4 - Verner W. Clapp, Chief Assistant Librarian, becomes Acting Librarian of Congress.

SEPTEMBER 8-19 - The Library and Princeton University cosponsor a "Colloquium on Islamic Culture in Its Relation to the Contemporary World" on the Princeton campus.

NOVEMBER 10 - The Library and the American Academy of Motion Picture Arts and Sciences announces the completion of experiments to convert the Library's early paper prints of motion pictures to durable, modern film.

1954

APRIL 22 - President Dwight D. Eisenhower nominates L. Quincy Mumford, director of the Cleveland Public Library and president-elect of the American Library Association, to be Librarian of Congress.

JULY 26 - The Senate Committee on Rules and Administration, chaired by William E. Jenner of Indiana, holds hearings on the Mumford nomination. Three representatives of the American Library Association testify in his favor. Senator Jenner submits an execu

tive report to the Senate favoring the nomination on July 28. The US Senate confirms the nomination on July 29, without objection.

AUGUST 31 - President Eisenhower approves an act of Congress modifying aspects of the copyright law and ratifying the adherence of the United States to the Universal Copyright Convention, signed at Geneva, Switzerland, on September 6, 1952.

SEPTEMBER 1 - In a ceremony held in the Library's Whittall Pavilion, L. Quincy Mumford takes the oath of office as the eleventh Librarian of Congress. The oath, sworn on a Bible published in Philadelphia by Robert Aitken in 1782, is administered by Harold H. Burton, associate justice of the US Supreme Court. The Library has a book collection of approximately 10 million volumes, a staff of 1,800, and a total appropriation in fiscal year 1954 of $9.5 million.

SEPTEMBER 13 - The Library receives the Brady-Handy photographic collection, containing more than 3,000 negatives made by Civil War photographer Mathew B. Brady and several thousand by his nephew Levin C. Handy. The collection is a gift from Mr. Handy's daughters.

This photograph of Mary Todd Lincoln—taken between 1855 and the years she served as first lady (1861 1865)—is from the Brady-Handy Collection, which was donated to the Library in 1954.

Houdini at the Wintergarten, a poster from Berlin, 1933, advertises a performance by the great illusionist Harry Houdini. It forms part of the McManus-Young Collection of publications and pictorial material related to magic, presented to the Library in 1955.

1955

JUNE 6 - The Joint Library Committee concurs with Librarian Mumford's recommendation that the Library's "Books for the Blind activities" remain in the Library of Congress and not be transferred to the Department of Health, Education, and Welfare.

AUGUST 12 - With President Eisenhower's approval of the inclusion of presidential libraries in a new National Archives system of presidential libraries, the Library of Congress no longer receives official presidential papers. The Manuscript Division continues to maintain active custody of the papers of 23 presidents, from George Washington through Calvin Coolidge.

OCTOBER - The 20,000-item John J. and Hanna M. McManus and Morris N. and Chelsey V. Young collection of printed, manuscript, and pictorial materials related to magic, is donated to the Library. The pictorial materials include posters, dust jackets from magic books, scrapbooks, portraits, carnival photographs, and Houdiniana.

1956

JUNE 13 In response to an inquiry from the Council of the American Association for State and Local History, Librarian Mumford reasserts the Library of Congress position with regard to the acquisition of manuscripts. Because the Library "has a duty to the nation . . . it cannot abdicate the collecting of manuscripts of national importance to scholarship in favor of any association or any other repository."

AUGUST - The president approves an act that expands the functions of the Armed Forces Medical Library and designates it as the National Library of Medicine. The Librarian of Congress is named as an ex officio member of its board of regents.

SEPTEMBER 19 - Librarian Mumford announces the resignation, after a 33-year Library of Congress career, of Chief Assistant Librarian Verner W. Clapp.

1957

With a grant from the Rockefeller Foundation, the Library initiates a research project to study the preservation of sound recordings. The report, *Preservation and Storage of Sound Recordings*, is published in 1959.

MAY 21 - Defending a proposed increase in the Library's budget, Representative Clarence Cannon of Missouri, chairman of the House of Representatives Committee on Appropriations, praises the Library as "convincing proof" that Americans are "a people of culture, learning, and scientific culture equal if not superior to any on the globe" and expresses his hope that no congressional budget action will "retard the continued growth and development of this national institution."

AUGUST 16 - President Eisenhower approves an act authorizing the Library's Presidential Papers Program. The Library will arrange, index, and microfilm the presidential collections in its custody "in order to preserve their contents against destruction by war or other calamity and for the purpose of making them more readily available for study and research."

DECEMBER 19 - Librarian Mumford announces the appointment of six eminent writers as Library of Congress honorary consultants for the next three years: playwright Maxwell Anderson, short story writer Eudora Welty, poets Elizabeth Bishop and John Crowe Ransom, and critics R.P. Blackmur and Cleanth Brooks. He also explains that the title "honorary consultant" is now used as the title for all non-salaried Library advisors.

1958

JANUARY - The Librarian establishes an interdepartmental Committee on Mechanized Information Retrieval to study the "problem of applying machine methods to the control of the Library's general collections."

JANUARY 17 - The Library Space Committee, organized by Librarian Mumford to consider future space needs, including the possibility of constructing a third major Library building, holds its first meeting. After further study, on August 13 the Architect of the Capitol submits the requirements and cost estimates for such a third building to the Joint Library Committee for consideration.

JUNE 26 - The Library receives a $55,000 grant from the Council on Library Resources for a one-year test of "cataloging-in-source," a project that will enable publishers to print Library of Congress cataloging information in their books.

AUGUST 25 - The Library establishes a new policy regarding its use by high school students: each student must submit a letter signed by his or her school principal certifying the student's need to use the collections.

AUGUST 27 - President Eisenhower approves an appropriation that includes $60,000 for the preservation of early motion pictures in the Library's collections.

SEPTEMBER 2 - The president approves an act establishing a national cultural center as a bureau of the Smithsonian Institution, later named the John F. Kennedy Center for the Performing Arts. The Librarian of Congress will serve as an ex officio member of the new center's board of trustees.

SEPTEMBER 6 – The president approves an amendment to the Agricultural Trade Development and Assistance Act of 1954 (popularly known as Public Law 480), which authorizes the Library of Congress to use US-owned foreign currency to acquire books, periodicals, and other research materials from around the world to benefit the Library and other libraries and research centers in the United States.

DECEMBER 28 – The Library announces a $200,000 grant from the Council on Library Resources that will enable it to establish and publish the *National Union Catalog of Manuscript Collections*, a national inventory of important manuscript collections.

1959

FEBRUARY 12 – The Library marks the sesquicentennial of the birth of Abraham Lincoln by opening a year-long exhibition in his memory, one of the most comprehensive displays of historical material about Lincoln ever assembled. Vice President Richard M. Nixon, members of Congress, and several noted Lincoln scholars attend the opening.

DECEMBER 7 – The Carnegie Corporation announces a $200,000 grant to the Library to establish and operate, for a period of five years, an African section. The new unit is being created, Librarian Mumford notes, "because of increased interest in African studies and to more fully exploit the Library's outstanding Africana collections."

PART THREE

★

FOR THE WORLD
1960–2016

This photograph of the Madison
Building with its colorful banners
appeared on the cover of the journal
of the American Library Association in
September 1988.

INTRODUCTION

Having weathered two world wars, expanded its collections, and constructed a second building, the Library approached the 1960s on firm footing. On April 22, 1954, President Dwight D. Eisenhower nominated L. Quincy Mumford, director of the Cleveland Public Library and president-elect of the American Library Association, to become the Librarian of Congress. About halfway through what turned out to be Mumford's 20-year term, it was clear that a new global era of growth had been inaugurated, one featuring accelerated technological change; increased funding for libraries and for research materials in the United States and abroad; continuation of post–World War II interest in international affairs, especially in relations with Russia and the Communist world, along with Africa and Asia; and a national concern for civil rights, prompted in part by racial violence and the assassinations of President John F. Kennedy, Senator Robert F. Kennedy, and Reverend Dr. Martin Luther King, Jr.

The introduction of automation into the Library's cataloging procedures (1958–66) and the initial development of the Library's overseas acquisitions programs (1958–65) contributed to the institution's unprecedented rate of growth between 1954 and 1975. In those 21 years, the Library's book collection increased from approximately 10 million to approximately 17 million volumes, the staff from 1,600 to 4,500, and the annual appropriation from $9.5 million to $116 million. In collaboration with Congress and the Office of the Architect of the Capitol, in 1958 Librarian Mumford initiated planning for a third major Library of Congress building on Capitol Hill. The James Madison Memorial Building was authorized in 1965 and construction began in 1971. The Library's occupancy of the James Madison Memorial Building in 1980 was a highlight of Daniel Boorstin's administration.

Boorstin, who became Librarian in 1975, obtained congressional approval to create the American Folklife Center in 1976 and the Center for the Book, an office to promote books and reading, in 1977. Next came a Library of Congress Performing Arts Library at the Kennedy Center, a joint project of the two organizations. In 1980 he established a Council of Scholars, a formal link between the Library and the world of scholarship. In 1983, the Library opened the Mary Pickford Theater in the Madison Building, which was an important step in enhancing public access to the Library's remarkable motion picture collection.

Librarian of Congress James H. Billington, who took office in 1987, developed a different, long-range approach to expanding the Library's functions and outreach. He sought and obtained congressional approval for the Library's first development office and the creation, in 1980, of its first private-sector support group, the James Madison Council. To help share the Library's resources more widely, Billington initiated several projects to test new technologies. The culmination in late 1994 was his announcement of a pilot National Digital Library, supported primarily by private funds, which would create several million digital items from the Library's Americana collections and make them widely accessible through the World Wide Web. Under Billington's guidance, the Library moved forward on several fronts: creating the John W. Kluge Center, which encouraged the use of the Library's wide and varied collections by scholars; opening *Treasures of the Library of Congress*, a rotating exhibition of the its rarest and most significant international items; and establishing a popular annual National Book Festival.

Dr. Carla D. Hayden broke the mold when she became the first African American and first woman Librarian of Congress in 2016. She inherited what is now a global institution. In her inaugural address, Hayden envisioned the Library as a place "where you can touch history and imagine your future. This Library of Congress, a historic reference source for Congress, an established place for scholars, can also be a place where we grow scholars, where we inspire young authors, where we connect with those individuals outside the limits of Washington and help them make history themselves." This is the exciting future of America's national library.

By 2007 the National Book Festival—which began in 2001 on Capitol Hill—was being held on the National Mall, with more than 120,000 in attendance. The 70 participating authors and illustrators spoke about their new books in 7 different themed pavilions, while the Pavilion of the States highlighted books and authors from all 50 states and 4 US territories.

1960

JANUARY 19 - The Africana Section is established.

MARCH - In a report on the cataloging-in-source experiment undertaken in 1958 with funding from the Council on Library Resources, the Library concludes that a permanent, full-scale cataloging-in-source program cannot be justified in terms of financing, technical considerations, or utility.

MAY 9 - Librarian Mumford announces that, because of "the crowded space situation in the Library," the Government Printing Office bindery, after being located in the Library for nearly 60 years, has been returned to the Government Printing Office. However, small "repair stations" for manuscripts, maps, prints and photographs, rare books, newspapers, and books in the general collections are retained in the Library.

JUNE - The Library publishes *A Guide to the Study of the United States of America: Representative Books Reflecting the Development of American Life and Thought*, a 1,193-page volume that identifies and describes more than 10,000 individual titles.

JUNE - The Library publishes the first issue of the *World List of Future Meetings*, which attempts to meet "the growing need by officers of the Government and by scholars and research persons generally for an up-to-date comprehensive listing of international meetings."

JULY 12 - President Eisenhower approves the Legislative Branch Appropriations Act for fiscal year 1961. The new law appropriates $75,000 to prepare preliminary plans and cost estimates for a third Library building and additional funds to rent 62,500 square feet of temporary storage space in the Washington, DC, area for its overflowing collections.

1961

MARCH - The Library publishes *Archive of Recorded Poetry and Literature: A Checklist*, the first detailed inventory of the holdings of the archive.

MARCH 13 - Librarian Mumford establishes the Office of Information Specialist to study the "automation of the bibliographic functions of the Library" and guide both the plans for data processing and its integration into the Library's organization.

APRIL 23 - The Library announces a $100,000 grant from the Council on Library Resources "for a survey of the possibilities of automating the organization, storage, and retrieval of information." Gilbert W. King, director of research for the International Business Machines Corporations, will head the six-person survey team.

JULY 10 - Librarian Mumford sends Congress a comprehensive report from the Register of Copyrights on the proposed revision of the US copyright law.

JULY 31 - President John F. Kennedy approves an act authorizing the Library to arrange, transliterate, index, and microfilm the vital statistics portions of its collection of the original records of the Russian Orthodox Greek Catholic Church in Alaska.

AUGUST 10 - President Kennedy approves the Legislative Branch Appropriations Act for fiscal year 1962, which includes the first appropriation to the Library for the acquisition of foreign research materials under the provisions of Public Law 480, as amended on September 6, 1958.

1962

MAY 24 - Senator Claiborne Pell of Rhode Island, a member of the Joint Library Committee, introduces into the Congressional Record a memorandum prepared at his request "on the subject of the Library of Congress and connected matters." Written by Douglas W. Bryant, associate director of the Harvard University Library, the memorandum addresses "what the Library of Congress does and what it ought to do for the Government and the Nation generally." In his memorandum, dated May 1, 1962, Bryant urges further expansion of the national role of the Library of Congress and the recognition of such a role through legislation and the establishment of a "National Library Advisory Board (if not a National Research Library Foundation)" in the executive branch. Librarian Mumford replies to this memorandum on September 28 and strongly defends the Library's location in the legislative branch of the American government. He asserts that, "the Library of Congress today performs more national library functions than any other national library in the world."

SEPTEMBER 19 - President Kennedy approves an act that extends the period of copyright protection for certain works pending the enactment of a general revision of the copyright law.

OCTOBER 22 - Librarian Mumford establishes a Children's Book Section in the Library's Reference Department. The creation of such a section was recommended as a result of a study undertaken by Frances Clarke Sayers in 1952, but Congress did not approve its establishment until 1962. The section's purpose is not to serve children directly but instead to provide reference and bibliographic services to specialists and the general public or, in the words of its first head, Virginia Haviland, "to serve those who serve children." It opens in March 1963 and is renamed the Children's Literature Center in 1978.

OCTOBER 22-24 - More than 30 poets take part in the Library's first National Poetry Festival, which is supported by the Bollingen Foundation. The general theme, "Fifty Years of American Poetry," marks the fiftieth anniversary of *Poetry* magazine.

1963

FEBRUARY 18 - The Library announces that it has undertaken a comprehensive program to microfilm approximately 500 foreign newspapers in lieu of binding them.

JUNE 6 - The House of Representatives Committee on Appropriations recommends an increase in the Library's fiscal year 1964 budget. In its report, it notes that "a third building is badly needed—now." It also cautions against the recently renewed suggestion that the Library "ought to be officially designated as the National Library and its administration shifted to the Executive Branch."

1964

JANUARY 15 - The Library's first computer, a rented IBM 1401 to be used for payroll, budget, and fiscal work, is installed in the Library's newly established Data Processing Office.

JANUARY 22 - The Library releases *Automation and the Library of Congress*, the feasibility study sponsored by the Council on Library Resources. The survey team, headed by Gilbert W. King, concludes that the automation of bibliographic processing, catalog searching, and document retrieval is technically and economically feasible in large research libraries. The authors urge the establishment of an automation program at the Library and recommend that the Library, "because of its central role in the American library world as the national library," take the lead in the automation venture. The Library begins the development of "system specifications" for its internal operations and also for services to other libraries.

Staff at work in the Library's Data Processing Office, 1960s.

In the 1960s, librarians turned to computers to help manage the overflow of books and archival material.

MARCH - The Bibliographical Society of America publishes *Incunabula in American Libraries*, a census of fifteenth-century books in North American libraries compiled and edited by Frederick R. Goff, chief of the Library's Rare Book Division. The census determines that the Library's collection of 5,616 incunabula is the largest in North America, followed by the Henry E. Huntington Library and Harvard University, with 5,314 and 2,910 incunabula, respectively.

MAY 4 - The Main Reading Room is closed for cleaning and restoration, and for the installation of new lighting and a new heating, air-conditioning, and ventilating system. It reopens on August 16, 1965.

JUNE - The General Services Administration makes warehouse facilities in Middle River, Maryland, several miles east of Baltimore, available to the Library "for the storage of equipment and material not frequently needed."

JULY 20 - A comprehensive bill for the general revision of the US copyright law is introduced in Congress. The bill is a result of nine years of work by the Copyright Office.

AUGUST - Librarian Mumford establishes the Information Systems Office, which will be responsible for the Library's program "to utilize mechanical and electronic equipment in library processes."

AN ESSENTIAL RESOURCE IN A TIME OF GRIEF

On November 22, 1963, while riding in a motorcade in Dallas, John F. Kennedy, the 35th president of the United States, was fatally shot. Late that evening, Roy P. Basler, director of the Library's Reference Department, received a call at home from White House Special Assistant Arthur M. Schlesinger. Explaining he was making a request on behalf of the president's widow, Jacqueline Kennedy, Schlesinger asked Basler, a Lincoln specialist, for help in obtaining details about the lying-in-repose of President Lincoln in the East Room of the White House in 1865. Though in shock, Mrs. Kennedy was looking for a historical precedent of a state funeral that would honor a beloved fallen leader and console a grief-stricken nation. Basler promised assistance, either from his personal books or from the collections of the Library. He also gave Schlesinger the home phone number of David C. Mearns, chief of the Manuscript Division, another Lincoln specialist, on the chance that he also might be able to give an immediate answer without needing to take a trip to the Library.

But the two librarians soon realized that they needed to consult the nineteenth-century newspapers and magazines most likely to contain the necessary details. Mearns volunteered to make the trip to the Library, asking that he be authorized to take with him James I. Robertson, Jr., executive director of the US Civil War Centennial Commission, and James O. Sutton, head of the Library's Newspaper and Periodicals Division. The three men met at the Library's Annex shortly before 11 p.m. There had not been time to request light service in the stacks, so they searched the collections with flashlights. After the trio located excellent photographs in *Leslie's Weekly* and marked precise accounts in several newspapers, Mearns called Schlesinger with the results. The requested information was delivered to the Northwest Gate of the White House that night. According to his account in the David C. Mearns Papers in the Manuscript Division, Mearns "reached home about half past one."

The funeral procession for John F. Kennedy crossed Memorial Bridge on the way to Arlington National Cemetery.

The immediate aftermath of the Kennedy assassination began a remarkable four days, not only in the lives of individual Americans, but also in the life of the Library of Congress. On confirmation of the president's death on November 22, the Library had closed at 3:15 p.m., leaving only a staff of two reference librarians on duty. The next day, Saturday, November 23, Acting Librarian Robert C. Gooch reopened the exhibit areas in the Main Building from 9 a.m. until 10 p.m., their normal hours. Sixteen staff members provided emergency service, answering questions, mostly from radio and television reporters or from out-of-town newspapers.

In the early hours of Sunday, November 24, Deputy Librarian Rutherford D. Rogers, who had returned from a trip to Chicago, received an urgent request from the State Department Library for detailed accounts of the funeral processions of presidents Washington, Lincoln, Grant, and Theodore Roosevelt, asking for delivery before 8 a.m. the next day. Another special team was assembled to transcribe the information from contemporaneous newspaper accounts, photocopy the transcriptions, and deliver them to the State Department ahead of the deadline.

The Library's exhibit halls were opened as usual on Sunday, November 24. At 10:30 a.m. the Library was informed that newly sworn President Lyndon B. Johnson soon would be attending President Kennedy's funeral mass at St. Mark's Episcopal Church, across Third Street from the Library's Annex Building. The Fifth Precinct of the Metropolitan Police Department asked that as many Library of Congress guards as could be spared be posted on Third Street. The Library temporarily closed the Main Building and eight of the nine guards were assigned to work with the Metropolitan Police.

Late in the afternoon, the Library received another request from the White House. This one asked for the words and music of an Irish song, "O'Donnell Aboo," to be used at the president's funeral. Music Division chief Harold Spivake called staff member Irving Lowens, who came to the Library and found a copy of the song. However, the White House wanted multiple copies and the volume he located was under copyright protection. Eventually, Lowens found a pre-1900 sheet-music version of which multiple copies could be made, and copies were dispatched to the White House. Ultimately, however, the piece was not used.

President Kennedy's casket arrived and was taken into the Capitol. Long viewing lines began to form in the late afternoon. Because of the cold weather and the Library's proximity to the Capitol, Library officials decided to keep the west basement doors of the Main Building open all night to allow those waiting to seek refuge from the cold and to use the rest rooms. Those doors remained open until the normal closing time of 10 p.m. on Monday, November 25. More than 4,000 people entered the Main Building that weekend, 950 of them during the long night hours between 10 p.m. Sunday and 9 a.m. Monday.

On Monday, a skeletal staff of nine, headed by Reference Department Director Basler, reported for duty. Basler received permission to invite those staff members into the Librarian's office at 11 a.m. to join him in watching the funeral of President Kennedy on television.

On Tuesday, November 26, the Library resumed its normal services and hours.

In the Library's 1964 annual report, Librarian of Congress L. Quincy Mumford proudly noted: "Probably no single event in these past ten years has shown the use and work of a great library than (has) the death of President John Fitzgerald Kennedy."

NOVEMBER – The Library receives the first installment of the gift of the records of the National Association for the Advancement of Colored People (NAACP), a private archive of more than one million items.

1965
JANUARY 11 – The Library hosts and cosponsors a conference on machine-readable catalog copy; the other sponsors are the automation committee of the Association of Research Libraries and the Council on Library Resources.

MARCH 11 – The Library and the Bureau of the Budget announce the establishment of the Federal Library Committee "to provide more effective planning, development, and operation of federal libraries." Its secretariat will be at the Library.

JUNE – The Library issues "A Proposed Format for a Standardized Machine-Readable Catalog Record," by information specialist Henriette D. Avram. The important study leads to the development of the Library's Machine-Readable Cataloging (MARC) system.

JUNE – Mr. and Mrs. Walter C. Louchheim, Jr., of Washington, DC, donate funds to the Library to distribute tapes of the Library's music concerts to educational and commercial broadcasters nationwide. Three years later they establish the Katie and Walter Louchheim Fund to support musical performances and poetry readings.

JULY 21 – The Library receives a grant of $75,300 from the Council on Library Resources to establish a Center for the Coordination of Foreign Manuscript Copying.

SEPTEMBER 29 – President Lyndon B. Johnson approves the National Foundation on the Arts and Humanities Act of 1965. The new law creates a Federal Council on the Arts and the Humanities; the Librarian of Congress is designated an ex officio member of the council.

OCTOBER 19 – President Johnson approves a Supplemental Appropriations Act for fiscal year 1965, which authorizes $75 million for the construction of a third Library of Congress building, "to be named the James Madison Memorial Building and to contain a Madison Memorial Hall." The structure will be located across Independence Avenue, directly south of the Main Building.

NOVEMBER 8 – The president approves the Higher Education Act of 1965. Title II, Part C, of the act gives the Library a mandate to provide new and unparalleled services to the nation's academic libraries. It authorizes the Office of Education to transfer funds to the Library to acquire all library materials currently published throughout the world that are of value to scholarship, and to provide and distribute cataloging and bibliographic information about these materials promptly after receipt.

This 1936 photo from the National Association for the Advancement of Colored People (NAACP) Collection shows a banner reading "A Man Was Lynched Yesterday." Between 1920 and 1938, as black people were subjected to mob violence throughout the country, the NAACP often hung this flag at their Fifth Avenue Headquarters to protest racism. The NAACP began donating its archives to the Library in 1964.

DECEMBER - A joint conference with the Association of Research Libraries on the need for a national preservation program leads the Library to reassess its program and begin to assume a leadership role on the national level. A position of assistant director for preservation is established, and between 1967 and 1978, Frazer G. Poole spearheads a new, centralized Library preservation program.

1966

JANUARY 13 - At a conference at the British Museum national librarians from several countries meet with Library of Congress officials to discuss the development of procedures for the Library's new acquisitions and cataloging program, authorized by the Higher Education Act of 1965. The endeavor will be known as the National Program for Acquisitions and Cataloging (NPAC).

JANUARY 21 - The Library receives a grant of $87,650 from the Council on Library Resources to support the secretariat of the new Federal Library Committee for three years.

JANUARY 21 - The Council on Library Resources gives the Library a $130,000 grant for investigations that will lead to a pilot program for the distribution of cataloging information in machine-readable form. The Library will also study the feasibility and value of providing such service on a wider scale and on a continuing basis. The new project is christened MARC (Machine-Readable Cataloging).

MAY 2 - Mrs. Adrian Van Sinderen of Washington, Connecticut, places in the custody of the Library the last copy remaining in private hands of the Bay Psalm Book of 1640—the first extant book known to be published in English-speaking North America. She retains ownership of the book during her lifetime but bequeaths it to the Library.

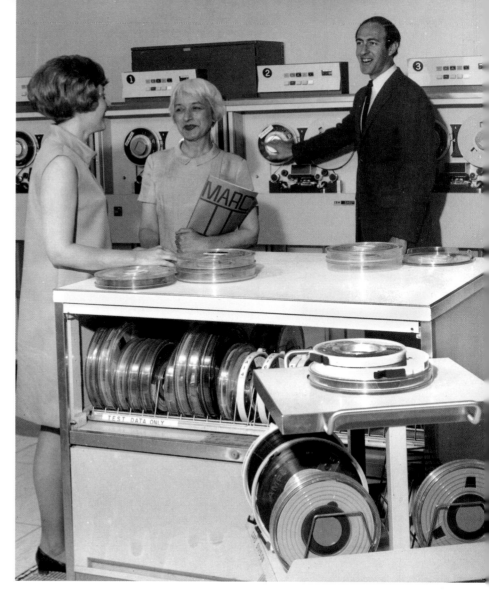

Henriette Avram (center), the director of the Library's Machine-Readable Cataloging (MARC) Pilot Project in 1968, conferring with two colleagues in the Information Systems Office.

MAY 13 - President Johnson approves the second Supplemental Appropriations Act for fiscal year 1966, which includes $300,000 for the acquisition and cataloging of library materials in selected countries by the Library of Congress under the provision of Title II, Part C, of the Higher Education Act of 1965. The new National Program for Acquisitions and Cataloging (NPAC), opens its first shared cataloging office in Europe in London on June 24, working in cooperation with British publishers and the British National Bibliography. In October the Library opens its first NPAC regional office in Rio de Janeiro to serve as a focal point for acquiring South American publications.

OCTOBER 23 - The Library announces that it has received a generous gift from the Martha Baird Rockefeller Fund for Music, which will enable it to transfer its earliest recordings of American folk music to magnetic tape for future preservation.

NOVEMBER - A pilot project to test the feasibility of distributing machine-readable cataloging data to other libraries begins. The Library sends weekly distributions of MARC tapes to 16 participating institutions.

The Bay Psalm Book of 1640, a book of psalms metered for singing, was the first book printed by the settlers of the Massachusetts Bay Colony. The tools and press used in printing had been brought over with them on a ship from England. It was placed in the Library's custody in 1966.

Chilean poet Pablo Neruda recorded his poetry for the Library's archives on June 20, 1966. Neruda won the Nobel Prize for Literature in 1971.

1967

JANUARY - The American Library Association (ALA) publishes the *Anglo-American Cataloging Rules: North American Text*, prepared by the ALA, the Library of Congress, the Library Association (Great Britain), and the Canadian Library Association, with financial support from the Council on Library Resources.

JANUARY 31 - A pilot project by the Library, in cooperation with the Association of Research Libraries, to study techniques for the preservation of deteriorating or "brittle" books commences. It focuses on works published since about 1870 on paper that disintegrates with age.

MAY 19 - Jane Engelhard of Far Hills, New Jersey, presents a gift of $10,000 to the Library for a revolving fund. The new Jane Engelhard Fund will be used to expand the Library's facsimile publications program and to support other publications that describe the Library's collections and services.

AUGUST 25 - Members of the Joint Library Committee and Library of Congress officials unveil a model and the plans for the future Library of Congress James Madison Memorial Building.

1968

JANUARY - The Library publishes *The MARC II Format: A Communications Format for Bibliographic Data*, prepared by Henriette D. Avram, John F. Knapp, and Lucia J. Rather of the Information Systems Office.

The Blue Eagle, one of the motion pictures selected for acquisition and preservation as a result of a 1967 cooperative agreement with the American Film Institute, was promoted as a "Fighting Drama of Adventure, Courage, Loyalty and Strength on the High Seas."

The National Library of Medicine, the National Agricultural Library, and three divisions of the American Library Association adopt the MARC format as the standard.

SEPTEMBER 19 - The Library and the American Film Institute conclude a cooperative agreement for the further development of the Library's national motion picture collection. The Institute gives the Library an initial grant of $125,000 toward acquisition of American film classics not in the collection, with priority given to films made between 1912 and 1942.

In 1967 the Library revealed an architectural drawing by architectural firm DeWitt, Poor & Shelton of the planned James Madison Memorial Building, the Library's third major structure on its Capitol Hill campus.

OCTOBER 3 - In its report to President Lyndon B. Johnson, the National Advisory Commission on Libraries recommends the "recognition and strengthening of the role of the Library of Congress as the National Library of the United States and the establishment of a Board of Advisors for the Library."

1969

MARCH 27 - With the mailing of the first computer tapes containing cataloging data, the MARC Distribution Service is inaugurated.

MARCH 29–31 - The Library moves the Copyright Office from its crowded quarters on Capitol Hill to a temporary location at Crystal City in Arlington, Virginia.

MAY 23 - At the opening of its exhibition commemorating the 150th anniversary of the poet Walt Whitman's birth, the Library announces that it will acquire the Charles Feinberg collection of Whitman materials, which includes more than 20,000 items. Anonymous benefactors will purchase it for the Library.

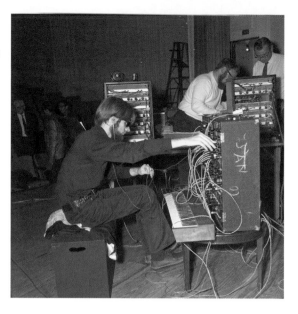

In 1970 the Library used the McKim Fund to establish a festival of chamber music. This performance from the 1970s incorporated a Moog synthesizer.

More than 20,000 items related to the poet Walt Whitman, seen here in an 1887 photograph, are part of the Charles Feinberg Collection.

OCTOBER 17 - After a four-week move, the Geography and Map Division settles in rental quarters on Pickett Street in Alexandria, Virginia. Approximately 3.5 million maps are transported in approximately 4,000 five-drawer steel map cases.

DECEMBER 29 - Antiquarian book dealer Hans P. Kraus of New York City donates to the Library a notable collection of manuscripts relating to the history and culture of Spanish America in the colonial period.

1970

FEBRUARY - The Library announces plans to establish a preservation research laboratory that, in addition to basic research, will also seek to develop solutions to preservation problems for libraries and archives throughout the United States. A grant of $70,000 from the Council on Library Resources will be used to purchase scientific equipment for the laboratory.

MARCH 16 - President Richard M. Nixon approves an act increasing the authorization for appropriations for the James Madison Memorial Building to $90 million, with an added proviso: "Nothing contained in the Act of October 19, 1965 (79 Stat. 986) shall be construed to authorize the use of the third Library of Congress building authorized by such Act for general office building purposes."

MARCH 26 - The McKim Fund, a new endowment received by bequest of the late Mrs. W. Duncan McKim, will be used to support the composition and performance of chamber music for violin and piano.

This 1968 image shows author Ralph Ellison signing a copy of *To Heal and to Build: The Programs of Lyndon B. Johnson* for Lady Bird Johnson. Ellison wrote an essay for the volume. The first lady inscribed the photograph, "To Ralph Ellison in whose time and talent helped make this book possible." It is part of the Library's Ralph Ellison Papers.

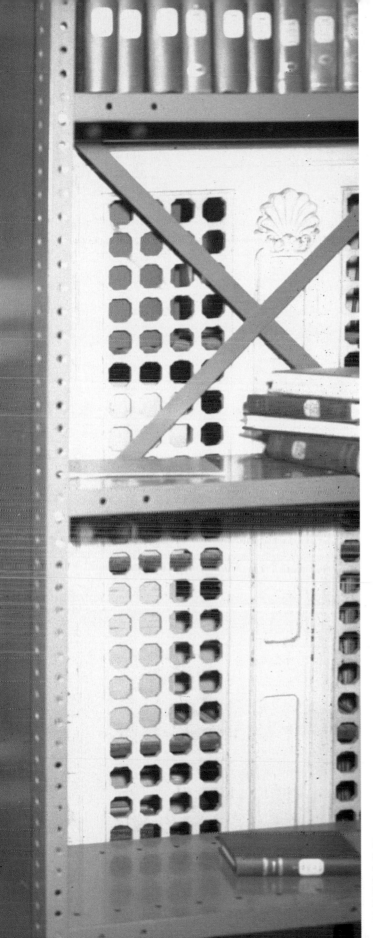

In the 1970s, the Library's stacks became increasingly crowded while Library officials and staff members waited for the completion of the Madison Building.

OCTOBER 26 - President Nixon approves the Legislative Reorganization Act of 1970. The new law changes the name of the Legislative Reference Service to the Congressional Research Service (CRS), effective January 3, 1971. The duties of the service are expanded, with increased emphasis placed on policy research and analysis and on direct services to committees and individual members of Congress. On January 11, 1971, the Library establishes the first branch of CRS in the Rayburn House Office Building.

1971

APRIL 22 - The Architect of the Capitol awards the contract for the first phase of the construction of the James Madison Memorial Building.

MAY 27 - The House Office Building Commission, chaired by Representative Carl Albert, the Speaker of the House, recommends that no further action be taken on the appropriation of funds for a third Library building until the location of a fourth House office building has been determined.

JUNE 1 - The House of Representatives Committee on Appropriations, chaired by Representative George Andrews of Alabama, recommends an appropriation of $67,391,250 for operating expenses for the Library for fiscal year 1972, and $71,090,000 for the Architect of the Capitol for construction of the superstructure of the James Madison Memorial Building. President Nixon approves the appropriations on July 9.

JUNE 4 - In a debate in the House of Representatives on the legislative branch appropriations bill for fiscal year 1972, the House rejects by a vote of 69 to 48 an amendment that would delete the recommended appropriation for the James Madison Memorial Building.

JUNE 20 - The Library announces that it has received matching grants of $200,000 each from the National Endowment for the Humanities and the Council on Library Resources to support a new program of providing cataloging data to be printed in the books themselves. The project will be known as the Cataloging in Publication (CIP) program. The program is launched on July 13 with the selection by lot of the first 27 participating publishers.

JUNE 23-28 - Approximately 25 staff members alleging racial discrimination on the part of the Library engage in a work stoppage. Eleven of the employees are dismissed.

JUNE 25 - At its 90th annual conference, the American Library Association approves a membership resolution calling for an inquiry into and report on allegations that the Library "discriminates on racial grounds in recruitment, training, and promotion practices." Later in the year, on November 9, Librarian Mumford informs the American Library Association that the Library will not present testimony before the staff ALA Library of Congress Inquiry Team that is investigating the charge of racial discrimination. He makes this statement at the request of Representative Wayne

The father in this 1971 *New Yorker* drawing could have reassured his young daughter that, indeed, the Library of Congress did have a copy of *The Poky Little Puppy.* The Children's Literature Center at the Library assists users in gaining access to all children's materials dispersed throughout the institution. The Library holds approximately 500,000 children's books and related items, such as boxed and board games, sound recordings, maps, and illustrations.

*"Just think! Every book that's ever been published in the United States
is right here in the Library of Congress."
"Even 'The Poky Little Puppy'?"*

L. Hays of Ohio, chairman of the Joint Library Committee, who states that "the American Library Association is infringing on and usurping the oversight responsibilities of Congress in making an investigation of an Agency under the exclusive jurisdiction of Congress."

OCTOBER 15 - President Richard Nixon approves an amendment to the copyright law that will make it possible, for the first time, to register claims for sound recordings.

1972
JANUARY 25 - The ALA Library of Congress Inquiry Team concludes that there was "a pattern of actions for which it could conceive no other motivation than racial discrimination." That is countered on January 27 by Librarian Mumford, who protests the lack of specifics as well as the conclusions of the ALA Inquiry Team, which he feels "fails to recognize the Library of Congress' accomplishments in the area of race relations."

MAY 29 - In accordance with the recommendations of the Association of Research Libraries, the Library assumes responsibility for coordinating a national program for the microfilming of foreign newspapers.

JULY - The Library transfers its collection of 50,000 volumes of US newspapers to the Library's warehouse in Alexandria, Virginia. The volumes now can be served to patrons only on 48-hour notice.

AUGUST 1 - In cooperation with the Brookings Institution, the Congressional Research Service begins a series of seminars on public policy issues for members of Congress. The first seminar, held in the Whittall Pavilion, concerns US relations with China.

1973
JANUARY 29-30 - The Library sponsors a conference on "The Teaching of Creative Writing," which is supported by the Gertrude Clarke Whittall Poetry and Literature Fund.

FEBRUARY 23 - Librarian Mumford approves a new employment opportunity plan for fiscal year 1973, inaugurating a comprehensive affirmative action program for the Library under the provisions of the Equal Employment Opportunity Act of 1972. On April 13, he announces the appointment of a Federal Women's Program Coordinator, who will be responsible for advising the Library administration about special concerns regarding the employment and advancement of women on the Library's staff. From June 5 to 7, five members of the American Library Association, accompanied by Executive Director Robert Wedgeworth, visit the Library and confer with the Librarian and other officials regarding the institution's affirmative action program.

SEPTEMBER 21 - Officials from the Library meet in Toronto with representatives from other institutions to plan a concentrated effort to create a comprehensive national serials database in machine-readable form.

DECEMBER 30 - President Nixon issues an executive order exempting Librarian Mumford from mandatory retirement until December 31, 1974.

1974

JANUARY 23 - The council of the American Library Association accepts without dissent the report of the membership team of five library directors from around the country who visited the Library of Congress on June 5-7, 1973, for consultation regarding the Library's new affirmative action program. The report notes the extensive efforts being made by the Library to combat racial discrimination but recommends further efforts and the monitoring of the Library's progress by the ALA and the other organizations.

MARCH 8 - Librarian Mumford; Senator Howard W. Cannon of Nevada, chairman of the Joint Library Committee; and Architect of the Capitol George M. White participate in an informal ceremony for the laying of the cornerstone of the Library of Congress James Madison Memorial Building.

MAY - The Library publishes *Films and Other Materials for Projection*, which is the first Library of Congress book catalog produced by computer-aided composition techniques.

MAY 24 - The Library announces that its Cataloging in Publication (CIP) program is absorbing the LC pre-assigned number program, which itself began in 1953 as part of the Library's All-the-Books Program.

JULY - The Library's National Serials Data Program receives a grant of $150,000 from the National Science Foundation for the development of an automated national database in science and technology.

DECEMBER - The Library and the Caroline and Erwin D. Swann Collection of Caricature and Cartoon reach agreement about future Swann Collection donations to the Library. The first installment from this unique archive, dedicated to the preservation of original comic art by caricaturists and cartoonists from the eighteenth to the twentieth century, arrives in September 1975. Major installments are added in 1977 and 1979. The Swann Foundation continues to provide acquisitions and programming support. The Swann Gallery in the Jefferson Building opens on February 25, 1998.

In this illustration from the 1920s, from the Library's Swann Collection of Caricature and Cartoon, a fashionably dressed flapper stands with one hand on her hip and a cigarette in the other hand. The first installment of the Swann Collection came to the Library in 1975.

March 10th 1876

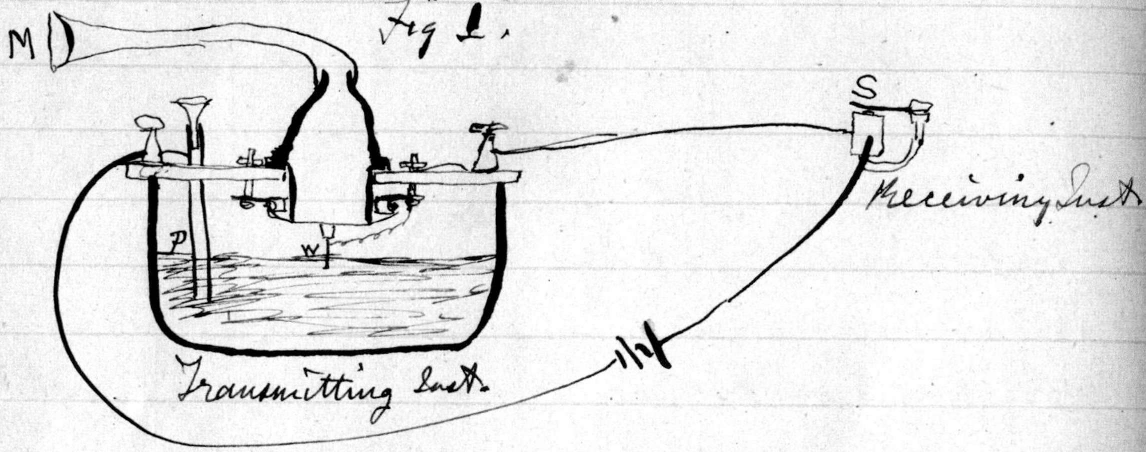

Fig I.

M   S

Receiving Inst

Transmitting Inst.

1. The improved instrument shown in Fig. I was constructed this morning and tried this evening.

P is a brass pipe and W the platinum wire M the mouth piece — and S the armature of the Receiving Instrument.

Mr. Watson was stationed in one room with the Receiving Instrument. He pressed one ear closely against S and closed his other ear with his hand. The Transmitting Instrument was placed in another room and the doors of both rooms were closed.

I then shouted into M the following sentence: "Mr. Watson — Come here — I want to

DECEMBER 16 - The Library announces that it has received a grant of $106,132 from the Council on Library Resources for the expansion of the automated bibliographic services provided by the Library through its MARC system.

DECEMBER 31 - After a 20-year career as Librarian of Congress, L. Quincy Mumford retires. Deputy Librarian John G. Lorenz becomes Acting Librarian of Congress.

1975

JANUARY 18 - At a meeting of the Association of Research Libraries, Processing Department Director William J. Welsh and John C. Rather, chief of the Technical Process Research Office, discuss the future of catalog control at the Library. They express the hope that an automated system of cataloging control using the MARC database will be available by 1979.

FEBRUARY - The Library publishes *Procedures for Salvage of Water-Damaged Library Materials*, prepared by the Preservation Office. The booklet inaugurates a new series, LC Publications on Conservation of Library Materials.

APRIL 24 - To celebrate its 175th anniversary, the Library opens its American Revolution Bicentennial exhibit, *To Set a Country Free*. Also on view are two commemorative exhibits about the history of the Library.

JUNE 2 - In ceremonies held in the Library's Whittall Pavilion, the heirs of Alexander Graham Bell donate the distinguished inventor's manuscripts to the Library. The collection of approximately 130,000 items is presented by Melville Bell Grosvenor, grandson of the scientist and chairman of the board of the National Geographic Society.

JUNE 28 - The Library receives a contract award of $52,000 from the National Commission on Libraries and Information Science for a study to define the role of the Library of Congress in the evolving national network for library and information science.

JUNE 30 - President Gerald R. Ford nominates historian and author Daniel J. Boorstin, senior historian at the Smithsonian Institution, to be Librarian of Congress.

JULY - The National Commission on Libraries and Information Science releases its report *Toward a National Program for Library and Information Services: Goals for Action*. The commission emphasizes that the participation of the Library of Congress is crucial to the development of its proposed national program and notes that "new legislation may be needed to designate the Library of Congress as having responsibility for integral parts of the National Program." Moreover, the commission states its belief that the Library of Congress should be designated as the US National Library.

Alexander Graham Bell made this drawing of a telephone and detailed his first phone conversation with Mr. Watson in this March 10, 1876, entry from his journal, now in the Alexander Graham Bell Papers, which were donated to the Library in 1975.

JULY 4 - At its 94th annual conference, the American Library Association adopts a resolution opposing the nomination of Daniel J. Boorstin for Librarian of Congress because "Dr. Boorstin's background, however distinguished it may be, does not include demonstrated leadership and administrative qualities which constitute basic and essential characteristics necessary in the Librarian of Congress." On July 30 and 31, the Senate Committee on Rules and Administration, chaired by Howard W. Cannon of Nevada, begins its hearings on the Boorstin nomination. Representatives of the American Library Association and Library of Congress labor unions oppose the nomination. Senator Cannon delays the continuation of the hearings until September 10, after the congressional recess.

SEPTEMBER 10 - After additional testimony from the nominee, the Senate Committee on Rules and Administration concludes its hearings on the Boorstin nomination, reporting in favor of the Boorstin nomination on September 25. The vote is unanimous. On September 26, the Senate confirms, without debate, the nomination of Daniel J. Boorstin for the post of Librarian of Congress.

NOVEMBER 12 - In a ceremony held in the Library's Great Hall and attended by President Gerald R. Ford and Vice President Nelson A. Rockefeller, Daniel Boorstin takes the oath of office as the 12th Librarian of Congress. Presiding officer for the ceremony is Representative Lucien N. Nedzi of Michigan,

chairman of the Joint Library Committee. Boorstin takes the oath, which is administered by Carl Albert, the Speaker of the House of Representatives, on the Thomson Bible from the Jefferson collection. The Library of Congress has a book collection of nearly 11 million volumes, a staff of 4,500, and an appropriation in fiscal year 1976 of more than $116 million.

1976

In the movie *All the President's Men*, directed by Alan J. Pakula, Watergate investigative reporters Bob Woodward and Carl Bernstein, portrayed by actors Robert Redford and Dustin Hoffman, visit the Library in pursuit of White House records. The most dramatic scene is filmed from within the upper dome of the Main Reading Room, looking down 160 feet on the diminutive researchers.

Fannie Lee Teals showed off her bicentennial quilt at an event hosted by the American Folklife Center in 1977.

JANUARY 2 - President Gerald Ford approves an act of Congress that creates the American Folklife Center in the Library of Congress. The center's general purpose is "to preserve and present American folklife."

JANUARY 16 - Librarian Boorstin creates an 11-person staff Task Force on Goals, Organization, and Planning to carry out a one-year review that will focus on recommendations for the Library's future. More than 150 staff members serve on Task Force subcommittees, and private foundations support the participation of more than 75 distinguished individuals from outside the Library who represent eight of the institution's key constituencies: arts, humanities, law, libraries, media, publishers, science and technology, and social sciences. The Task Force submits 33 staff recommendations and suggestions from the outside advisors to the Librarian in January 1977. A new Office of Planning and Development reviews the recommendations and uses them as guidelines for a major reorganization in 1977–78.

FEBRUARY 12 - At a press conference, Boorstin displays the extraordinary historical items he found in the wall safe in his office shortly after he moved in. Among the treasures were a pair of gold-rimmed spectacles, a pair of folding spectacles, a watch fob, a pocketknife, a handkerchief, and a wallet containing a Confederate five-dollar bill and newspaper clipping—all recovered from Abraham Lincoln's pockets on the evening of his assassination.

APRIL 13 - In a ceremony at the Jefferson Memorial marking the birthday of Thomas Jefferson, President Ford approves an act to change the name of the Library of Congress Annex Building to the Library of Congress Thomas Jefferson Building. The dedication ceremony takes place on the morning of September 21, 1976, in cooperation with the American Library Association. An afternoon symposium, chaired by Jefferson scholar Dumas Malone, features talks by Frederick R. Goff, former chief of the Library's Rare Book Division, and historian Merrill D. Peterson.

JULY 22 - In an address at the annual conference of the American Library Association, held in Chicago, Librarian Boorstin explains why he thinks public libraries in our county are threatened and offers his suggestions, emphasizing "some of the ways in which we as librarians may make wider and more effective use of the characteristic products of the Age of Broadcasting toward our more traditional purposes."

OCTOBER 19 - Congress approves the Copyright Reform Act of 1976, which creates the American Television and Radio Archive in the Library of Congress. The Library is charged with the development and maintenance of "an ongoing collection of television and radio broadcasts that document the history of those media since their inception."

THE CENTER FOR THE BOOK
IN THE LIBRARY OF CONGRESS

The Library of Congress Center for the Book, which comprises the Young Readers Center and the Poetry and Literature Center, promotes books and libraries, literacy and reading, and poetry and literature. Since its founding in 1977, the Center has developed a diverse range of events, series, lectures, partnerships, prizes, contests, and awards, and has established affiliate centers in the 50 states, the District of Columbia, and the US Virgin Islands.

This poster commemorates the immensely popular exhibition *Building a Better Mouse: Fifty Years of Animation*, which opened at the Library on November 21, 1978.

DECEMBER 16 - Librarian Boorstin opens a planning conference for the Library's forthcoming national preservation program, which will be developed with funding from the Council on Library Resources. He notes: "If the preservation problem, the brittle books problem, is one of cataclysmic proportions, it does offer us the opportunity of cataclysmic grandeur, to save the record of our civilization, past and future."

1977

SEPTEMBER 5 - In an address to librarians at the 1977 annual conference of the International Federation of Library Associations meeting in Brussels, Belgium, Boorstin focuses on the role of the librarian in the new technological age.

OCTOBER 13 - President Jimmy Carter approves an act of Congress creating the Center for the Book in the Library of Congress "to stimulate public interest and research in the role of the book in the diffusion of knowledge." President Carter notes that he signed the bill to affirm his "commitment to scholarly research and to the development of public interest in books and reading."

OCTOBER 20 - In remarks at the first meeting of the national advisory board of the Center for the Book, Boorstin notes that the Library of Congress, "as the national library of the most technologically advanced nation on earth (has) a special duty . . . to see that the book is the useful, illuminating servant of all other technologies, and that all other technologies become the effective, illuminating acolytes of the book."

1978

NOVEMBER 21 - The groundbreaking and extremely popular exhibition *Building a Better Mouse: 50 Years of Animation*, featuring items from the Library's Walt Disney Collection, opens. It remains on view until January 31, 1979.

During a visit to the Library on September 11, 1979, the Dalai Lama looked at rare Tibetan items in the collection.

1979

MARCH - In hearings in both the House and Senate, subcommittee members consider the Library's request for $3.5 million to begin planning for the renovation of the Jefferson Building, once the new Madison Building opens.

NOVEMBER 19 - In a talk entitled "Gresham's Law: Knowledge or Information?" presented at the White House Conference on Library and Information Services in Washington, DC, Librarian Boorstin emphasizes the distinction between knowledge and information, the importance of the distinction, and the dangers to libraries and other institutions that fail to recognize it.

1980

APRIL 24 - The James Madison Memorial Building is dedicated. Senator Harry F. Byrd of Virginia speaks about "James Madison—The Man," and Senator Claiborne Pell, chairman of the Joint Library Committee, and Vice Chairman Lucien N. Nedzi address the topic "The Library of Congress—In Service to Congress and the People."

MAY 28 - The Madison Building opens to the public. Measuring more than 2,100,000 square feet, it ranks among the largest public buildings in Washington, DC.

Walter Hancock carved the heroic 11-foot-tall white Carrara marble statue of James Madison at the end of Madison Memorial Hall.

"KNOWLEDGE WILL FOREVER GOVERN IGNORANCE" —THE MADISON MEMORIAL

The father of the US Constitution believed in the power of knowledge to uphold democracy—and he believed that books would preserve such knowledge. So, it was only fitting that the Library's third building would be named for James Madison and serve as the only national memorial to the country's fourth president.

In the late 1950s, crowded stacks in the once-spacious Annex building, plus an increasing collection growth rate, made it clear that a third major Library building would soon be needed. On August 13, 1958, the Architect of the Capitol submitted a detailed statement to the Joint Library Committee about a future structure. Congress appropriated planning funds for today's James Madison Memorial Building in 1960. Ultimately, two separate Capitol Hill projects were successfully united in 1965 to bring this project to fruition: the creation of a James Madison Memorial and the construction of a third Library of Congress building. Construction was authorized the same year and work began.

However, life in a democracy can be complicated. On May 27, 1971, the US House Office Building Commission, chaired by Speaker of the House Carl Albert, recommended that no further action be taken on the appropriation of funds for a third Library building until a location of a fourth House of Representatives building had been determined. On June 4, 1971, in a debate in the House on the legislative branch appropriation for fiscal year 1972, the House rejected by a vote of 69 to 48 an amendment that would have deleted the recommended appropriation for the Library's James Madison Memorial Building. Thus work finally moved ahead. The cornerstone was laid on March 8, 1974, and the building was dedicated on April 24, 1980—the Library's 180th anniversary. The next year, on November 20, 1981, President Ronald Reagan dedicated Madison Memorial Hall on the building's ground floor.

Modern in style, the Madison Building was designed by the firm of DeWitt, Poor & Shelton,

Associated Architects. When it opened, it was one of the three largest public buildings in the Washington, DC, area (the others being the Pentagon and the FBI buildings), containing 2,100,000 square feet with 1,500,000 feet of assignable space. It houses both administrative offices and several special collection reading rooms and their related collections. Administrative offices include the Office of the Librarian, the Congressional Research Service, the Copyright Office, the Law Library, and National and International Outreach. The reading rooms are those for manuscripts, geography and maps, music, government publications and newspapers, and prints and photographs. There is a small reference area for motion pictures, broadcasting, and recorded sound, but the major reading rooms and the collections for these disciplines are part of the Packard Campus at Culpeper, Virginia.

Two quotations from James Madison adorn the marble exterior walls of the building, on either side of the main entrance on Independence Avenue. On the right side is a quote that speaks of liberty and learning being dependent on one another: "WHAT SPECTACLE CAN BE MORE EDIFYING OR MORE SEASONABLE, THAN THAT OF LIBERTY & LEARNING, EACH LEANING ON THE OTHER FOR THEIR MUTUAL AND SUREST SUPPORT?" On the left is a quote about knowledge and democracy: "KNOWLEDGE WILL FOREVER GOVERN IGNORANCE: AND A PEOPLE WHO MEAN TO BE THEIR OWN GOVERNORS, MUST ARM THEMSELVES WITH THE POWER WHICH KNOWLEDGE GIVES." A four-story bronze relief, *Falling Books* by Frank Eliscu, dominates the main entrance. Off the entrance to the immediate left is the James Madison Memorial Hall, which features a heroic, 11-foot marble statue of Madison by Walter K. Hancock. The work shows Madison in 1783 when, at the age of 32, he developed a list of books "proper for the use of Congress." His right hand holds a volume of the *Encyclopedie Methodique*, which was published in Paris between 1782 and 1832. Eight quotations from Madison concerning government and individual rights were incised by Constantine L. Seferlis in Madison Hall's teakwood panels. Madison also is honored by a bronze medallion profile, hanging above the doors to the Manuscript Reading Room. A second medallion, this one showing Madison at his writing desk, is above the entrance to the Manuscript Division offices. Both medallions are by Robert Alexander Weinman.

On January 24, 1783, James Madison chaired a committee of delegates to the Continental Congress, which recommended a list of 250 titles for a library for the Congress. The motion to adopt the committee report was defeated primarily because of the "inconvenience of advancing even a few hundred pounds." Madison was disappointed but understood. In later years he developed a personal library of several thousand volumes. He was more a user of books than a collector; his library was a workshop that provided the knowledge and information he needed as a legislator, pamphlet writer, presidential advisor, cabinet member, and, finally, president. He had hoped to give his library to the University of Virginia, but instead it had to be sold to settle claims on his estate. In 1980, with the dedication of the Madison Memorial Library, James Madison and his bookish heritage finally had a permanent home.

Falling Books, a four-story bronze relief by sculptor Frank Eliscu, is installed above the Madison Building's entrance.

JUNE 10 – The Library announces that the three Library of Congress buildings on Capitol Hill now bear the names of the three presidents involved in the early establishment of the institution. The original 1897 Library building is now the Library of Congress Thomas Jefferson Building. The second building, opened in 1939, is now the Library of Congress John Adams Building, named in honor of the second US president, who signed the bill creating the Library of Congress on April 24, 1800.

Together with the new James Madison Memorial Building, the nation's memorial to the fourth president, they reunite on Capitol Hill most of the Library's facilities, services, and collections. On June 13, President Carter signs into law the act of Congress that renames the two older buildings.

The James Madison Memorial Building, the third major Library Building on its Capitol Hill campus, opened its doors to the public in 1980.

President Ronald Reagan dedicated Madison Memorial Hall on November 20, 1981.

JULY 16 - The demolition of the temporary partitions and utilities on the second floor of the Great Hall in the Jefferson Building begins, inaugurating the building's planned renovation.

NOVEMBER 14 - Boorstin announces the establishment of a Council of Scholars, a group of 23 distinguished professionals representing a wide range of academic fields. They will explore and assess how the Library's collections support their respective disciplines. Their first meeting, held on November 19, is devoted to the topic "Creativity: Its Many Faces," and includes a public lecture by Boorstin, a symposium, and the opening of an exhibition.

1981

JANUARY 1 - Filing of cards into the Library's main card catalog stops and the online cataloging of the Library's collections officially begins. The card catalog, perhaps the world's largest, consists of approximately 22 million cards filed alphabetically by author, title, and subject into 27,000 drawers. It is relocated and is retained for reference use in a stack adjacent to the Main Reading Room.

1982

APRIL 21 - The US Postal Service issues a new 20-cent stamp commemorating the Library of Congress. The design is based on an 1898 photograph of the newly opened Library building. Librarian Boorstin and Postmaster General William F. Bolger speak at the first day of issue ceremony in the Library's Coolidge Auditorium.

An 1898 photograph illustration of the Library's Jefferson Building is featured on this 20-cent US postage stamp issued on April 21, 1982.

1983

MARCH 26 - The Library opens the exhibition *The American Cowboy* in the two-story exhibit gallery on the first floor of the Madison Building. The exhibition, supported by United Technology Corporation, travels to museums in Texas, Colorado, California, and Alberta, Canada.

JULY 14 - Congress appropriates $750,000 to restore the west exterior terrace and steps of the Thomas Jefferson Building.

NOVEMBER 18 - The Senate agrees to a bill sponsored by Senator Charles McCurdy Mathias, Jr., of Maryland, which authorizes a study of the changing role of the book, to be conducted by the Librarian of Congress under the auspices of the Library of Congress Center for the Book.

1984

MARCH 7 - The 21-person Advisory Committee on the Book in the Future, appointed by Boorstin, meets at the Library, along with project consultants. Librarian Boorstin's conclusions are published internally by the Joint Library Committee in December. A major point is that our democracy, built on books and reading, "is now threatened by the twin menaces of illiteracy and aliteracy." The individual views of each advisor and supplementary materials are compiled in a volume published by the Library in 1987.

OCTOBER 10 - "A Nation of Readers," the national reading theme of the Library's Center for the Book for 1993–94, is also the subject of a new 20-cent commemorative stamp issued by the US Postal Service in cooperation with the Library. The first day of issue ceremony takes place in the Coolidge Auditorium.

Computer terminals became
part of the workstation at
the central desk in the Main
Reading Room in the mid-1980s.

OCTOBER - The Architect of the Capitol receives an appropriation of $81.5 million for the renovation and restoration of the Jefferson and Adams Buildings, to include the cleaning and conservation of the murals in the Jefferson Building.

DECEMBER 7 - *Books and Other Machines*, an exhibition suggesting how the adaptable, portable, flexible book is invigorated by new technologies, opens in the Thomas Jefferson Building.

1985

OCTOBER 29 - In remarks launching the seventh season of the Library of Congress/CBS Television "Read More About It" book project, Boorstin celebrates an unusual convergence: "We dare not be without the latest view of the world, brought to us by television. Nor dare we be without those other countless vistas which all civilization has prepared for us over the centuries—in books."

DECEMBER 20 - Congress approves the Arts, Humanities, and Museums Amendments of 1985, which recognize that the position of Consultant in Poetry to the Library of Congress, established in 1937, is equivalent to that of Poet Laureate of the United States and therefore establishes in the Library of Congress the position of Poet Laureate Consultant in Poetry. Boorstin names Robert Penn Warren, who served as Consultant in Poetry to the Library of Congress in 1944–45, as the first US Poet Laureate Consultant in Poetry. Warren holds the position from 1986 to 1987.

THE FIRST PRESIDENTIAL LIBRARY

The papers of Andrew Jackson, 7th president of the United States, were the first presidential papers to come to the Library, in 1903. Many more would follow.

ANDREW JACKSON.
Seventh President of the United States.

Today more than 15 Presidential Library-Museums dot the American landscape in more than a dozen states, raising awareness of the personalities and politics that have shaped American history. But few people know that the Library of Congress Manuscript Division is the nation's oldest and most comprehensive presidential library. While recently opened and planned libraries, such as those honoring presidents Bill Clinton in Little Rock, Arkansas; George W. Bush in Dallas, Texas; and Barack Obama in Chicago, Illinois, hold papers of a single chief executive, the Manuscript Division has in its custody the papers of 23 presidents, including the men who founded the nation, wrote its fundamental documents, and led it through the great crisis of its existence. The collections range chronologically from George Washington through Calvin Coolidge and include more than two million individual items.

The Library began acquiring presidential papers soon after the Jefferson Building opened its doors in 1897. So imposing was the new structure that it seemed to be designed especially for the papers of a president. It was "the natural and fitting repository for presidential papers," declared the descendants of American journalist and politician Francis P. Blair, who in 1903 gave the Library its first presidential collection, the Andrew Jackson Papers.

In his first State of the Union message on December 3, 1901, President Theodore Roosevelt proclaimed that the Library of Congress, as "the one national library of the United States," had "a unique opportunity to render to the libraries of this country—to American scholarship—service of the highest importance." Soon after the Jackson Papers arrived at the Library, Roosevelt followed those words with action. By executive order on March 9, 1903, he transferred from the State Department to the Library of Congress the papers of presidents George Washington, Thomas Jefferson, James Madison, and James Monroe, along with the papers of Alexander Hamilton and Benjamin Franklin.

In subsequent years, the Manuscript Division assiduously acquired other presidential papers, obtaining some by purchase—the papers of James Polk and Andrew Johnson, for example—and many others by gift—including those of Martin Van Buren, Grover Cleveland, William McKinley, Woodrow Wilson, and Calvin Coolidge.

No gift was pursued with more patience and diligence than the papers of Abraham Lincoln. Librarian of Congress Herbert Putnam first approached the president's son, Robert Todd Lincoln, about the donation of his father's papers in 1901. Agreement was reached in 1919. However, Robert Todd Lincoln decided to seal President Lincoln's papers, closing them to all researchers until 21 years after his own death. This delay produced rumors that the documents would reveal the complicity of members of Lincoln's cabinet in his assassination. The papers were opened with great fanfare on July 26, 1947; the results were important for historians, but disappointed those hoping the documents contained any scandalous secrets. There were none.

The Abraham Lincoln papers were unsealed in 1947. The event was highly anticipated by scholars and the public alike. The papers were subsequently part of a popular Library exhibition.

The Library of Congress presidential papers collection holds items that are among the most important individual manuscript treasures in the nation. In the Washington Papers are Washington's diaries, his commission as commander-in-chief of the American army, and his annotated copy of the United States Constitution. Jefferson's papers contain his rough draft of the Declaration of Independence, with marginalia by Benjamin Franklin and John Adams. Madison's papers include the incomparable notes on the Constitutional Convention, the principal source for understanding the composition and meaning of the Constitution. In Lincoln's papers are the first draft of the Emancipation Proclamation, two drafts of the Gettysburg Address, and the holograph copies of his first and second inaugural addresses. The Woodrow Wilson Papers contain the original draft of Wilson's Fourteen Points concerning the World War I Peace Treaty.

The size of each presidential collection varies from a handful of documents —631 in the Zachary Taylor Papers—to the voluminous—more than 675,000 items in those of William Howard Taft. On August 16, 1957, President Dwight Eisenhower approved an act of Congress authorizing the Presidential Papers Program in the Library of Congress. The Library was charged with arranging, indexing, and microfilming the papers in its possession "in order to preserve their contents against destruction by war or other calamity for the purpose of making them more readily available for study and research." The funds were made available in 1958.

Microfilming was then the leading technology, and the Presidential Papers Program allowed the Library to successfully sell positive copies of the microfilm to libraries and scholars and to make its role as a presidential library better known. A new electronic technology was on the horizon, however. In 1990, the Library inaugurated American Memory, a pioneering effort that made digitized versions of some of its unique resources available throughout the country, particularly to teachers and their students. The Library's microfilmed Presidential Papers collection became a key resource for American Memory, which in its early years included the papers of Abraham Lincoln, George Washington, and Thomas Jefferson. A five-year project, American Memory proved that students, researchers, and the public would use digitized primary resources if access were available. Subsequently, the list of presidential papers available online has grown to include those of James Madison, James Monroe, Martin Van Buren, John Tyler, Zachary Taylor, and William Henry Harrison. Moreover, to provide the most complete record of each presidency, the Manuscript Division continues to acquire—through gift and purchase—additional original documents and reproductions for each of its 23 presidential collections.

1986

FEBRUARY 10 - In extended testimony before a congressional appropriations committee, Boorstin bluntly describes the severe effects that recent budget cuts are having on the Library, calling this "a time of crisis in Congress's Library, in the Nation's Library." His plea results in the restoration of a substantial portion of the recently cut appropriation.

DECEMBER 10 - Boorstin announces that he will resign as Librarian of Congress on June 15, 1987.

1987

APRIL 17 - President Ronald Reagan nominates James H. Billington, director of the Woodrow Wilson International Center for Scholars and a specialist in Russian history, to be Librarian of Congress.

MAY - The Library receives the first installment of the Moldenhauer Archives, a collection of autograph music, manuscript, letters, and documents—and the most significant composite gift of musical documents ever received by the Library. The archive is donated through a bequest by Hans Moldenhauer.

MAY 6 - Librarian Boorstin accepts the invitation of the Senate Committee on Rules and Administration, issued with the approval of President Reagan, to remain in office until his successor is confirmed and ready to assume the responsibilities of Librarian of Congress.

JULY 14 - The Senate Committee on Rules and Administration, chaired by Wendell H. Ford, holds hearings on the nomination of James H. Billington to be Librarian of Congress. While believing that "the position as head of the world's largest library" should be "filled from the ranks of distinguished librarians," the American Library Association recommends in its testimony an agenda for the Library of Congress in the years ahead and expresses its desire to maintain a close working relationship with the new Librarian. Billington's appointment is confirmed on July 24.

SEPTEMBER 14 - In a ceremony held in the Library's Great Hall and attended by President Ronald Reagan, James H. Billington takes the oath of office as the 13th Librarian of Congress. Senator Wendell H. Ford presides over the ceremony, and Thomas S. Foley, Majority Leader, House of Representatives, offers formal greetings. The oath of office, taken on the Library's copy of the 1782 Aitken Bible, the first complete Bible printed in the independent United States, is administered by William H. Rehnquist, the Chief Justice of the United States. President Reagan provides remarks to which the new Librarian of Congress responds. The Library of Congress collection consists of more than 85 million items, including 14 million books, has an appropriation of more than $235 million, and a staff of 4,983 employees.

DECEMBER - Billington initiates a comprehensive review and planning process to chart the Library's future. The review includes four components: an internal staff Management and Planning Committee (MAP), an external National Advisory Committee, regional forums with local library communities, and a review by a management consulting firm. He also asks the General Accounting Office to perform an audit.

DECEMBER - The Main Reading Room closes for renovation.

1988

JANUARY - Billington gives the 27-person MAP Committee a three-fold charge: to find ways to increase the Library's effectiveness in serving the Congress, the federal government, the nation's libraries, scholars, the entire creative community, and all citizens; to review the Library's legislative, national, and international roles and responsibilities; and to recommend broad goals the Library should achieve by the year 2000 and practical steps to obtain them. The MAP Committee presents its vision for the Library's future in a 300-page report dated November 1988 that contains 108 separate recommendations. During the months following, the committee's recommendations are incorporated into a new strategic plan that goes into effect on October 1, 1989.

MARCH - With congressional approval, Librarian Billington establishes the Library's first Development Office.

APRIL 13 - Billington gives the opening address for the exhibition *Legacies of Genius* in Philadelphia. In this talk he succinctly summarizes his hope that the Library can move simultaneously in two general directions: "in more deeply"—to strengthen the Library, its staff, and its services; and "out more broadly"—to make the Library's riches available to even "wider circles of our multi-ethnic society."

SEPTEMBER 27 To make certain the Library plays a leadership role in ensuring the survival, conservation, and public availability of the nation's film heritage, Congress approves the National Film Preservation Act of 1988. The legislation establishes the National Film Preservation Board (NFPB) and the

As honorary chair of the Library's "Year of the Young Reader" national reading program, First Lady Barbara Bush read to young people in the Library's Great Hall in March 1989.

National Film Registry. Every year, beginning in 1989, the Librarian of Congress, with assistance from members of the NFPB and the general public will choose 25 films that are "culturally, historically, or aesthetically significant" for the National Film Registry, and these films are given priority in Library preservation efforts and treatment. Among the first 25 films selected are *The Best Years of Our Lives* (1946), *Casablanca* (1942), and *Citizen Kane* (1941). Through subsequent authorizations and expansions of the act, a National Film Foundation is created and the Library receives authority to expand is national film preservation program.

DECEMBER 5 - At a White House ceremony, President Reagan signs a proclamation designating 1989 as the "Year of the Reader," a theme promoted by the Library's Center for the Book.

1989

JANUARY 30 - In response to a request from new First Lady Barbara Bush, Librarian Billington and John Y. Cole, the director of the Center for the Book, meet with Mrs. Bush at the White House to discuss how she might help with the Center's forthcoming "Year of the Young Reader" campaign. She agrees to become honorary chairperson and launches the campaign in March by reading aloud to a group of Washington, DC, school children in the Library's Great Hall.

1990

JANUARY - With approval from Congress, Librarian Billington establishes the James Madison National Council, a private-sector group that will further the Library's mission by providing financial support for digital initiatives, publications, exhibitions, acquisitions, staff development, internships, and fellowships that advance scholarship. The first official meeting takes place on January 25th.

FEBRUARY - The Library announces its new American Memory project, the first important step in fulfilling Librarian Billington's goal of finding new ways of disseminating to the nation the "substantive content" of the Library's collections. American Memory will make 15-20 American history collections available to libraries and other institutions on optical media. Drawing on the foundation of the Library's 1982–88 Optical Disk Pilot Project, the start-up period for American Memory is planned for 1990–95, during which enhancements to the existing electronic format will be developed through prototype systems and creative repackaging. Early planning for American Memory is supported by gifts from the private sector.

JULY 17 - President George H.W. Bush issues a proclamation designating the 1990s as the "Decade of the Brain," an effort "to enhance public awareness of the benefits to be derived from brain research." The Library and the National Institute for Mental Health (NIMH) announce a joint initiative supported

by the Charles A. Dana Foundation to advance the proclamation. The endeavor will include six symposia between 1991 and 1995, a 1996 celebration of the 50th anniversary of the National Mental Health Act, and a series of public and congressional programs from 1997 to 1999. In 1995, the Library and NIMH publish a book, *Neuroscience, Memory, and Language*, containing 11 papers from the symposia.

1991

MARCH 22 – The Library announces a new Junior Fellows program for college juniors and seniors and graduate students. This privately funded program will pay a monthly stipend for each two-to-six-month fellowship. Librarian Billington cites several fellowship objectives: making the Library's unique collections better known, helping the Library make available previously unexplored materials, and "exposing bright young Americans to the challenging career opportunities at the Library of Congress and other research libraries."

JUNE 3 – The newly restored Main Reading Room in the Jefferson Building reopens, boasting bright colors and its first carpet. The card catalog has been replaced with a new central reference desk and 226 new and refurbished reading desks. The Computer Catalog Center features workstations that incorporate end panels from the original card catalogs.

Folk singer Burl Ives presented a "Year of the Young Reader" concert at the Library on September 21, 1989. Afterwards he donated his guitar to the Library for its collection.

Raisa Gorbachev, wife of the president of the Soviet Union, opened an exhibit of rare Russian manuscripts at the Library on May 31, 1990.

Main Reading Room staff posed for a photograph on June 3, 1991, to mark the opening of their newly restored space, the first tangible result of a 1984 appropriation to renovate and restore the Jefferson and Adams Buildings.

1992

MARCH 30 - Librarian Billington announces new security measures to protect the Library's collections. Patrons are required to obtain a Library Identification Card with their photograph and there will no longer be public access to the stacks in the general collections or the Law and Serials Divisions. Access to the collections is still fully available; however, Library staff will deliver materials directly to patrons in those reading rooms.

JUNE 17-JULY 16 - The Library presents its first online exhibition, *Revelations from the Russian Archives*. The exhibit features once-secret documents spanning the entire Soviet era, from the October Revolution of 1917 to the failed coup of August 1991.

JUNE 26 - Congress approves the National Film Preservation Act of 1992. The new law reauthorizes the National Film Registry and National Film Preservation Board established in 1988. It also directs the Librarian of Congress to 1) study and report to the Congress on the current state of film preservation and restoration activities, including the work of the Library and other major film archives in the United States and 2) establish a comprehensive national film program for motion pictures in conjunction with other film archivists and copyright owners.

1993

JANUARY 8 - The Library's renovated Great Hall opens to the public. A major exhibition, *Rome Reborn: The Vatican Library and Renaissance Culture*, is on view until April 30. Both the exhibition and the accompanying illustrated book are developed and produced in association with the Biblioteca Apostolica Vaticana.

AMERICAN MEMORY: LINCOLN

Photomosaic by Robert Silvers

JANUARY 23 – Billington announces that the Joint Library Committee has approved online access to the Library's automated information files through the Internet beginning in April.

APRIL – The Library of Congress Information System (LOCIS), which includes an online computer version of the Library's bibliographic data that had been developed during the 1970s, becomes available on the Internet.

JUNE – The Newspaper and Periodical Reading Room opens the Library's first public workstation with Internet access.

JULY 14 – Billington and Vice President Al Gore co-chair the Library's first major conference on electronic library resources, "Delivering Electronic Information in a Knowledge Based Democracy."

1994
JANUARY 5 – Billington announces the donation by the Public Broadcasting System of its television program archives, spanning four decades and including more than 40,000 videotapes and films.

JUNE 22–30 – The Library's World Wide Web site debuts at the American Library Association's annual conference in Miami, Florida.

SEPTEMBER 8 – The Library follows its 1993 Vatican Library exhibition in the renovated Jefferson Building with a second exhibition in its Great Libraries series: *Creating French Culture: Treasures from Bibliothèque nationale de France.*

OCTOBER 13 – With support from $13 million in donations from the private sector, the Library launches its National Digital Library (NDL) Program. The NDL, with American Memory as its flagship project, will make substantial portions of the Library's Americana collections available to the public through digital and electronic conversion. A public-private partnership, the NDL not only will be the institution's pioneering online educational outreach program, but also will serve as the springboard for subsequent digital projects for the next several years. By the end of 2004, more than eight million items are available, ranging from the papers of US presidents and Civil War photographs, to the early films of Thomas Edison and the first baseball cards.

OCTOBER 21 – The Library announces the first 10 participants in its new Leadership Development Program. Supported by a $1 million gift from John W. Kluge, chairman of the James Madison Council, the program is designed "to help revitalize librarianship while providing new oppor-

This digitally produced poster image of Abraham Lincoln was created as part of the public announcement of the creation of the Library's National Digital Library Program, which made parts of the Library's Americana collections available through digital and electronic conversion. Designed by Robert Silvers, the portrait is composed from a montage of 1,320 small images of scenes from the Civil War.

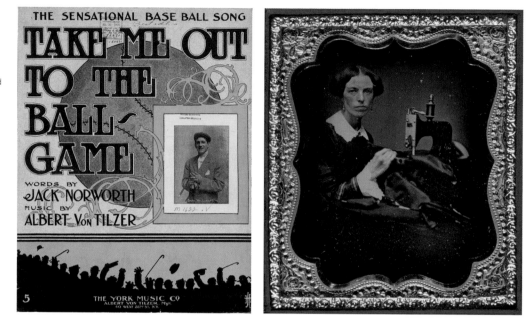

Dozens of treasures were featured in the 1997 exhibition *American Treasures of the Library of Congress*, including the sheet music for "Take Me Out to the Ball Game" and a beautiful nineteenth-century daguerreotype of a woman sewing.

tunities for members of minority groups who will be playing an increasing role in America's cultural and educational institutions."

NOVEMBER - The Library's National Reference Service begins a pilot project to respond via e-mail to reference inquiries received over the Internet.

DECEMBER 8-9 - The Library features its extensive New Deal Arts collections in a public symposium, "The Best of Times for American Culture." Twenty-one participants and firsthand observers of the projects—most of them in their seventies and eighties—accept the Library's invitation for two days of interviews, discussions, and reminiscing.

1995

JANUARY 5 - THOMAS.gov, a website providing free public access to US federal legislative information, debuts as a bipartisan initiative of Congress. The system is named in honor of Thomas Jefferson, one of the Library's principal founders. It is officially retired on July 5, 2016, yielding to Congress.gov.

1996

MARCH 6 - The Learning Page is established as a companion website to American Memory. Designed to introduce K–12 educators to the Library's resources and to support teacher professional development programs, it is a key component in the development of what will evolve into the Library's Educational Outreach Division.

"Whether we are reflecting on the Library's past or looking into its possible futures, we invoke the spirit of the founder of our collections, Thomas Jefferson, who, in his far-reaching curiosity, built a personal library that became the Nation's Library. It is a model that in its scope and depth still inspires us as our power to store and disseminate the numbers, words, and images that comprise the world's tangible memory outstrips our ingenuity in using that power."

— Librarian of Congress James H. Billington, 1997

MAY 7 - The consulting firm of Booz, Allen & Hamilton submits a management review of the Library to the General Accounting Office, a review requested in August 1995 by the Senate Appropriations Committee. Noting that the Library's mission "has been a topic of intermittent debate for nearly 200 years," after considering several scenarios, the report endorses the Library's current dual mission of service to both the Congress and the nation and urges the institution to begin serving each more effectively by "performing as a national Information/ Knowledge Broker."

JULY - The Global Legal Information Network (GLIN), a federation of government agencies that contribute national legal information to the GLIN database, debuts on the Law Library's website.

1997
Billington focuses on the significance of Thomas Jefferson's legacy in the opening sentences of his brief preface to a new Library booklet, *The Coolidge Legacy*, by historian Cyrilla Barr about the magnificent musical legacy left to the Library by Elizabeth Sprague Coolidge: "Whether we are reflecting on the Library's past or looking into its possible futures, we invoke the spirit of the founder of our collections, Thomas Jefferson, who, in his far-reaching curiosity, built a personal library that became the Nation's Library. It is a model that in its scope and depth still inspires us as our power to store and disseminate the numbers, words, and images that comprise the world's tangible memory outstrips our ingenuity in using that power."

APRIL 1 - Today in History, a presentation illuminated by items from the Library's digital collections, debuts on the Library's website.

MAY 1 - The entire Thomas Jefferson Building reopens to the public in its fully restored state for the first time since the completion of a major renovation and restoration that began in 1984. The centerpiece is the opening of the exhibition *American Treasures of the Library of Congress*, which also marks the 100th anniversary of the opening of the Jefferson Building in 1897. The exhibition is made possible by a grant from the Xerox Foundation. A Festival of Cultures on May 4 marks the opening of the space to the public.

1998

The family of entertainer Bob Hope donates Hope's personal papers, radio and television broadcasts, and other materials to the Library, including his carefully organized 88,000-page Joke File, arranged by subject. The gift includes an endowment to support the Bob Hope Gallery of American Entertainment, which will open in the Jefferson Building on May 9, 2000. The inaugural exhibition in the gallery, *Bob Hope and American Variety*, celebrates Hope's career in the context of vaudeville in America. The Bob Hope Foundation continues to provide administrative and programming support.

1999

APRIL 13 - An evening reception in the Great Hall of the newly restored Jefferson Building celebrates the exceeding of a recent fund-raising goal for the National Digital Library (NDL), which receives 75 percent of its funding from private sources, and the recent addition of multimedia materials to the NDL. The new materials include the Alexander Graham Bell Family Papers of some 1,400 items; *An American Time Capsule: Three Centuries of Broadsides and Other Printed Ephemera*, which includes 28,000 primary source items dating from the seventeenth century to the present; and *Hispano Music and Culture of the Northern Rio Grande: The Juan B. Rael Collection*, an online presentation of a multi-format ethnographic field collection documenting religious and secular music of Spanish-speaking residents of rural Northern New Mexico and Southern Colorado. The new acquisitions make more than 40 electronic collections available in a public-private partnership that augments the $15 million in public funding dedicated to the National Digital Library Program.

The family of Bob Hope donated the entertainer's personal papers, radio and television broadcasts, and other materials to the Library in 1998. This scene is from Bob Hope's 1942 movie *My Favorite Blonde*.

Designers Ray and
Charles Eames,
photographed by John
Bryson, seated on a
rug in their home, in
1959. Their famous
Eames chairs are seen
in the background.
The Eameses were
the subject of a major
Library exhibition
in 1999.

The Library's major bicentennial exhibition featured items from the Alfred Whital Stern Collection, including Abraham Lincoln's death mask.

APRIL 14 – The Library announces the start of a nationwide search to locate duplicates of volumes from the personal library of Thomas Jefferson that were destroyed by a fire in the US Capitol on Christmas Eve, 1851. The quest is part of the Library's Gifts to the Nation project to celebrate the 200th anniversary of the Library in 2000.

MAY 20 – The Library opens an exhibition, *The Work of Charles and Ray Eames: A Legacy of Invention*, in the Jefferson Building. It is the first posthumous retrospective of the Eameses' work and brings together the sources of their inspiration, the personal documents of their lives, and the finished products of their genius. It draws heavily on the photographs, drawings, and documents from the Library's collection of more than one million items donated by Ray Eames after her death in 1988. The first comprehensive archive of an influential American design firm to come to the Library, the Eames collection focuses on graphic art, textiles, furniture, and architectural and exhibit design.

AUGUST 24 – The National Library for the Blind and Physically Handicapped launces Web-Braille, which allows braille readers to read more than 2,700 book files in digital braille.

DECEMBER 21 – The Library debuts the Meeting of Frontiers website, which includes more than 2,500 items that describe the parallel experiences of the United States and Russia in exploring and settling their frontiers and the meeting of those frontiers in Alaska and the Pacific Northwest. It is the Library's first major digital project involving international material and extensive cooperation with foreign institutions, and "the first component of an international digital library that will build upon the Library's National Digital Library Program." Available in English and Russian, it is the first bilingual project on the Library's website.

Deputy Librarian of Congress Donald Scott and Librarian Billington admired the Library's bicentennial stamp.

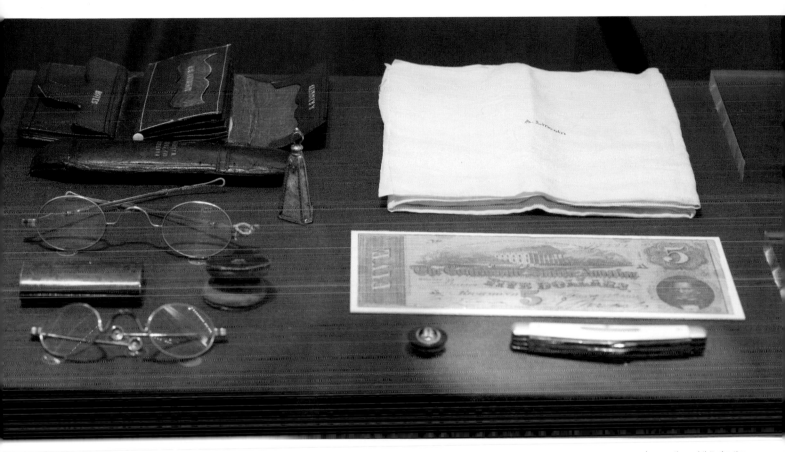

2000

APRIL 24 – The bicentennial of the
Library of Congress begins at 9:30 a.m.
and lasts into the evening. Writers,
musicians, scholars, and members of
the public join the Library in celebrating its 200th anniversary. Events
include first-day ceremonies for a new
Library of Congress postage stamp and
commemorative coin; the launch of
a new website, America's Library, for
young people and their families; the
opening of a new exhibition displaying
a reconstruction of Jefferson's library,
arranged according to his original classification scheme; and an exhibition
saluting the book *The Wizard of Oz*. In
addition, the Library presents its first
Living Legend awards to outstanding
individuals who have made significant
contributions to America's diverse cultural, scientific, and social heritage.
Award recipients over the years include
Julian Bond, Gloria Steinem, Stephen
Jay Gould, Mario Vargas Llosa, Julia
Child, Yo-Yo Ma, and Billie Jean King.

Among the exhibits for the
occasion of the Library's
bicentennial was a display
of the contents of President
Lincoln's pockets the night
he was assassinated.

Library of Congress Living Legend Pete Seeger performed at the bicentennial celebration in 2000.

Some cast members of the popular children's television show *Sesame Street* attended the Library's bicentennial party.

JULY - The National Research Council releases *LC21: A Digital Strategy for the Library of Congress*, a study commissioned by the Library. The report outlines and recommends that the Library pursue an aggressive strategy of creating, acquiring, describing, and preserving electronic resources. In October the Library establishes the position of Associate Librarian for Strategic Initiatives to address the Library's technology infrastructure and policies and to collaborate with the public and private sectors. In support of the report's recommendation, on December 20 Congress appropriates $99.8 million for the Library "to develop a nationwide collecting strategy for digital material" through a National Digital Information Infrastructure and Preservation Program (NDIIPP).

OCTOBER 5 - Members of the Joint Library Committee and Librarian Billington announce that Metromedia president John W. Kluge has donated $60 million to establish the John W. Kluge Center in the Library of Congress and the John W. Kluge Prize in the Human Sciences. It is the largest private monetary donation ever given to the Library.

OCTOBER 23-26 - The changing role of national libraries in the digital environment is discussed by librarians from 21 nations at a Library of Congress bicentennial symposium, "National Libraries of the World: Interpreting the Past, Shaping the Future."

OCTOBER 27 - Congress approves the creation of the Library of Congress Veterans History Project, which will collect, preserve, and make accessible the personal stories of American veterans who served their country from World War I to the present day. Collections will be housed within the American Folklife Center.

NOVEMBER 9 - To make certain the Library plays a leadership role in the preservation of the nation's audiovisual heritage, Congress approves the National Recording Preservation Act of 2000, which creates the National Recording Preservation Board (NRPB) and the National Recording Registry. A National Recording Foundation also is created. The NRPB includes representatives of most of the national organizations concerned with sound, audio, and music, as well as a number of "at large" experts. Each year since 1998, the NRPB and members of the public have chosen 25 recordings that are "culturally, historically, or aesthetically significant" for the National Recording Registry and thus for priority preservation by the Library. The NRPB will play a major role in the development of the Library's comprehensive National Recording Preservation Plan, which is issued in December 2012. In 2014, the NRPB begins to form a Radio Preservation Task Force (RPTF), which has expanded across the country to include academic, archival, curatorial, and other radio experts who serve as research associates. On February 26–28, 2016, the RPTF organizes and hosts the first national conference on radio preservation at the Library and the University of Maryland.

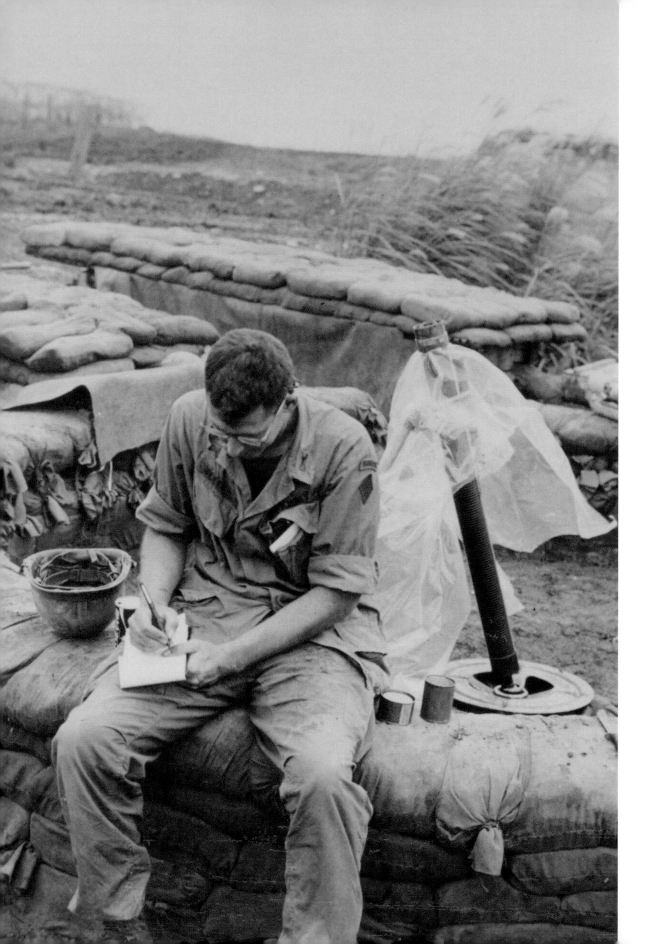

NOVEMBER 18 – To help alleviate book overcrowding in the Library's Capitol Hill buildings, the Library opens its first high-density book-storage facility at Fort Meade, Maryland. The first in a series of such facilities at Fort Meade, it provides storage for 1.2 million books and periodicals, an environmentally safe atmosphere, and electronically controlled security and fire control. Service to Capitol Hill reading rooms is provided twice a day. On July 2, 2003, Congress appropriates additional funds for off-campus collection storage and for the design of storage space. It also authorizes the transfer of 100 acres from the US Army at Fort Meade to the Architect of the Capitol for use by the Library of Congress.

2001

JUNE 7 The Library opens its first gallery permanently dedicated to its international collections. A rotating exhibition in the Jefferson Building, *World Treasures of the Library of Congress*, will draw on the Library's foreign collections to explore a series of universal themes. The first theme, "Beginnings," presents a broad range of materials that relate to the origins of civilizations and cultures.

First Lieutenant James F. Scott took a moment to compose a letter home from Alpha 4 Fire Base in Vietnam. In addition to oral histories, the Veterans History Project collects original manuscripts, such as correspondence, as well as photographs, military papers, diaries and journals, and creative works. Since 2000, the Veterans History Project has archived more than 100,000 individual veterans' narratives, and over one-third of these have digitized content, viewable online.

SEPTEMBER 8 – The first National Book Festival, developed in cooperation with First Lady Laura Bush, is held in the Library's Jefferson and Madison Buildings and on the east plaza and lawn of the Capitol. A crowd of approximately 30,000 enjoys presentations by more than 60 prominent authors, illustrators, storytellers, and poets. The annual festival moves outdoors to the National Mall in 2002 and to the Walter E. Washington Convention Center in 2014.

NOVEMBER – The Digital Reference Section is created to provide reference services related to the Library's online collections.

In the company of several participating authors, Librarian Billington and First Lady Laura Bush opened the first National Book Festival in front of the Jefferson Building on September 8, 2001.

Billy Collins, Library of Congress Living Legend and US Poet Laureate from 2001 to 2003.

2002

JANUARY 4 - Poetry 180 debuts online. A project initiated by Poet Laureate Billy Collins (2001–03), Poetry 180 offers high-school students a daily poem to be read aloud each day during the school year.

JUNE - The Library's Ask a Librarian online service debuts. It allows researchers to submit questions directly to staff in each of the Library's reading rooms and receive expert research assistance, typically within five business days.

NOVEMBER 12-14 - The Library hosts "The Civil War and American Memory," a major symposium on the Civil War that features discussions and presentations by 36 leading scholars from across the country. Sponsored

The Library's exceptionally strong Civil War collections were the foundation for this 949-page reference book published in 2002 and a major symposium in November 2002, "The Civil War and American Memory."

by the Library's Publishing Office, the symposium celebrates the recent publication by Simon & Schuster of *The Library of Congress Civil War Reference*, a 949-page illustrated trove of information on the antebellum period, the war, and the aftermath of the conflict, drawn from the Library's unparalleled Civil War collections.

NOVEMBER 25 - The Herb Block Foundation donates to the Library the archives of Herb Block, one of America's most influential political commentators and the editorial columnist for the *Washington Post* for 55 years. Included are more than 14,000 original cartoons and voluminous files of records, correspondence, photographs, and preparatory sketches. The Library formally announces the donation on March 11, 2003, with a special exhibition, *Herblock's Gift: The Herb Block Foundation Collection*. The new Herblock gallery in the Jefferson Building's Graphic Arts Galleries opened on March 18, 2011. The foundation continues to provide acquisitions and programming support.

2003

JANUARY 2 - Librarian Billington announces the first annual selection of 50 recordings for preservation as part of the National Recording Registry, created by the National Recording Preservation Act of 2000.

MAY 7 - The John W. Kluge Center for Scholars officially opens. Special events include a performance by singer Tony Bennett in the Library's majestic Main Reading Room and the premiere of a "new" composition by John Philip Sousa, "The Library of Congress March," reconstructed from manuscript sketches and orchestrations in the Library's Sousa collection.

MAY 20 - The personal stories of American veterans become widely available as the Veterans History Project goes online on the Library of Congress website.

JUNE 18 - The Library announces the $10 million purchase of the only known copy of the 1507 world map by Martin Waldseemüller, which contains the first use of the word *America* as a designation for a portion of the New World. Acquisition of the map was made possible by the generosity of Congress and of a small group of private donors.

The archives of longtime *Washington Post* political cartoonist Herbert L. Block (Herblock), seen here at the drawing board in his studio, were donated to the Library in 2002.

This image of the devastating terrorist attack on New York City on September 11, 2001, is from the September 11 Digital Archive.

SEPTEMBER 10 - The Library acquires its first major born-digital collection, the September 11 Digital Archive, which contains more than 13,000 written accounts, recordings, videos, and photographs of the terrorist attacks on New York City; Washington, DC; and Western Pennsylvania.

OCTOBER 1 - The Library's American Folklife Center agrees to become the archive for the interviews produced by the StoryCorps oral history project. In 2005, StoryCorps launches a Mobile Booth at the Library and its weekly broadcast debuts on National Public Radio's *Morning Edition*.

In June 2003, the Library announced the purchase of the only known copy of the 1507 world map by Martin Waldseemüller, which contains the first use of the word *America* as a designation for a part of the New World.

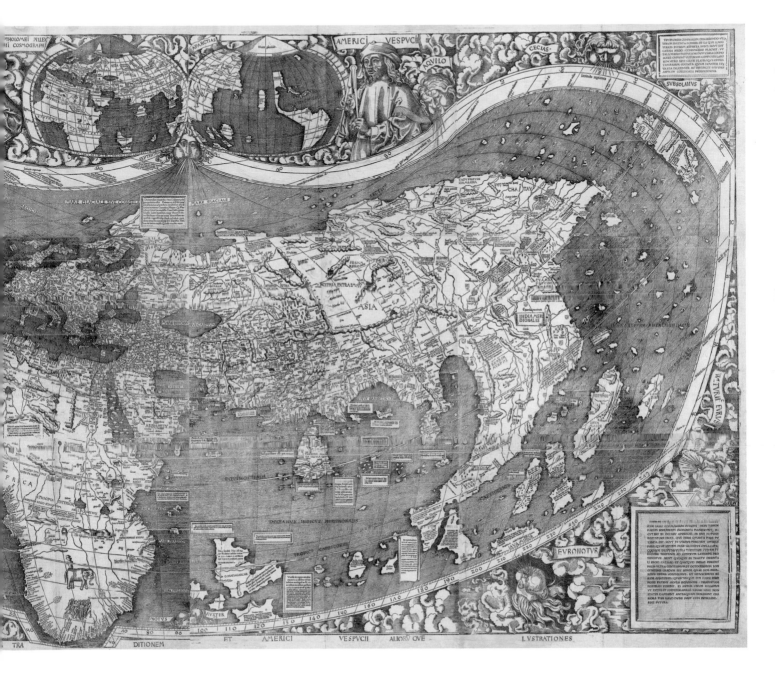

Among the annual selection of recordings to be preserved as part of the National Recording Registry was Sam Cooke's "A Change is Gonna Come" from 1965, chosen for the Registry in 2006.

This painted ceramic jaguar sculpture, from AD 600–900, is part of the Jay I. Kislak Collection, acquired in 2004.

NOVEMBER 5 – The Library announces that the first recipient of the $1 million John W. Kluge Prize for Achievement in the Study of Humanity is philosopher and historian Leszek Kołakowski of Poland. Billington explains that the prize honors lifetime accomplishment in the humanities and social sciences, "areas of scholarship for which there are no Nobel Prizes."

2004

In the film *National Treasure* and its sequel, *National Treasure: Book of Secrets* (2007), actor Nicolas Cage leads a team of treasure-seekers in plots focused on two historical documents: the Declaration of Independence in the former and the diary of John Wilkes Booth in the latter. Both movies feature dramatic scenes in the Main Reading Room of the Jefferson Building.

MARCH – The Library acquires the ethnological collection of folklorist Alan Lomax, which supplements the folklife collection amassed for the Library during the 1930s and early 1940s.

APRIL – The Jay I. Kislak Early Americas Collection is donated to the Library. Its more than 3,000 items, including rare books, manuscripts, historic documents, and maps and art, contain some of the earliest records of the indigenous peoples of North America.

2005

AUGUST 2 – Congress approves the Library of Congress Digital Collections and Educational Curricula Act of 2005, requiring the Library to teach educa-

In 2005, StoryCorps converted an Airstream trailer into a traveling recording studio—the MobileBooth—and launched its first cross-country tour. Each year, StoryCorps visits cities and towns across the country to record the stories of the people who live there. The audio files are archived in the Library's American Folklife Center.

Paul Simon was the first recipient of the Gershwin Prize for Popular Song.

tors and librarians how to incorporate its digital collections into educational curricula. The new law leads to the 2008 creation of the Teaching with Primary Sources (TPS) program, providing the basis for a new multistate effort with individual universities, consortia, and other partners.

2006

OCTOBER 17 - Novelist David Baldacci presents a public program at the Library about *The Collectors*, his twelfth consecutive *New York Times* bestseller. The plot is triggered by the murder of the director of the Library's Rare Book and Special Collections Division. The Library's Main Reading Room is featured on the book's front cover and the endpapers feature pages of the Bay Psalm Book (1640), one of the institution's "top treasures."

2007

MARCH 1 - The Library announces that Paul Simon is the first recipient of the Gershwin Prize for Popular Song, presented to a composer or performer for his or her lifetime achievement in song composition. Subsequent winners of the annual prize include Stevie Wonder (2009), Paul McCartney (2010), Burt Bacharach and Hal David (2012), Carole King (2013), Billy Joel (2014), Willie Nelson (2015), and Smokey Robinson (2016).

THE LIBRARY'S POP PERSONA

Popular novelist David Baldacci has been one of the most frequent speakers at the Library's annual National Book Festival, appearing in 2003, 2005, 2007, 2009, and 2015. He visited the Library of Congress several times while writing *The Collectors* (2006), a thriller set partially in the Library that became his twelfth consecutive *New York Times* bestseller. Here he signs a book for a fan at the 2007 National Book Festival.

Throughout its 200-plus-year existence, the Library of Congress has faithfully chronicled American culture, so much so that the institution itself has become a symbol of who we are—free people who cherish knowledge. Its physical grandeur, priceless treasures, and accessibility to the public have won it a following in Hollywood, publishing, and the popular music industry. And it has extended its influence beyond its walls, through online exhibits, live-streamed events, and websites for educators,

students, and researchers. No longer simply the "book palace" of Librarian Spofford's dreams, it is a festival site, concert venue, protector and conserver of manuscripts and ephemera, and sometimes even a movie set.

Perhaps two dozen major films have been set in part at the Library of Congress. Six of the most popular are *Mr. Smith Goes to Washington* (1939), *Born Yesterday* (1950), *All the President's Men* (1976), *National Treasure* (2004), *National Treasure: Book of Secrets* (2007), and *J. Edgar* (2011). Whether it be an idealistic senator (*Mr. Smith*), the self-educated girlfriend of a mobster (*Born Yesterday*), the *Washington Post* reporters who broke the story of the Watergate cover-up (*All the President's Men*), an amateur historian who unveils secrets in the founding documents (both *National Treasures*), or an FBI director who was once employed at the Library as a messenger and clerk (*J. Edgar*), all these characters knew that the Library of Congress could aid them in their quests. With open access, miles of resources, and an untarnished reputation as a protector of democracy, it has played a small but heroic role in American cinema.

The Library manages to hold onto its integrity in popular literature, but often there is blood on the floor. Mystery novels that depict the Library of Congress—and occasionally its staff members—in some detail include Steve Berry's *The Lincoln Myth* (2014); David Baldacci's *The Collectors* (2006); two titles by former Library of Congress staff member Charles A. Goodrum, *Best Cellar* (1987) and *A Slip of the Tong* (1992); and Margaret Truman's *Murder at the Library of Congress* (1999). Clearly there is more going on in the stacks than meets the eye in these intriguing tales of mayhem.

When it is not appearing in dramatic scenes, the Library is creating them. It hosts an annual book festival that, since its inception in 2001, has become wildly popular. The more than 100,000 attendees at the 2016 festival heard from 120 writers, poets, and illustrators. Herman Wouk, Stephen King, John Grisham, Toni Morrison, E.L. Doctorow, Louise

Erdrich, and Marilynne Robinson are among the novelists featured in recent years, along with strong contingents of graphic novelists. Since 2014, the festivals have also featured poetry slams that draw great crowds. Additionally, Poets Laureate Robert Pinsky, Robert Haas, Billy Collins, Rita Dove, Ted Kooser, Natasha Trethewey, and Juan Felipe Herrera have created special poetry projects that reach beyond their offices at the Library to inspire students and readers nationwide.

There has been a consistent "soundtrack" at the Library throughout its history. The Archive of American Folk Song, established in 1928, only three years after the first chamber music concert series took place in the Coolidge Auditorium, served as the core of today's American Folklife Center. The Library commissioned Aaron Copland's *Appalachian Spring*, which premiered at the Library in 1944. A reprise performance of that work in 2016 was still exhilarating after more than 70 years. In addition to manuscripts by George and Ira Gershwin, the Music Division has rich collections of manuscripts from American composers John Philip Sousa, Victor Herbert, Irving Berlin, Richard Rogers, Oscar Hammerstein II, Jerome Kern, and Leonard Bernstein, among others. And beginning in 2007, the Gershwin Prize for Popular Song, awarded by the Library to notable performers, has honored Paul Simon, Stevie Wonder, Paul McCartney, Carole King, and Willie Nelson, among others. In performances that have literally rocked the walls, these artists have delighted Library audiences and those who watched them broadcast on PBS.

The Library will continue to document and collect popular culture well into the future. Through special exhibitions and acquisitions, it will add to its amazing trove and offer it for the study and enjoyment of all visitors and users. And there is no doubt that creators of film and fiction will find future inspiration in what started out as a book room in the US Capitol but is now a beloved icon of American history and culture.

The Library is the setting for several scenes in the 1950 film *Born Yesterday*.

The new Packard Campus for Audio-Visual Conservation opened in 2007.

MARCH 21 - Chronicling America, the National Digital Newspaper Program website of historical newspapers, debuts online.

APRIL 24 - The Library's first public blog is established and debuts online.

JULY 26 - The new Packard Campus for Audio-Visual Conservation, located on a 45-acre site in Culpeper, Virginia, is officially transferred to the Library by the Packard Humanities Institute. The Institute provided $155 million for the design and construction of a four-building facility, the largest private gift ever made to the Library. The new buildings house a preservation research facility and most of the Library's recorded sound and moving-images collections, comprising more than six million items.

2008

JANUARY 3 - Children's book author Jon Scieszka is appointed the first National Ambassador for Young People's Literature. The position was created "to raise awareness of the importance of young people's literature as it relates to lifelong literacy, education, and the development and betterment of the lives of young people." The Librarian of Congress selects the National Ambassador, based on recommendations from a committee representing many segments of the book community. Ambassadors serve a two-year term. The Library's Center for the Book and the Children's Book Council administer the National Ambassador initiative, which is supported by private funds. Subsequent National Ambassadors are Katherine Paterson (2010–11), Walter Dean Myers (2011–13), Kate DiCamillo (2014–15), and Gene Luen Yang (2016–17). In addition to appearances around the country, each participates in the National Book Festival.

Gene Luen Yang, a writer of graphic novels and comics, became the National Ambassador for Young People's Literature in 2016. He was accompanied at his inauguration by former ambassadors Kate DiCamillo (2014-15) and Jon Scieszka (2008-9). Yang will travel nationwide over the course of his two-year term promoting his platform, "Reading Without Walls," which shows kids and teens that reading is a vital part of their lives

SEPTEMBER 10 - Librarian Billington presents the first Library of Congress prize to a distinguished novelist, the Library of Congress Lifetime Achievement Award for the Writing of Fiction, to Herman Wouk. This initial award inspires subsequent annual awards, each presented in connection with the National Book Festival. From 2009 to 2012, the Library of Congress Creative Achievement Award for fiction is given to John Grisham (2009), Isabel Allende (2010), Toni Morrison (2011), and Philip Roth (2012). Recipients of the Library of Congress Prize for American Fiction are Don De Lillo (2013), E.L. Doctorow (2014), Louise Erdrich (2015), and Marilynne Robinson (2016).

SEPTEMBER 19 - National Treasures, Local Treasures: The Library of Congress at your Fingertips, an educational program that brings the resources of the Library of Congress to selected cities across the country, debuts at the Broward County Library in Fort Lauder-

dale, the home of the Florida Center for the Book. Hosted in 2008 by affiliated state centers in five states, National Treasures, Local Treasures introduces Library of Congress state-oriented resources and includes demonstrations by Library educational specialists about how to bring their state's history alive with rare primary source materials available on the Library of Congress website. Each program includes special guests from the state, including local authors and library directors, and members of Congress. In addition to the Broward County Library, the hosts are the Denver Public Library (October 27), the Dallas Public Library (November 24), the San Francisco Public Library (December 11), and the Los Angeles Public Library (December 12).

2009

JANUARY 27 - The Library launches its Twitter feed.

APRIL 7 - The Library's YouTube channel, created June 9, 2007, goes public.

APRIL 21 - In Paris, Librarian Billington announces the launch of the World Digital Library (WDL), an international collaborative project with support from UNESCO and others. Working with and drawing on the resources of cultural institutions around the world, the WDL makes available online copies of professionally curated primary source material freely available in multiple languages. Resources and formats vary widely and include rare books, maps, manuscripts, musical scores, prints, photographs, and film. WDL partners

In April 2009 Librarian Billington announced the launch of the Library's World Digital Library.

Representative Debbie Wasserman Schultz and her young children, seen here, and Representative Robert Aderholt and his young son helped open the Young Readers Center in the Jefferson Building in 2009.

are mainly libraries, archives, or other institutions that contribute to the project in other ways—for example, by sharing technology, or by convening or co-sponsoring meetings of working groups—or that support the project financially. The partnership now includes works from more than 180 organizations in 81 countries and offers more than 12,000 items to educators, scholars, and the general public.

OCTOBER 29 - Billington opens the Young Readers Center in the Jefferson Building, the first Library space devoted to the reading interests of children and teens.

2010

MARCH - Collector Thomas Liljenquist donates to the Library more than 500 ambrotype and tintype photographs of both Union and Confederate soldiers during the Civil War. The images are displayed at the Library from April 12 through August 12, 2011, at an exhibition, *Last Full Measure: Civil War Photographs from the Liljenquist Family Col-*

lection. The family continues to add to this collection.

JULY 2 - The Library announces that a recent hyperspectral imaging of Thomas Jefferson's rough draft of the Declaration of Independence has "clearly confirmed past speculation" that Jefferson made an important word correction in his writing of the document. Scientists in the Library's Preservation and Testing Division have verified that he changed the phrase "our fellow subjects" to "our fellow citizens."

SEPTEMBER 26 - A specially designed 18-wheel truck containing information and facsimile treasures from the Library begins a one-year tour to cities and towns across America. The first stop is on the grounds of the Handley Regional Library in Winchester, Virginia. By the time the tour concludes on September 21, 2011, at the Culpeper County Library in Culpeper, Virginia, the *Gateway to Knowledge* rolling exhibition visits 40 locations in 34 states. It is made possible through the support of Abby and Emily Rapoport and other members of the Library's James Madison Council.

2011

J. Edgar, director Clint Eastwood's biographical film about longtime FBI director J. Edgar Hoover stars actor Leonardo DiCaprio. Hoover worked at the Library of Congress for five years before joining the Department of Justice. The movie includes a scene featuring the card catalog area in the Main Reading Room, and implies that Hoover's obsession at the FBI with both recordkeeping and investigative work were influenced by his brief Library of Congress career.

Poised to depart from the Jefferson Building, the "Gateway to Knowledge," an 18-wheeler containing information and facsimile treasures from the Library, began a one-year tour across America in 2010-11.

This Civil War-era image of an African American Union soldier with his wife and children is from the Liljenquist Collection, which the Liljenquist family began donating to the Library in 2010.

The Library launched its National Jukebox interactive website in May 2011, making thousands of historic sound recordings—such as the Victor Talking Machine Company's "Bandana Days—One Step"—available to the public.

MAY 10 - The Library launches its National Jukebox, an interactive website that allows users to play thousands of historic sound recordings—many of them unavailable to the public for more than a century. The more than 10,000 previously out-of-print recordings cover popular music, opera, comedy, religious music, and political speeches produced by the Victor Talking Machine Company. The National Jukebox is a collaboration between the Library and Sony Music Entertainment.

2012

JUNE 14-16 - The Library hosts its first "Mostly Lost" film workshop to tap the collective knowledge of film scholars and archivists for information about unknown or little known silent or early sound motion pictures. Films are screened before an audience of "detectives," who are encouraged to call out anything—actors' names, locations, set details—that might aid in identification of the work. The popular workshop, hosted in the state-of-the art theater at the Packard Campus for Audio-Visual Conservation in Culpeper, Virginia, becomes an annual event.

Poet Laureate Natasha Trethewey (2012–14) signed copies of her book at a 2013 reading.

JUNE 25 - The Library opens *Books That Shaped America*, an exhibition of books selected by subject specialists and curators throughout the Library. Its purpose, according to Librarian Billington, "is to stimulate a national conversation on books written by Americans that have influenced our lives, whether they appear on this initial list or not." Many of the 88 books are first editions from the Rare Book and Special Collections divisions and rarely on view. Members of the public are encouraged to comment on the books in a survey on the Library's 2012 National Book Festival website and to nominate other titles for subsequent additions of the exhibit. On June 16, 2016, *America Reads*, a follow-up exhibit, recognizes the public's choice of 65 books that have had a profound effect on American life. Forty of these books are chosen directly by the public. An additional 25 titles are selected by the public from a list created for the 2012 *Books that Shaped America* exhibition.

SEPTEMBER 13 - Natasha Trethewey, the 19th Poet Laureate Consultant to the Library of Congress and US Poet Laureate, opens the Library's 2012–13 literary season, which also marks the 75th anniversary of the Library's Poetry and Literature Center. Trethewey's first term is noteworthy for her "Office Hours," during which she meets with the general public in the Library's Poetry Room—harkening back to a tradition established by her predecessors in the consultant's post from 1937 to 1986. On June 10, 2013, the Librarian appoints her to a second term. Her signature Poet Laureate project in 2013–14 will be a regular appearance on *PBS NewsHour*'s Poetry Series, featuring on-location poetry-related reports in various US cities, conducted with *NewsHour* Senior Correspondent Jeffrey Brown.

Rachel Carson's *Silent Spring*, a groundbreaking book on environmental science published in 1962, was one of 88 books selected by Library of Congress specialists and curators for the 2012 exhibition *Books That Shaped America*.

The Library of Congress acquired the personal papers of American astronomer, astrobiologist, and popular scientist Carl Sagan in 2012. The Sagan collection was donated by writer (most notably of the TV series *Family Guy*), producer, and director Seth MacFarlane, and is officially designated The Seth MacFarlane Collection of the Carl Sagan and Ann Druyan Archive. Carl Sagan is shown here in 1979 with a Viking Lander model.

A visitor took advantage of an open house day on February 18, 2013, in the Library's Main Reading Room to photograph the interior of the dome 160 feet above her. The Library hosts approximately two million public visitors each year.

2013

SEPTEMBER – The Library announces the availability of the Braille and Audio Recording Download (BARD) online service through its National Library Service for the Blind and Physically Handicapped. BARD permits patrons to download braille and talking books to their mobile devices without cost.

SEPTEMBER 22 – The Library announces the first recipients of the Library of Congress Literacy Awards, organizational prizes initiated and funded by philanthropist David M. Rubenstein. Awards go to Reach Out and Read (Rubenstein Prize, $150,000), 826 National (American Prize, $50,000), and PlanetRead (International Prize, $50,000).

2014

JULY 29 – The Library opens to the public and makes available online a collection of approximately 1,000 pages of correspondence between 29th US President Warren G. Harding and his mistress, Carrie Fulton Phillips. The letters had been locked in a vault in the Library's Manuscript Division since their donation to the Library in 1972.

President Barack Obama, along with Michelle Krowl of the Manuscript Division, viewed the original manuscript of President Abraham Lincoln's Second Inaugural Address on March 8, 2015. Accompanied by his two daughters, the president made a private visit to the Jefferson Building to examine the manuscript, which the Library placed on display for four days to commemorate the 150th anniversary of Lincoln's speech.

Congressman John Lewis of Georgia, a major figure in the American Civil Rights movement, visited the Library's 2014 exhibition *The Civil Rights Act of 1964: A Long Struggle for Freedom.*

JULY 29 - The Library launches an online site for its collection of World War I sheet music.

NOVEMBER 6 - The Library opens a 10-week exhibition, *Magna Carta: Muse and Mentor*, which celebrates the 800th anniversary of the first issue of Magna Carta. The 1215 Magna Carta, on loan from England's Lincoln Cathedral, is the centerpiece of the exhibition, accompanied by rare materials from the Law Library of Congress and other divisions. The exhibition's focus is on how this great charter of rights and liberties stands at the heart of English and American law and has influenced the legal systems of many other democratic nations. *Magna Carta: Muse and Memory* also celebrates the 75th anniversary of the Lincoln Magna Carta's first visit to the Library of Congress.

2015

APRIL 7 - The American Archive of Public Broadcasting (AAPB), a collaboration launched in 2013 among the Library of Congress, WGBH Boston, and the Corporation of Public Broadcasting, launches its website. The project saves and makes digitally accessible significant at-risk historical public television and radio programs before they are lost to posterity. By the summer of 2016, approximately 68,000 items comprising 40,000 hours of programming from the late 1940s to the present have been digitized for long-term preservation.

APRIL 15 - The Library places online a selection of recordings from its Archive of Recorded Poetry and Literature, a series of audio recordings of renowned poets and prose writers reading from their works. Highlights include Robert Frost interviewed by fellow Library of Congress Consultant in Poetry Randall Jarrell in 1959; Kurt Vonnegut giving a lecture in the Library's Coolidge Auditorium in 1971; and Nobel Laureate Czeslaw Milosz reading with Paul Muldoon in 1991. The archive, established in 1943 when Allen Tate was Consultant in Poetry, contains nearly 2,000 recordings of poets and prose writers.

SEPTEMBER 3 - The Library marks the 15th anniversary of its National Book Festival, which was first held on September 8, 2001—three days before the terrorist attacks on the World Trade Center, Western Pennsylvania, and the Pentagon. This anniversary event, which also honors Thomas Jefferson, the Library's primary founder, attracts more than 100 leading writers and a record number of book lovers to the Walter E. Washington convention Center. It is the second year at the indoor center following 13 successful years on the National Mall. Author headliners include David McCullough, who participated in the first festival in 2001, and Louise Erdrich, winner of the 2015 Library of Congress Prize for American Fiction.

SEPTEMBER 16 - The Library launches an online selection of records from its Archive of Hispanic Literature on Tape, a series of audio recordings of renowned poets and prose writers reading from their work in their native languages. The archive, which began in 1943, contains nearly 700 recordings of poets and prose writers participating in sessions at the Library of Congress and at other locations in Spain and Latin America.

SEPTEMBER 30 - Librarian James H. Billington retires, telling the staff "it has been the great honor and joy of my life to lead the Library of Congress for 28 of my 42 years of public service in Washington," and praising his colleagues at "this amazing American institution." As the 13th Librarian of Congress, Billington doubled the size

A participant went behind the scenes at a Library tour during the 2014 Summer Teacher Institute.

DO NOT ENTER
LC STAFF AND AUTHORIZED
STACK PASS HOLDERS
ONLY
MAY ENTER

of the Library's traditional collections while simultaneously creating a massive new digital Library of Congress. He also established the National Book Festival; the John W. Kluge Center and its Nobel-level John W. Kluge Prize for Achievement in the Study of Humanity; the Library's four-building, state-of-the art audio-visual conservation center in Culpeper, Virginia; the Gershwin Prize for Popular Song; and other programs to "get the champagne out of the bottle" for the American public.

OCTOBER 1 - Deputy Librarian of Congress David H. Mao becomes the Acting Librarian of Congress.

2016

FEBRUARY 1 - The Library releases statistics for fiscal year 2015. Its collection now comprises more than 162 million physical items in a wide variety of formats. In fiscal year 2015, it added 1.7 million physical items to its permanent collections; registered more than 443,000 copyright claims; and responded to more than one million reference requests from Congress, the public, and other federal agencies.

FEBRUARY 24 - President Barack Obama nominates Carla D. Hayden, chief executive officer of the Enoch Pratt Free Library in Baltimore, Maryland, to be the 14th Librarian of Congress.

Singer and songwriter Willie Nelson was the 2015 recipient of the Library of Congress Gershwin Prize for Popular Song. The all-star tribute featured performances by Nelson, as well as Edie Brickell, Leon Bridges, Rosanne Cash, Ana Gabriel, Jamey Johnson, Alison Krauss, Raul Malo of The Mavericks, Neil Young, Promise of the Real, Buckwheat Zydeco, and past Gershwin Prize honoree Paul Simon.

FEBRUARY - The Library completes the digitization of thousands of manuscripts and photographs that once belonged to civil rights icon Rosa Parks and makes the collection available online to the public.

APRIL 20 - Carla D. Hayden testifies before the Senate Committee on Rules and Administration regarding her nomination by President Obama to become the 14th Librarian of Congress. On June 9, the committee votes unanimously to forward Hayden's nomination to the full Senate with the recommendation that it be approved. On July 13, the US Senate confirms Carla D. Hayden by a vote of 74 to 18.

SEPTEMBER 14 - Carla D. Hayden is sworn in as the 14th Librarian of Congress. She is the first woman and the first African American to hold the position. The Library's collection of more than 162 items includes more than 38 million cataloged books and other print materials in 470 languages; more than 70 million manuscripts; the largest rare book collection in North America; and the world's largest collection of legal materials, films, maps, sheet music, and sound recordings. In fiscal year 2016, the Library employed 3,149 permanent staff members and operated with a total 2016 appropriation of $642.04 million, including the authority to spend $42.13 million in receipts. Since its founding in 1990, the James Madison Council has sponsored more than 350 projects and initiatives. Its financial support has exceeded $223 million, approximately 54 percent of the private funds raised by the Library during this period.

In 2015, school children from the Rosa L. Parks Elementary School, in Prince Georges County just outside Washington, DC, came to the Library to look at items from the newly acquired Rosa Parks Collection.

On September 14 in the Library's' Great Hall, with her mother holding a copy of the Library's Lincoln Bible, Carla D. Hayden take the oath of office to become the 14th Librarian of Congress. Chief Supreme Court Justice John G. Roberts, Jr., (left) administers the oath as Speaker of the House Paul D. Ryan observes.

On August 25, 2016, the Library's Communications Office recorded a welcome photo and video in the Great Hall for Carla D. Hayden, the new Librarian of Congress.

APPENDIX

THE LIBRARIANS OF CONGRESS

On April 24, 1800, when President John Adams approved an appropriation "for the purchase of such books as may be necessary for the use of Congress," no mention was made of the position of librarian. Oversight of the Library of Congress was to be provided by a Joint Library Committee. On January 16, 1802, President Thomas Jefferson approved an act of Congress providing details about the new institution's governance and use. It stipulated that the president would appoint the Librarian—not Congress. The librarian's pay was not to exceed $2 a day. No special qualifications for the position were prescribed. No term of office for the Librarian of Congress was specified until 2016, when Congress approved a term of 10 years, with the possibility of one 10-year extension.

On February 19, 1897, President Grover Cleveland approved the reorganization and expansion of the Library of Congress in its new Capitol Hill building as part of the Library's fiscal year 1898 appropriation. Included in the legislation was a new provision stating that the president's appointment of a Librarian of Congress was to be approved by the Senate. Moreover, the Librarian of Congress, not the Joint Library Committee, was given sole authority and responsibility for administering the institution, including selection of the staff.

Now used primarily for ceremonial purposes, this ornate room was the office of the Librarian of Congress from 1897 until 1980, when the official office was moved to the Madison Building.

George Watterston

JOHN J. BECKLEY
1802–1807

President Thomas Jefferson decided that the clerk of the House of Representatives would also serve as the Librarian of Congress. On January 29, 1802, he appointed clerk John J. Beckley, a political ally, to serve also as first Librarian of Congress. Beckley, a lawyer, served concurrently in the two positions until his death.

Beckley made several suggestions regarding possible acquisitions by the Library to Jefferson and to members of the Joint Library Committee. He also assisted in the publication of the Library's first catalog in 1802.

John Beckley was born in England on August 4, 1757, and was sent to Virginia eleven years later to work as a scribe for a mercantile firm. He died on April 8, 1807. His son Alfred inherited a large tract of unsettled land in what today is West Virginia and built the first house in a village that became the city of Beckley, named by Albert to honor his father.

PATRICK MAGRUDER
1807–1815

President Jefferson briefly considered separating the clerkship and Library positions but did not, deciding to again appoint the clerk of the House of Representatives to the post of Librarian of Congress. On November 6, 1807, he notified the new House clerk, Patrick Magruder, that he would begin serving as Librarian the next day, November 7.

Magruder, a lawyer who had served one term as a member of the Ninth Congress, carried out his daily tasks as Librarian when needed, but did not show as much interest in the Library as his predecessor. Magrud-

er's term as Librarian was tainted by scandal after the British burned the Capitol and destroyed the Library on August 24, 1814, a day when he was absent. Congress held him responsible for failing to protect the Library as well as its financial records. He resigned on January 28, 1815. Patrick Magruder died on December 24, 1819, and is buried with his wife at Sweden, the family estate near Petersburg, Virginia.

GEORGE WATTERSTON
1815–1829

The acquisition of Thomas Jefferson's personal library in early 1815 prompted President James Madison to name the first full-time Librarian of Congress on March 21, 1815. He was George Watterston, a local novelist, poet, and journalist, whose first task was to organize and publish a Library catalog based on Jefferson's library. He also adopted Jefferson's library classification scheme for use by the Library. Watterston was an ardent nationalist who advocated both a national role for and a separate building to house the Library, which he considered "the Library of the United States." An outspoken Whig, his librarianship came to an abrupt end on May 28, 1829, when newly elected President Andrew Jackson, a Democrat,

replaced him with another Democrat, John Silva Meehan.

Watterston was born on October 23, 1783, on a ship in New York harbor. He died in Washington on February 4, 1854. His obituary notice in the *National Intelligencer* does not mention his years as Librarian of Congress, instead emphasizing his close identification with the Washington Monument Society.

JOHN SILVA MEEHAN
1829–1861

A local printer, editor, and newspaper publisher, John Silva Meehan served as Librarian of Congress from May 28, 1829, until May 24, 1861, when the newly elected president, Abraham Lincoln, a Republican, replaced him with another Republican. Meehan was an efficient but passive Librarian who demonstrated none of Watterston's ambition for the institution. Polite and cheerful, he carefully followed the suggestions of respective chairmen of the Joint Library Committee, especially Senator James A. Pearce, the conservative and scholarly chairman from 1846 until 1862. Pearce favored the Library's relatively narrow legislative role. In the late 1850s, he and Meehan agreed to relinquish several government-wide functions

John Silva Meehan

the Library had acquired in early years: the distribution of public documents, the international exchange of books and documents, and copyright deposit. Pearce tried but failed in his attempt to prevent Meehan's dismissal by President Lincoln in 1861.

John Silva Meehan was born in New York City on February 6, 1790, and died in Washington in his residence on Capitol Hill, not far from the Library of Congress, on April 24, 1863—the Library's 63rd anniversary.

JOHN G. STEPHENSON
1861–1864

A physician from Terre Haute, Indiana, Stephenson was active in Indiana politics and an early Lincoln supporter. With endorsements from Senator Henry S. Lane of Indiana and others, he sought and on May 24, 1861, obtained a patronage appointment as Librarian of Congress from President Abraham Lincoln. He assumed his duties on June 3 and soon, to the dismay of Senator Pearce, who had not been consulted, dismissed several members of the small staff. However, in September he hired the well-qualified Ainsworth Rand Spofford as Assistant Librarian.

John G. Stephenson

Ainsworth Rand Spofford

Spofford administered the Library during Stephenson's absences during the Civil War, including his service as a volunteer aide-de-camp during the battles of Chancellorsville and Gettysburg. On December 22, 1864, Stephenson submitted his resignation as Librarian, effective December 31, 1864.

John G. Stephenson was born in Lancaster, New Hampshire, on March 1, 1828, and died on November 12, 1883, in Washington, DC. He is buried in Washington's Congressional Cemetery.

AINSWORTH RAND SPOFFORD
1864–1897

A bookseller, journalist, and editor from Cincinnati, Spofford served as Assistant Librarian from 1861 until December 31, 1864, when Lincoln appointed him Librarian of Congress. On December 22, 1864, the day that Librarian Stephenson submitted his resignation, Spofford forwarded to President Lincoln eight letters and a petition signed by members of Congress endorsing his application for the librarianship.

As Librarian of Congress, Spofford gained the confidence of Congress and over a period of more than three decades almost single-handedly transformed the Library of Congress from a library devoted primarily to serving Congress into a national institution that also served the American public. His effort was made easier by the death in late 1862 of conservative Senator James A. Pearce, the dominant force on the Joint Library Committee since the mid-1840s. The new chairman, Senator Jacob Collamer from Vermont, was supportive of Spofford's efforts, as were his successors. Spofford's major achievements were the centralization of US copyright registration and deposit at the Library in 1870 and, over an eleven-year period, persuading Congress to construct the Library's first separate building, which opened in 1897.

Ainsworth Rand Spofford was born in Gilmanton, New Hampshire, on September 12, 1825. He moved to Cincinnati in 1845, where he became a bookseller and literary entrepreneur. In January 1859 he became associate editor and chief editorial writer for the *Cincinnati Daily Commercial*. In mid-September 1861, when he was in Washington, DC, to report on the first Battle of Bull Run, he visited the Library of Congress and met Librarian Stephenson.

In 1897, nearing the end of his long career, he stepped down as Librarian of Congress and then was appointed Chief Assistant Librarian on July 1, 1897, by the new Librarian of Congress, John Russell Young. He died on August 11, 1908, and is buried in Washington's Rock Creek Cemetery.

JOHN RUSSELL YOUNG
1897–1899

On June 30, President William McKinley nominated journalist and former diplomat John Russell Young to be Librarian of Congress. The reorganization of the Library approved on February 19, 1897, required Senate confirmation of a president's choice as Librarian of Congress, and on June

30, Young became the first Librarian to be so confirmed. He took office on July 1, 1897, and immediately appointed former Librarian of Congress Ainsworth Rand Spofford as the Chief Assistant Librarian.

Young presided over the opening of the new Library building on November 1, 1897, an occasion widely praised in the press. The transfer of more than 800 tons of material from the old Library in the Capitol building was completed on November 20, and on the Thanksgiving holiday more than 4,700 visitors toured the new building. During the next year Young efficiently directed an administrative reorganization that included the hiring of additional staff and the reclassification of the collections. He used his extensive diplomatic experience and contacts to solicit materials for the Library, determined to make it "a true library of research." However, on January 17, 1899, he succumbed to a lingering illness and died. He was buried in his home state of Pennsylvania.

John Russell Young

Herbert Putnam

HERBERT PUTNAM
1899-1939

During the congressional recess, on March 13, 1899, President McKinley appointed Herbert Putnam, director of the Boston Public Library and incoming president of the American Library Association, to be 8th Librarian of Congress. Putnam took the oath of office on April 5, 1899, and was confirmed by the Senate without debate on December 6, 1899.

The first experienced librarian to hold the post, Putnam expanded Spofford's national library concept and the Library of Congress itself during his 40-year tenure. He worked closely with the American Library Association to inaugurate new cataloging, bibliographic, and interlibrary loan services to libraries across the nation. Another important initiative was to begin building the Library's international collections. He also was responsible for establishing the 1925 Library of Congress Trust Fund Board, which enabled the Library to accept and administer private gifts and bequests.

Putnam shaped the Library's administrative direction and presided over steady growth. By 1938, when he informed President Franklin D. Roosevelt that he was ready to retire, the Library had a staff of more than 1,100, a book collection of six million volumes, and an annual appropriation of

approximately $3 million. The position of Librarian Emeritus was created for him on June 20, 1938, but the president asked him to stay on until a successor could be found. He did not assume the position of Librarian Emeritus until October 1, 1939, the day before his successor assumed his duties.

In 1939 the American Council of Learned Societies honored Putnam—and his "collaborators and associates"—for making the Library of Congress "an indispensable instrument on the American continent for the promotion of learning and the increase of knowledge."

Herbert Putnam was born on September 20, 1861, at his parents' home in New York City. He died on August 14, 1955, in Woods Hole, Massachusetts.

ARCHIBALD MACLEISH
1939-1944

On June 7, 1939, President Franklin D. Roosevelt nominated writer and poet Archibald MacLeish to become Librarian of Congress. Senate Library Committee hearings were held on June 13 and 19. The American Library Association opposed the nomination because it felt "the Congress and the American people should have a librarian . . . who not only is a gentleman and a schol-

Archibald MacLeish

Luther H. Evans

ar but who also is the ablest library administrator available." However, the committee reported favorably on June 20, and on June 29 the Senate confirmed the nomination by a vote of 63 to 8, with 25 not voting. MacLeish took the oath of office on July 10 at his local post office in Conway, Massachusetts.

A wartime librarian, MacLeish promoted the Library of Congress and librarians in general as "agents of democracy." He also initiated a major reorganization of the Library, developing new statements of the institution's objectives, along with "Canons of Selection," guiding principles for its growing collections. In addition to serving Congress, he believed, like Putnam before him, that the Library should be a "reference library for the people." Archibald MacLeish resigned on December 19, 1944, to become the US Assistant Secretary of State for Public and Cultural Relations.

Archibald MacLeish was born on May 7, 1892, in Glencoe, Illinois. He died in Boston, Massachusetts, on April 20, 1982.

LUTHER H. EVANS
1945–1953

President Harry S. Truman nominated Luther H. Evans, then serving as Acting Librarian of Congress, for the position of Librarian of Congress on June 18, 1945. The Senate Library Committee held hearings on the nomination on June 28 and submitted its favorable report. The entire Senate approved the nomination without objection on June 29. Evans took the oath of office on June 30, 1945.

A political scientist, Luther Evans was working at the National Archives when newly appointed Librarian MacLeish brought him to the Library of Congress, where he soon became

MacLeish's Chief Assistant Librarian. As Librarian of Congress, Evans unsuccessfully advocated greater growth of the Library's national services and recognition of its national role. However, the growth of the Library remained steady during his administration. Evans gradually increased the Library's presence on the international scene through the Library of Congress Mission to Europe from 1945 to 1947, which obtained multiple copies of European publications from the war period. His personal interest in international affairs remained strong throughout his librarianship. He resigned as Librarian of Congress on July 5, 1953, to become the director-general of UNESCO.

Luther Evans was born on October 13, 1902, at his grandmother's farm near Sayersville, Bastrop County, Texas. He died on December 23, 1981, in San Antonio, Texas.

L. QUINCY MUMFORD
1954–1974

On April 22, 1954, President Dwight D. Eisenhower nominated L. Quincy Mumford, director of the Cleveland Public Library and president-elect of the American Library Association, to be Librarian of Congress. The first Librarian of Congress to graduate from a professional library school (with a BS in library science from Columbia University, 1929), Mumford was a popular

choice among librarians. The Senate held hearings on July 26 and confirmed the nomination, without objection, on July 29. Librarian Mumford took the oath of office in the Library's Whittall Pavilion on September 1, 1954.

During his 20 years of service, L. Quincy Mumford guided the Library through an impressive period of expansion. In 1958, he initiated planning for the third Library of Congress structure on Capitol Hill, the Madison Building. Also in 1958 he launched a new era when he established an interdepartmental Committee on Mechanized Information Retrieval. He was able to use funds from the Higher Education Act of 1965 to establish several new overseas offices to acquire and catalog materials for the Library and other research libraries. On the congressional side, he supported the Legislative Reorganization Act of 1970, which broadened the responsibilities of the Legislative Reference Service and changed its name to the Congressional Research Service. He retired on December 31, 1974.

Lawrence Quincy Mumford was born on December 11, 1903, on a farm near Ayden, in Pitt County, North Carolina. He died in Washington, DC, on August 15, 1982.

Daniel J. Boorstin

DANIEL J. BOORSTIN
1975-1987

On June 30, 1975, President Gerald R. Ford nominated Daniel J. Boorstin, author, historian, and former director of the Smithsonian Institution's National Museum of History and Technology, to be Librarian of Congress. The nomination was supported by the Authors League of America but opposed by the American Library Association because the nominee "was not a library administrator." Senate hearings were held on July 30–31 and September 10, 1975; on September 26, 1975, the full Senate confirmed the nomination without debate. Daniel J. Boorstin took the oath of office in the Library's Great Hall on November 12, 1975.

Boorstin's initial and continuing emphasis was on greater public visibility for the Library and more interaction between the institution and the organizations and individuals it served. He saw one of his principal roles as Librarian "to be a catalyst, an avenue between the world of ideas and what goes on at the Library." Several of the offices he created, including the American Folklife Center (1976), the Center for the Book (1977), and the Council of Scholars (1980), were public-private partnerships assisted by advisory boards and private funding.

Boorstin retired in 1987 to devote more time to writing and lecturing. He became Librarian of Congress Emeritus on August 4, 1987.

Daniel J. Boorstin was born in Atlanta, Georgia, on October 1, 1914. He died on February 28, 2004.

JAMES H. BILLINGTON
1987-2015

On April 17, 1987, President Ronald Reagan nominated historian James H. Billington, director of the Woodrow Wilson International Center for Scholars at the Smithsonian Institution, to be the 13th Librarian of Congress. The Senate held hearings on July 14, 1987. The American Library Association neither endorsed nor opposed the nomination, but presented an agenda that it hoped the Library would follow in the years ahead. Billington was confirmed on July 24. He took the oath of office in the Library's Great Hall on September 14, 1987.

At his swearing-in ceremony, Billington explained that he planned to move the Library "out more broadly" and "in more deeply." These two themes indeed continued throughout his 29 years as Librarian. The first was to be accomplished by making the Library's resources more widely available, especially by using new technologies "to share the substantive content" of the Library's unparalleled collections. The second meant strengthening the Library's catalytic role as a leader in "turning information into knowledge," eventually "distilling it into wisdom." His major achievements included the creation of the Library's first development office; the James Madison Council, the Library's first private-sector support group; the National Digital Library (1994); the John W. Kluge Center for Scholars (2000); and the World Digital Library (2009).

James H. Billington was born on June 1, 1929, in Bryn Mawr, Pennsylvania. He retired from the Library of Congress on September 30, 2015.

James H. Billington

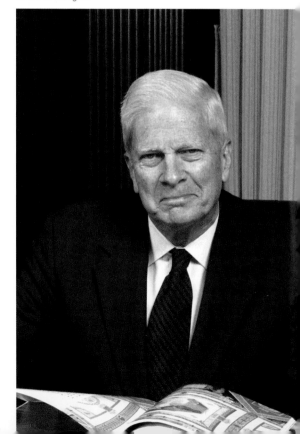

CARLA D. HAYDEN
2016–

On February 24, 2016, President Barack Obama nominated Carla D. Hayden, chief executive officer of the Enoch Pratt Free Library in Baltimore, Maryland, and a former president of the American Library Association, to be the 14th Librarian of Congress. The Senate Committee on Rules and Administration held hearings on the nomination on April 20, and the Senate majority confirmed her nomination on July 13 by a vote of 74 to 18.

Hayden—the first woman and first African American to become Librarian—took the oath of office in the Library's Great Hall on September 14, 2016. Participants in the ceremony included congressional leadership and US Supreme Court Chief Justice John G. Roberts, Jr., who administered the oath on the Bible from the Library's collections used by President Abraham Lincoln at his second inauguration more than 150 years ago and by President Barack Obama at his two inaugurations.

Carla D. Hayden

FURTHER READING

DONOR

Alan Bisbort, Linda Barnett Osborne, and
Sharon M. Hannon. *The Library of Congress: The
Nation's Library, Washington, D.C.*, revised edi-
tion. London: Scala Publishers, 2012.

John Y. Cole. *For Congress and the Nation: A
Chronological History of the Library of Congress
through 1975*. Washington, DC: Library of
Congress, 1979.

John Y. Cole and Jane Aikin, eds. *Encyclo-
pedia of the Library of Congress: For Congress, the
Nation and the World*. Lanham, MD: Bernan
Press, 2004.

John Y. Cole and Henry Hope Reed, eds.
*The Library of Congress: The Art and Architecture
of the Thomas Jefferson Building*. New York:
Norton, 1997.

James Conaway. *America's Library: The Story of
the Library of Congress*. New Haven, CT: Yale
University Press, 2000.

William Dawson Johnston. *History of
the Library of Congress, Volume I, 1800–1864*.
Washington, DC: Government Printing
Office, 1904.

Library of Congress. *Librarians of Congress,
1802–1974*. Washington, DC: Library of
Congress, 1977.

Carl Ostrowski. *Books, Maps, and Politics:
A Cultural History of the Library of Congress,
1783–1861*. Amherst, MA: University of
Massachusetts Press, 2004.

Jane Aikin Rosenberg. *The Nation's Great
Library: Herbert Putnam and the Library of
Congress, 1899–1939*. Urbana: University
of Illinois Press, 1993.

Margaret E. Wagner, ed. *American Treasures of the Library of Congress*, introduction
by Garry Wills. New York: Harry N.
Abrams, 1997.

Julie C. Opperman is a publisher
and investor of Croatian origin.
She also continues the philan-
thropic efforts of the late Dwight
D. Opperman, an iconic figure in
the American legal community and
noted philanthropist.

PHOTO CREDITS

The images in this book are from the collections of the Library of Congress unless otherwise noted. Known information about these images, including creator, year, custodial division, collection name, and reproduction number, is listed below by page number. Many images in this book are from the Library's Prints & Photographs Division and can be viewed or downloaded from the Prints & Photographs Online Catalog (www.loc.gov/pictures). For reproductions of images from other divisions, contact Duplication Services (www.loc.gov/duplicationservices; 202-707-5640). The following abbreviations are used throughout the image credits:

AFC American Folklife Center
AMED African and Middle Eastern Division
Br-Ha Brady-Handy Photograph Collection
Coll. Collection
COM Office of Communications
DS Duplication Services
EUR European Division
G&M Geography & Map Division
HEC Harris & Ewing Collection
IPO Interpretive Programs Office
MBRS Music, Broadcasting & Recorded Sound Division
MSS Manuscript Division
MUS Music Division
NPCC National Photo Company Collection
NYWTS New York-World Telegram & Sun Newspaper Photograph Collection
P&P Prints & Photographs Division
CMHA Carol M. Highsmith Archive
PO Publishing Office
RBSC Rare Book & Special Collections Division
UNK Creator unknown

Cover: see p. 2
Back cover: UNK, 1895. P&P, LC-USZ62-101888

FRONT MATTER
2: Carol M. Highsmith, 2007. P&P, CMHA, LC-DIG-highsm-03188; **4**: Carol M. Highsmith, 1980–2006. P&P, CMHA, LC-DIG-highsm-12559; **6**: Carol M. Highsmith, 1980–2006. P&P, CMHA, LC-DIG-highsm-13970; **8**: Carol M. Highsmith, 1980–2006 P&P, CMHA, LC-DIG-highsm-16602

PART ONE: FOR CONGRESS
10: William Thornton, ca. 1800. P&P, LC-DIG-ppmsca-07219; **13**: Levin C. Handy, ca. 1897. P&P, LC-DIG-ppmsca-34896; **14**: After John Singleton Copley, 1850–1900. P&P, LC-DIG-ppmsca-15705; **15**: Charles Balthazar Julien Févret de Saint-Mémin, 1805. P&P, LC-DIG-ppmsca-31800; **17**: UNK, ca. 1853. P&P, LC-USZ62-1818; **18**: Peter S. Duval, 1846. P&P, LC-DIG-ppmsca-30581; **19**: George Munger, 1814. P&P, LC-DIG-ppmsca-23076; **20–21**: LC/David Sharpe, 2000. COM; **22**: Thomas Jefferson to Samuel Harrison Smith, May 8, 1815. MSS; **25**: After W.G. Doles, ca. 1898. P&P, LC-USZ62-59096; **26–27**: Alexander Jackson Davis, 1834. P&P, LC-DIG-ppmsca-09409; **28 left**: Augustus Köllner, ca. 1846–1855. P&P, LC-DIG-ppmsca-23165; **28 right**: N. Currier, 1844. P&P, LC-USZC4-6089; **29 left**: UNK. P&P, LC-USZ62-14760; **29 right**: John James Audubon and R. Havell, 1827–1838. P&P, LC-USZC4-894; **30**: Thomas U. Walter, 1852. P&P, LC-DIG-ppmsca-07220; **32 left**: UNK. P&P, LC-USZ62-13081; **32 right**: Mathew B. Brady, 1844–1860. P&P, Daguerreotype Coll., LC-USZ62-109982; **34**: H.C. Howard, 1860. P&P, LC-DIG-pga-01637; **35**: F. Sachse & Co., 1866. P&P, LC-DIG-pga-04078; **36**: MSS, LC Archives, PIO series; **37 left**: Mathew B. Brady, ca. 1865. P&P, LC-USZ62-91814; **37 right**: G.D. Wakely, 1866. P&P, LC-DIG-stereo-1s02418; **38**: UNK, 1880. P&P, Br-Ha, LC-DIG-cwpbh-03642; **39 left**: UNK, 1855–1865. P&P, Br-Ha, LC-DIG-cwpbh-01804; **39 right**: UNK, 1860–1880. P&P, LC-USZ62-117814; **40**: Smithmeyer & Pelz, 1873. P&P, LC-DIG-ppmsca-31513; **41**: G.F. Gilman, 1881. P&P, LC-DIG-pga-01369; **43**: Carol M. Highsmith, 1980–2006. P&P, CMHA, LC-DIG-highsm-13002; **45**: George West, 1844. MSS, Caleb Cushing Papers, oversize container #2; **46**: Joseph Ferdinand Keppler, 1885. P&P, LC-DIG-ds-04498; **47**: Abdullah Frères, 1880–1893. P&P, Abdul-Hamid II Coll., LC-USZC4-11658; **48**: P.J. Pelz, 1888. P&P, LC-DIG-ppmsca-25376; **49**: Frances B. Johnston, ca. 1900. P&P, LC-USZ62-6010; **50**: UNK, 1890. P&P, Washingtoniana Coll., LC-USZ62-73542; **51**: UNK, 1892. P&P, LC-USZ62-51462; **52**: Carol M. Highsmith,

2009. P&P, CMHA, LC-DIG-highsm-11661; **53**: UNK, 1894. P&P, LC-DIG-ppmsca-22306; **55**: W.K.L. Dickson, 1894. P&P, LC-DIG-ppmsca-13462; **56**: Carol M. Highsmith, 2007. P&P, CMHA, LC-DIG-highsm-01932; **57**: UNK, 1895. P&P, LC-USZ62-120935; **58**: Elihu Vedder, ca. 1896. P&P, LC-DIG-ppmsca-13482; **59**: UNK, 1896. P&P, LC-USZ62-40188; **60**: W. Bengough, 1897. P&P, LC-DIG-ppmsca-17588; **61**: Carol M. Highsmith, 2007. P&P, CMHA, LC-DIG-highsm-02072; **62**: Carol M. Highsmith, 2007. P&P, CMHA, LC-DIG-highsm-02015; **65**: Levin C. Handy, [1898?]. P&P, LC-DIG-ppmsca-25378

PART TWO: FOR THE NATION
66: Detroit Photographic Co., 1901. P&P, Photochrom Coll., LC-DIG-ppmsca-18147; **69**: Carol M. Highsmith, 2007. P&P, CMHA, LC-DIG-highsm-03193; **70**: Carol M. Highsmith, 2007. P&P, CMHA, LC-DIG-highsm-01927; **72**: Albrecht Dürer, 1504. P&P, LC-DIG-ppmsca-18945; **73**: UNK, ca. 1898. P&P, LC-USZ62-38245; **74**: UNK, 1901. P&P, Br-Ha, LC-DIG-cwpbh-03424; **75**: Frances B. Johnston, ca. 1899. P&P, Frances Benjamin Johnston Coll., LC-USZ62-4541; **76**: Detroit Photographic Co., 1898. P&P, Photochrom Coll., LC-DIG-ppmsca-18034; **79 left**: UNK, 1900. P&P, LC-DIG-ppmsc-04826; **79 right**: MSS, Daniel A.P. Murray Papers; **80**: UNK, ca. 1900. P&P, LC-USZ62-59275; **81**: P&P, BIOG FILE; **82**: UNK, 1900–1920. P&P, LC-USZ62-118630; **85**: Jack Delano, 1930–1950. P&P, LC-USZ62-100400; **87**: Underwood & Underwood, 1904. P&P, LC-DIG-stereo-1s05904; **88**: EUR; **89**: LC/Barbara Dash. RBSC; **91**: UNK, 1906. P&P, LC-DIG-ppmsca-35800; **93**: UNK, 1924. P&P, NPCC, LC-US762-111913; **95**: Harris & Ewing, 1912. P&P, HEC, LC-DIG-hec-01689; **96**: 15th century. AMED; **98**: UNK, 1914. P&P, LC-DIG-ppmsca-33995; **99**: UNK, ca. 1911. P&P, Robert M. La Follette, Sr., Papers, LC-USZ61-1553; **100**: Underwood & Underwood, ca. 1919. P&P, LC-USZ62-60729; **101**: UNK, 1922. P&P, NPCC, LC-USZ62-33031; **102**: UNK, 1919 or 1920. P&P, NPCC, LC-DIG-npcc-28564; **103 above**: 1920. P&P, U.S. GEOG FILE; **103 below**: UNK, ca. 1875. P&P, Br-Ha, LC-DIG-cwpbh-03798; **104**: UNK, 1922. P&P, NPCC, LC-DIG-npcc-06229; **105**: UNK. P&P, LC-USZ62-399; **106**: Harris & Ewing, 1938. P&P, HEC, LC-DIG-hec-24277; **107**: MUS, Coolidge Foundation Coll.; **109**: Harris & Ewing, ca. 1930. P&P, LOT 5760; **110**: UNK, 1925. P&P, NPCC, LC-DIG-npcc-26817; **111**: RBSC, Otto Vollbehr Coll; **114 and 115**: MUS; **116 above**: RBSC; **116 below**: UNK, 1929. P&P, NYWTS,

249

LC-USZ62-115443; **118**: Columbia Pictures, 1939. P&P, LC-DIG-ppmsc-03738; **119 left and right**: George and Ira Gershwin Coll., MUS; **120**: Carol M. Highsmith, 2007. P&P, CMHA, LC-DIG-highsm-03190; **121 left**: Carol M. Highsmith, 2007. P&P, CMHA, LC-DIG-highsm-02758; **121 right**: Carol M. Highsmith, 2007. P&P, CMHA, LC-DIG-highsm-02767; **122**: MSS, LC Archives, PIO series; **123**: UNK, 1938–1950. P&P, Lomax Coll., LC-DIG-ppmsc-00433; **125**: LC/ Shawn Miller, 2015. COM; **126**: U.S. Office of War Information, 1940-41. P&P, LC-USZ62-123290; **127**: 1941. Charles L. Todd and Robert Sonkin Migrant Workers Coll. (AFC 1985/001:PH16); **128**: Ludwig van Beethoven, 1820. Gertrude Clarke Whittall Foundation Coll., MUS; **129**: Carol M. Highsmith, 1980–2006. P&P, CMHA, LC-DIG-highsm-13238; **131**: RBSC, Rosenwald Coll.; **132 left**: Pix Inc., 1943. P&P, LC-DIG-ppmsca-17591; **132 right**: Press Association, Inc., 1944. P&P, LC-DIG-ds-09163; **133**: Dorothea Lange, 1936. P&P, FSA - OWI Coll., LC-DIG-fsa-8b29516; **134**: LC, 1944. MUS; **135**: LC/Shawn Miller, 2016. COM; **136**: Victor Kraft, 1946. MUS, Aaron Copland Coll., Box Number 492/11. Used by permission of The Aaron Copland Fund for Music, Inc.; **139**: UNK, 1916. P&P, LC-USZ62-113150; **141 left**: MSS, W. Somerset Maugham Papers; **141 right**: UNK, 1948. P&P, LC-USZ62-135719; **143**: Orville Wright and John T. Daniels, 1903. P&P, Papers of Wilbur and Orville Wright, LC-DIG-ppprs-00626; **144**: MSS, LC Archives, PIO series; **145**: DS, LC-USP6-6286-c; **146**: DS, LC-USP6-2891-a; **148**: J.S. Smith & Co., 1890. RBSC, Alfred Whital Stern Coll. of Lincolniana; **149**: MSS, LC Archives, PIO series; **151**: Mathew B. Brady, 1855–1865. P&P, Br-Ha, LC-DIG-cwpbh-01026; **152**: RBSC, McManus-Young Coll.; **155**: DS, LC-USP6-3598-c

PART THREE: FOR THE WORLD

156: LC, 1988. P&P, LC-DIG-ds-10201; **159**: LC/ Michaela McNichol, 2007. COM; **162**: LC, 1964. COM; **163**: UNK, 1966. P&P, NYWTS, LC-DIG-ppmsca-15437; **164**: Stanley Tetrick, 1963. P&P, LOOK Magazine Photograph Coll., LC-DIG-ppmsca-24295; **166**: UNK, 1936. P&P, Visual Materials from the NAACP Records, LC-DIG-ppmsca-39304; **168**: COM; **169 left**: RBSC; **169 right**: UNK, 1966. P&P, Biographical File Filing Series, LC-DIG-ppmsca-38574; **170**: H.C. Miner Litho. Co., 1926. P&P, LC-DIG-ppmsc-03732; **171**: Rudolph Assoc., 1966. P&P, Alfred Easton Poor Papers, LC-USZ62-116855; **172 left**: UNK, 1887. P&P, Charles E. Feinberg

Coll., LC-DIG-ppmsca-07550; **172 right**: LC, 1970. P&P, LC-DIG-ds-10195; **173**: Robert L. Knudsen, 1968. P&P, Ralph Ellison Papers, LC-USZ62-137238; **174**: DS, LC-USP6-5805c; **177**: Charles E. Martin/ *New Yorker*, April 24, 1971 © Condé Nast; **179**: Russell Patterson, ca. 1925. P&P, Swann Coll., LC-DIG-ppmsca-01589; **180**: Alexander Graham Bell, March 10, 1876. MSS, Alexander Graham Bell Family Papers, Box 271; **182**: Beverly J. Robinson, 1977. South-Central Georgia Folklife Project Coll. (AFC 1982/010), 6-17617-29a; **184**: Lancy Hidy, Center for the Book; **185**: IPO; **186**: LC, 1979. P&P, LC-DIG-ds-10199; **187**: Carol M. Highsmith, 2007. P&P, CMHA, LC-DIG-highsm-03189; **188**: Carol M. Highsmith, 2007. P&P, CMHA, LC-DIG-highsm-03177; **190**: Carol M. Highsmith, 2007. P&P, CMHA, LC-DIG-highsm-03169; **191**: MSS, LC Archives, PIO series; **192**: PO; **193**: DS, LC-USP6-9814-36; **194**: N. Currier, 1835–1837. P&P, LC-DIG-pga-05787; **195**: MSS, LC Archives, PIO series; **197**: LC, 1989. P&P, LC-DIG-ds-10202; **199**: LC, 1989. P&P, LC-DIG-ds-10203; **200**: LC, 1990. P&P, LC-DIG-ds-10205; **201**: LC, 1991. P&P, LC-DIG-ds-10209; **202**: Robert Silvers, 1994. P&P, LC-DIG-ds-04950; **204 left**: Jack Norworth and Albert Von Tilzer, New York Music Co., 1908. MUS; **204 right**: UNK, ca. 1853. P&P, Daguerreotype Coll., LC-DIG-ds-04496; **206**: MBRS; **207**: John Bryson, 1959. P&P, Charles and Ray Eames Coll., LC-USZ62-137158; **208–9**: Carol M. Highsmith, 2009. P&P, CMHA, LC-DIG-highsm-11597; **210**: LC, 2000. P&P, LC-DIG-ds-10211; **211**: Carol M. Highsmith, 2009. P&P, CMHA, LC-DIG-highsm-11617; **212 above**: LC, 2000. P&P, LC-DIG-ds-10212; **212 below**: LC, 2000. P&P, LC-DIG-ds-10210; **214**: UNK. Carol Scott Coll. (AFC 2001/001/11082), Photograph (PH01), Veterans History Project Coll.; **215**: DS, LC-USP61-090801; **216 left**: klcc.org; **216 right**: PO; **217**: UNK, ca. 1980. P&P, Herbert L. Block Coll., LC-DIG-ppmsca-22217; **218**: UNK, 2001. P&P, Coll. of Unattributed 9/11 Photographs, LC-DIG-ppmsca-02149; **219**: G&M; **220 above**: UNK, 1964. P&P, NYWTS, LC-USZ62-107994; **220 below**: G&M, Jay I. Kislak Coll.; **221 left**: LC/Steve Winick, 2005. AFC; **221 right**: LC/Scott Suchman, 2007. COM; **222**: LC/ Nancy Alfaro, 2007. COM; **223**: Columbia Pictures, 1950. P&P, LC-DIG-ppmsca-25371; **224**: LC/Shawn Miller, 2015. COM; **225**: LC/Shawn Miller, 2016. COM; **226 left**: Photo courtesy First Evenements, 2009; **226 right**: LC/Barry Wheeler, 2009. COM; **227**: LC/Abby Brack Lewis, 2010. COM; **228**: UNK, 1863–1865. P&P, Liljenquist Family Coll. of Civil

War Photographs, LC-DIG-ppmsca-36454; **229**: National Jukebox, MBRS; **230 left**: LC/Abby Brack Lewis, 2013. COM; **230 right**: Rachel Carson, 1962. IPO; **231**: © Bill Ray, 1980. MSS, Seth MacFarlane Coll. of the Carl Sagan and Ann Druyan Archive. Courtesy of Bill Ray and Druyan-Sagan Associates, Inc.; **232**: LC/Katherine Blood, 2013. P&P; **233**: Pete Souza, 2015. P030815PS-0117. Courtesy of the Barack Obama Presidential Library; **234**: LC/ John Harrington, 2014. COM; **235**: LC, 2014. COM; **236**: LC/Shawn Miller, 2015. COM; **238**: LC/Shawn Miller, 2015. COM; **239 above and below**: LC/ Shawn Miller, 2016. COM

APPENDIX

240: Carol M. Highsmith, 2007. P&P, CMHA, LC-DIG-highsm-03192; **242 above**: UNK, 1811. P&P, LC-USZ62-6007; **242 below**: P&P, John Silva Meehan Papers, LC-USZ62-43063; **243 above**: L.C. Handy Studios, ca. 1900. P&P, Br-Ha, LC-USZ62-23839; **243 below**: Anson, 1860–1865. P&P, LC-USZ62-57283; **244 above**: Frances B. Johnston, ca. 1900. P&P, Frances Benjamin Johnston Coll., LC-USZ62-92405; **244 below left**: Dinwiddie Studio, ca. 1895. P&P, LC-USZ62-6011; **244 below right**: UNK, 1939–1944. P&P, LC-DIG-ppmsca-17592; **245 above**: UNK, 1940–1960. P&P, LC-USZ62-123764; **245 below**: Harris & Ewing, 1964. COM; **246 left**: LC. COM; **246 right**: LC, 2005. COM; **247**: LC/Shawn Miller, 2016. COM

INDEX

Page numbers in *italics* refer to illustrations and their captions